Ideals of Feminine Beauty

Recent Titles in
Contributions in Women's Studies

IDEALS OF FEMININE BEAUTY

Philosophical, Social, and Cultural Dimensions

EDITED BY

Karen A. Callaghan

Contributions in Women's Studies,
Number 141

GREENWOOD PRESS
Westport, Connecticut • London

Library of Congress Cataloging-in-Publication Data

Ideals of feminine beauty : philosophical, social, and cultural
    dimensions / edited by Karen A. Callaghan.
        p.   cm.—(Contributions in women's studies, ISSN 0147–104X ;
    no. 141)
    Includes bibliographical references and index.
    ISBN 0–313–26136–9   (alk. paper)
    1. Feminine beauty (Aesthetics)   2. Femininity (Psychology)
    3. Sex role.   I. Callaghan, Karen A.   II. Series.
    HQ1219I53   1994
    305.42—dc20   93–39353

British Library Cataloguing in Publication Data is available.

Library of Congress Catalog Card Number: 93–39353
ISBN: 0–313–26136–9
ISSN: 0147–104X

First published in 1994

Greenwood Press, 88 Post Road West, Westport, CT 06881
An imprint of Greenwood Publishing Group, Inc.

Printed in the United States of America

The paper used in this book complies with the
Permanent Paper Standard issued by the National
Information Standards Organization (Z39.48–1984).

10 9 8 7 6 5 4 3 2 1

Contents

Introduction

Karen A. Callaghan

This book is about ideals of feminine beauty and women, specifically how the social, political, cultural and personal experiences of women have been constructed by beauty standards. The aim is *not* to discuss, in detail, historical or current notions of what is considered beautiful. Other writers have accomplished that task quite well. This collection focuses on the dynamics of how beauty norms have been developed and the integral role they continue to play in the construction of the feminine gender identity. The connections between beauty and femininity are intricate and contradictory. Beauty is a pleasurable experience, and yet also a source of pain and rejection as women contort (or fail to contort) their bodies and selves according to restrictive, idealized images.

For many years feminist writers, from Brownmiller to Wolf, have articulated the connection between patriarchical images of female beauty and women's oppression. Hence, beauty norms, along with many other issues, are identified as obstacles to liberation. In addition, contemporary theorists, such as Foucault, have identified the body and sexuality as the sites for "cultural power struggles" (Mascia-Lees & Sharpe 1992, 5). These discussions challenge essentialist explanations of femininity and beauty as natural, apolitical and ahistorical phenomena. The chapters in this book also support the view that beauty is a socially constructed mechanism of patriarchical social control.

As part of the modern tradition, however, the word *beauty* is understood to represent goodness, pleasure, truth, purity and the sublime. This view of beauty is underpinned by social ontological dualism, as epitomized by the Cartesian understanding of truth and reality (Murphy 1989). Truth, accordingly, is defined as a pure (objective) vision of reality, using pure in the sense of being purged of any temporal, relative and idiosyncratic claims. Consequently, viable knowledge is revealed only when the correct conceptual and analytical tools and techniques are used. In modern society, knowledge derived from scientific inquiry is considered primary or, as post-modernists would say, the "center," since reality is reflected as accurately as possible. Other forms of expression, those derived via non-scientific methodology, are considered peripheral (subjective), lacking the seriousness and gravity of objective information. Hence, a hierarchy of legitimate ideas and facts is established.

In the modern tradition, social arrangements can be justified only by objective claims. According to traditional sociological theories, society constitutes a reality *sui generis*. Social facts, such as norms, roles, customs and so on, legitimately exert a constraining, compelling and unifying influence on individuals (Durkheim 1938). To use Talcott Parsons' (1966, 5–29) terms, social order is presumed to have certain "functional prerequisites," which must be fulfilled for order and integrity to be assured. Consequently, conformity to social demands is paramount. The conforming person is considered the more reasonable, controlled and objective individual. A conforming person has the insight and maturity to recognize the inevitable parameters of the "real world," that is, the necessary boundaries within which reasonable, civilized social exchange can commence. Failure to conform may cause the wild, the unrestrained and the chaotic to emerge.

This dualistic, hierarchical view of social order perpetuates the inferiorization and oppression of certain categories of persons (Turner, Singleton & Musick 1984). The center-periphery distinction underpins traditional gender, race, age and class identities. Peripheral identities, like peripheral expressions, are secondary, marginal and often, by necessity, excluded or controlled as a threat to reasonable social exchange. Those who represent the primary, objective categories (male, white, elite, etc.) of reality are afforded a privileged status regarding control of social arrangements and, hence, of people. Oppressive social arrangements can be justified, in the modern view, as compliance with the demands of truth and reason. Subjugation is portrayed as impersonal and apolitical. Oppressors exercise their power and privilege not to realize self-serving ends, but to comply with possible biological, social or historical requirements for social order. Oppression becomes bureaucratized, that is, it becomes a required and rational task, which will yield long-term social benefits. Domination and subordination become institutional prerequisites for the sake of an efficient, orderly functioning society.

Patriarchy is one form of oppression, which has been legitimated on social, biological, religious and economic prerequisites. For women in patriarchical systems, beauty norms serve as a locus of control over the most fundamental aspects of identity—the self, the body and intersubjectivity. The gender hierarchy is sustained by beauty norms that define women's power, self-assertion and worth in terms that reify male dominance. Beautiful women are desirable, but also signify a threat to masculine freedom and autonomy and, therefore, must be controlled. Women who cannot or will not conform to beauty standards are deviant and must be excluded for their defects or rebellion. In addition, beauty standards invoke a cultural discourse regarding age, class and race and are used as a means of social control over those aspects of identity as well. Simply put, ideals of beauty are powerful interpretations of normative behavior (Wolf 1991). While all persons are expected to conform to social standards (some of which involve appearance), beauty images have special, contradictory consequences for women. They are a sophisticated means of social control and yet are often portrayed either as empowering to women or as being merely idiosyncratic preferences void of any political, economic or social power.

To understand the significance of beauty, then, the dynamics of patriarchical social control must be discerned. The chapters in this volume discuss beauty as a socially constructed normative standard, which supports a discourse of feminine oppression and male dominance. Specifically, three important ideas are suggested by the authors.

First, beauty ideals are not inherently oppressive. Beauty is *essentially* nothing; socially constructed beauty norms can express an array of ideas and sentiments. In patriarchical systems, beauty has, to varying degrees, involved feminine self-destruction, since the masculine has been defined as the pivotal center from which all normative expressions must emerge and to which they must return. Beauty norms imply that every aspect of the female body/appearance must be acted upon in order to be acceptable. Furthermore, feminine beauty is defined as primarily for men's pleasure. So the woman who strives to achieve an aesthetic ideal does so not for self-actualization or accomplishment, but for masculine approval. Women's achievements are defined, then, as naturally vicarious, other-directed. Although social conformity usually implies integration, women are integrated into social order only on masculine terms. Women are expected to be beautiful, but because it is a potential threat, the feminine must first be neutralized (made passive, weak and dependent) and then reformed (violated, desired, controlled) to reify the masculine order.

Second, although these dynamics represent a power struggle, their origin and potency are broader than what is implied by the current use of the term *political.* The patriarchical beauty discourse has been developed, refined and reformulated in the dominant philosophical, religious, social, political and economic texts and practices. So an array of ideological nar-

ratives is employed to portray gender hierarchicalization as a natural, necessary and inevitable order. As a means of social control, beauty standards
are most powerful when they can appear as historically and culturally
ubiquitous. Their artificiality is masked with the authenticity that the "natural" label affords any phenomenon.

Third, and finally, in the modern discourse of social control, the individual is not subjected primarily to brute force as a means of obtaining
conformity. Modern control is often achieved through the use of symbolic
manipulation, which creates the guise of free will and choice. For instance,
as women in the United States, and many other countries, gain political,
economic and individual power, how can beauty ideals continue to represent a patriarchical discourse that oppresses the feminine? Are women
not free to accept or reject these standards? These questions reflect a
simplistic understanding of modern hierarchical power. Individual women
may gain success, while the feminine is still inferiorized. Women are subject to double standards, discriminatory treatment and trivialization, which
the individual may be able to minimize if the correct behaviors, speech
and thinking are exhibited. Adherence to beauty norms is one sort of
compliance behavior that women can exhibit in order to demonstrate their
willingness not to challenge the gender hierarchy. Beauty, according to the
patriarchical discourse, is a cue that a woman is nonthreatening. However,
the woman who conforms to beauty standards is accepting a limiting and
disjointed autonomy. These norms are rooted in feminine oppression, and
their content implies passivity, self-denial and self-loathing.

PHILOSOPHY, RELIGION AND BEAUTY

In Western philosophical/religious thought, feminine beauty plays a special role in the construction of patriarchy. Beauty is associated with the
body, which as a material phenomenon should be controlled, manipulated
and transcended. Viewed as naturally feminine, women are also associated
primarily with their bodily existence (Bordo 1990, 143). This strongly emphasized connection between women and the body has sustained the inferiorization of the feminine.

In his chapter, Algis Mickunas notes that in the Western tradition, the
body became the "grave of the soul," as transcendent reflection accompanied the emergence of patriarchy. Mickunas associates different "cultural modes of reflection" with the status of feminine beauty, and hence
the role of women. The development of Western philosophy can be
viewed as an attempt to disarm and neutralize the power that femininity
acquired through the goddess cults. Patriarchy is possible only if what
Mickunas calls "rescendence" is suppressed and replaced with transcendent reflection. Rescendence is a reflective mode that emphasizes a "re-

turn to the origin," and hence celebrates the maternal, creation, fruition and eroticism. The rescendent feminine is understood as the connection between humanity and the cosmic forces and is respected accordingly. In this reflective mode, beauty is associated with the powerful, life-giving force, which the maternal/feminine represents.

Transcendent reflection allows patriarchy to emerge as a "limiting and lowering force," which emphasizes individualism, purity, spirituality and salvation. Rescendent beauty is, then, made a terrible, polluting vice, which must be purified and controlled. Hence, in patriarchy, women, the feminine and the maternal come to represent a threat to masculine transcendence and the accompanying social order.

The history of Western thought and practices regarding women is replete with examples of the "purification" of the terrible beauty. In his chapter, Ben Lowe documents the medieval and early modern European ideal of feminine beauty. Lowe notes that the emphasis on the control and manipulation of women's bodies is sustained by the Platonic ideal of pure, asexual beauty. The dominant European sensibility of this period viewed eroticism (aroused in men by female bodies) as sinful and required its violent containment. Lowe documents the various beauty "treatments" women were expected to undergo to become physically and, more important, spiritually pleasing. The female body was acceptable only through conformity to the masculine gaze. The potential violence of these dynamics is presented in Lowe's discussion of the European treatment of Amerindian women. These women represented the "terrible" feminine autonomy (beauty) of a prepatriarchical order. Their appearance and practices signified the absence of the European gender hierarchy. The reactions of the Europeans, including rape, murder, torture and enslavement, demonstrate that failure to conform to beauty standards represents rebellion against the dominant social order.

The chapters by Usha Zacharias and Amira Sonbol articulate the philosophical/religious construction of beauty within Hinduism and Islam, respectively. Zacharias notes that although Hinduism offers a complex view of masculinity and femininity, the fundamentalist interpretation reifies the masculine, patriarchical social order. In Hinduism, feminine beauty can assume the guise of the passive, obedient woman or the militaristic, powerful woman. However, either image is legitimate only if the masculine hierarchy is preserved.

In her chapter, Sonbol explores the complex relationship among Islam, beauty and westernization. In the history of Islam, many different images of feminine beauty have emerged. Sonbol illustrates how specific beauty images make sense only if the relevant sociohistorical context is understood. Again, the degree of conformity to beauty norms is understood to signify integration-rejection of social arrangements.

WOMEN, BEAUTY AND SELF-IMAGE/CONTROL

The modern, Western world view emphasizes individuality, personal freedom and rational/scientific knowledge. Hence, modern patriarchical control is organized in terms of these characteristics. John W. Murphy explains how modern forms of social control must appear to be "neutral," "civilized" and certainly devoid of any crude coercion. This form of dominance creates the sense that individuals are free to pursue their own aims and desires. Conformity results, however, since integration into the social order is possible only if persons "normalize" themselves according to prescribed images and roles. As "accomplices in their own repression," individuals have difficulties in identifying external agents of control. For Murphy, this form of control should be understood as "symbolic violence," since conformity is achieved partly through the manipulation of symbolic phenomena, especially social imagery and language.

As symbolic violence, beauty images are presented as either natural or individual preferences, not as the result of a gender power struggle. The much-touted use of scientific research and technologically sophisticated images allows beauty to be represented most effectively as a reality *sui generis.* As "objective" facts, how can rational persons reject modern images of beauty? Is this not a rejection of reality, a practice for which modern societies have severe consequences? In addition, the technology that allows the rapid, slick production and dissemination of beauty images serves to intensify the symbolic control. Women and men are surrounded with images that include the desirable shape, color, texture and language of beauty. These images are completely artificial representations of actual women, but as the effects of modern technology, they attain the status of objective reality. These are the results of symbolic violence: Real persons become only flawed imitations of the perfect *image.*

The issue of modern technological imagery is discussed also by Eric Mark Kramer in his chapter on pornography. Kramer examines the modern suppression of the feminine in terms of the "phallocentric bias" found in various images of popular culture, including pornography. In pornographic images, the desire-rejection of the feminine is obvious. Images of childlike women or actual children are used; violence and other forms of degradation are frequent. For Kramer, the popularity of pornography is evidence of how these images pander to the modern masculine ethos of radical individualism, control and capricious consumption. Sexuality expressed in these terms is brutal, sterile, acontextual, without any concern or desire for social, intersubjective relations. Beauty and desire are enmeshed and suggestive of submission, violation, passivity and weakness. Technological innovation allows the viewer to manipulate the images, as the imagery suggests women should be controlled.

These contradictory beauty standards are evident also in the feminine self-identity. As individual girls/women construct a self-concept, they must assimilate cultural ideals that inferiorize the feminine. Debra Gimlim re-examines the eating disorder anorexia nervosa as a manifestation of the contradictions of the patriarchical discourse of femininity. Typically, ano-rexia is explained as either psychological maladaptation or rebellion against repression. Gimlim suggests that anorexia is overconformity to the images that idealize feminine thinness and imply the nonperfectability of women's bodies. The anorectic woman attempts to "normalize" her body according to the most logical conclusion of patriarchical domination—the destruction of the feminine.

Catherine G. Valentine analyzes women's journal writings to illustrate the self-concept that incorporates modern individualism with the patriarchical inferiorization of the feminine. Valentine notes that in modern patriarchal systems women develop a "sense of self that is distorted and divided against itself, self-policing and self-destructive." A divided self-concept is another form of symbolic violence. To be rational, women must accept the ideal: a feminine identity that is peripheral to the masculine.

The study conducted by J. Greg Getz and Hanne K. Klein reveals the complex social relations involved in self-policing and self-normalization. Having one's hair styled appears and is defined as a very private, personal experience. Stylist and client work together to bring out the best in each individual. However, Getz and Klein demonstrate that the seemingly self-directed pursuits of clients are replete with modern patriarchical norms. Patrons appeal to the stylists to be made attractive, but this can only be achieved temporarily. To be beautiful, women must continually consume the salon services and products. As women age, their beauty normalization involves more cost and time, as often prescribed by the stylists. Hence, as women gain the attributes that modern society associates with power—age, experience, education and perhaps economic independence—symbolic violence intensifies. The modern desire for beauty, which reflects youth, both inferiorizes mature women and supports their attempts to remain youthful, that is, dependent, passive and physically small and weak.

The struggle of women to reject or redefine beauty images is the focus of the chapters by Maxine Leeds and Cheri K. Erdman. Leeds's study of young African-American women explores the relationship between beauty norms and the racial hierarchy. Many young women interviewed noted the use of beauty to express an authentic racial identity. However, Leeds contends that while the racial hierarchy is challenged seriously by the young women, the gender discourse remains relatively intact. "White" standards of beauty are critiqued verbally, but often covertly adopted in order to be feminine and attractive. The most salient evidence of the lack of serious, thorough beauty critique is the women's insistence that an authentic, black "look" is one that is natural, even though numerous processes and products are involved. Again, the legitimacy of beauty is predicated on the basis of a natural, apolitical origin. Patriarchical control is able to neutralize partially these women's critique of racial domination.

In a similar study, Erdman interviewed women who have, in effect, overcome Valentine's "divided self" by accepting their bodies as fat. Rather than engaging in constant self-criticism, these women have personally overcome the symbolic manipulation of the feminine body. Erdman identifies the personal strategies that can challenge the dominant narratives. These strategies involve neutralizing symbolic violence by reconceptualizing the self and/or replacing restrictive beauty images with affirmative ideals of women's worth and value.

CONCLUSION: AUTHENTIC BEAUTY

Beauty is not inherently oppressive. Patriarchical beauty norms, past and present, have been revealed as a carefully constructed narrative that creates artificial and hierarchical restrictions on the feminine appearance and other aspects of identity. In order to challenge essentialist views of beauty, the idea that femininity is an inferior category/identity must be dismissed. This can be accomplished only if the very basis of modern social order, social ontological dualism, is also rejected.

The subversion of dualism reveals the political nature of social order (Kristeva 1986). This maneuver allows the status of any phenomenon to be questioned, reviewed, debated and so on without the risk of social chaos and destruction. Gender relations can be analyzed as historical, intersubjective interpretations that have been enforced through various means. Biology, nature and/or social prerequisites are no longer acceptable justifications for hierarchical relations.

This post-modern form of critique assumes that the social order is a discursive act. Boundaries of legitimacy exist, but obviously as the result of intersubjective action, that is, the perpetual interaction between persons as they construct social arrangements. The negotiation of boundaries may involve coercion, manipulation and other control mechanisms, but the underlying dynamic is nonetheless intersubjectivity or, to use Kristeva's (1986, 37, 111) term, "intertextuality." What, however, are the implications of these assumptions for creating an authentic feminine sense of beauty?

First, if beauty is a discursive practice, then existing norms/images are always legitimately subject to interpretation and critique. Ideals of beauty have limited and political validity. They are not natural and universal, and they do not inherently signify worth, value or other attributes.

Second, when beauty is understood as an interpretive act, then the stage is set for competing images to emerge. Existing beauty norms will not fade away, but they can no longer claim an *a priori* legitimacy. Power that is won through symbolic manipulation of the feminine can be confronted with symbolic alternatives. Everyday "beauty" routines can be analyzed to reveal the underlying self-loathing and rejection of the feminine. In other words, beauty can be democratized and legitimately constructed to express a wide range of sentiments, ideals and the like.

Third, and finally, beauty images can represent nonhierarchical relations only when they represent sentiments that have been collectively defined and validated. Authentic legitimacy is grounded on community participation, not abstract, *a priori* assumptions. Hence, the construction of beauty norms and images can no longer rest in the hands of a self-selected few. Obviously, democratizing beauty is predicated on increased participation in many other institutions, including the economic and political systems.

In sum, femininity will be celebrated, rather than degraded, by beauty images that represent a freely constructed discourse that rejects hierarchical, oppressive gender relations. Although women face economic, political and other cultural challenges, beauty should not be ignored as a genuine obstacle to autonomy and equality.

WORKS CITED

Bordo, S. 1990. Feminism, Postmodernism and Gender-scepticism. In L. J. Nicholson (ed.), *Feminism/Postmodernism* (pp. 133–56). New York: Routledge Chapman and Hall.

Durkheim, E. 1938. *The Rules of Sociological Method.* New York: Free Press.

Kristeva, J. 1986. *The Kristeva Reader.* Ed. T. Moi. New York: Columbia University Press.

Mascia-Lees, F. E., and P. Sharpe (eds.). 1992. *Tattoo, Torture, Mutilation, and Adornment, The Denaturalization of the Body in Culture and Text.* Albany: State University of New York Press.

Murphy, J. W. 1989. *Postmodern Social Analysis and Criticism.* Westport, Conn.: Greenwood Press.

Parsons, T. 1966. *Societies.* Englewood Cliffs, N.J.: Prentice-Hall.

Turner, B., R. Singleton, Jr., and D. Musick. 1984. *Oppression.* Chicago: Nelson-Hall.

Wolf, N. 1991. *The Beauty Myth:* How Images of Beauty Are Used Against Women. New York: William Morrow.

PART I

PHILOSOPHY, RELIGION AND BEAUTY

1

The Terrible Beauty and Her Reflective Force

Algis Mickunas

A survey of feminine beauty in the great texts of the Western tradition reveals an absence of seriousness. This is not to say that these texts treat the matter lightly; to the contrary, the galaxy of writings analyzing and dissecting this beauty is inordinate. And yet analytical dissection abolishes the presence and force of beauty. This analytic assault disarms and robs it of its terrible danger. Indeed, penetrating analyses may be the easiest way of disarming a given phenomenon. Yet precisely the preoccupation with covering and hiding, with subjecting beauty to rules and prohibitions, is what reveals its presence (Sloterdijk 1983, 222). The most serious depictions, therefore, avoid and hide something very troubling. This is clearly the case with feminine beauty. Her beauty was so overpowering, so terrible, that it had to be hidden, purified and subdued to the extreme (Daly 1978, 180). Indeed, this chapter contends that Western philosophy, from Plato through Kant, has depicted feminine beauty in ways that attempted to ensure its timidity and "purity." Could philosophy, with its striving to transcend the fleeting, the material, the phenomenal and the erotic, ever concern itself seriously with feminine beauty?

Given this question, feminine beauty can hardly be grasped without a set of complex cultural relationships. The latter will be seen as reflecting the very force of, and the efforts to hide, her terrible beauty. However, the notion of reflection should mesh closely with the ways in which it actually appears in cultures, and not as it is constructed by an external and unpolluted posture.

Cultural studies reveal that reflection, even the modern Western type, assumes that one event or activity is either supervening over or subtending/pervading other events. This means that such events are articulated in diverse ways and need not be anthropomorphic. If there are modes of reflection that reveal human shape, they do not have to be given any preeminence. Excluded are metaphysical questions about whether cultural modes of reflection are instituted consciously/deliberately or are founded on theories of psycho-physiological compulsion (Daly 1978, 180). Such considerations are excluded because of the methodological requirements of strictly adhering to cultural phenomena. Emphasizing such adherence is called for to point out that even explanations of reflection might be an aspect of a socioculturally accepted mode of interpretation and thus are not necessarily universal.

It would be theoretically and methodologically misleading if this chapter took for granted that symbolic conceptions are transcultural. They, too, are a part of a given culture and must be located within cultural parameters. Even the claims of some of the more radical types of textual analyses, such as "deconstruction," must be understood to have a cultural location. Placing phenomena within a cultural field is one of the fundamental methodological principles employed by both phenomenology and hermeneutics. The difference between the two is that the former employs this methodological prerequisite explicitly, while the latter does this implicitly.

SIGNS OF REFLECTIVE SUBMERSION

The most encompassing mode of this reflection consists of signs related to the return to the origin. This return has a specific requirement: dissolution of the individual into life, or the original maternal energy. As origin, she is the dimension that does not function signitively as does a concept or an object, but exercises a magnetic pull, an all-pervasive attraction against whose temptations the individual must guard. The pull to dissolution is commonly manifested by the feminine; as the queen of heaven and earth, she cannot be resisted. Most desired, she is also the most terrible. The hetare, loved and despised for her attraction, was enshrined; Samiramis, Kandake, Dido, Kleopatra and Verma are manifestations of life-giving forces. Her beauty is no longer that of appearance. The latter is a mere artifice of allurement, a momentary mask that some cultures require either to milden or to intensify the presence of her force. The latter is the very beauty of life giving and renewing and may appear as both a procreative drive and an erotic attraction.

All that she produces, nonetheless, she threatens to engulf, take back, devour and dissolve. All that attractive beauty, the promise of life and joy, is coupled with this terrible submersion. She is the cradle, the womb and the origin of all formations and transformations, a primordial source of sustenance. She carries the lust to birth and the dark mystery that never yields itself to light (Gimbutas 1991, 222, 256). This mystery pervades the sacral fruitfulness, as she calls to song and rite, orgy and celebration. In any attempt to decipher the origin, depths are encountered that cannot be avoided. Here are met the cults of creation and not salvation. Ancient Dionysian rites call for no salvation and no salvific oil. The signs are those of theatrics, superfluity, metaphor and disregard of norm, but there are no signs of distance, appeal, supplication and nonparticipation. In this pantheism, all growth is a force of reverie. Eros is divine, and all divinities are erotic, with all their fatal attractions. In a fundamental sense, her fruitfulness is intertwined with sacrality, and her beauty is celebrated in awe and reverence. Every act of fruition has cosmic significance and exists at the nexus of the powers of fruition and the world. Through the maternal, the human is an extension, a prolongation and an enhancement of the vital forces; the exchange of powers between the human and the cosmic events is taken for granted. Thus, the acts of eros and libido are not yet erotic or sexual in the modern sense, but are cosmically vivifying. Here the sexual act is a self-dissolving sacrifice, designed to empower life and not to exhibit aesketic self-denial.

This reflectivity is one of rescendence, a pull of dissolution, and not of transcendence, which promises an escape from the dangers of the terrible beauty. One's sexuality is not destined to make one separate, satisfied or singular in the exclusivity of one's partner, but is constituted by submergence into the vital/living center; this reflection yields no distance. This is how the signs of sexual self-emulation should be read, that is, the rituals of the orgiastic cults in which the priests or seers sacrifice their phallus. The loss is not an ascetic surrender for achieving transcendence, but a vivification of the origin, which pervades all fruitfulness. The rescending reflection is an identification with the origin into which one merges. For example, the great festival of Astare in Hieropolis reveals rows of males castrating themselves in a wild reverie in honor of the goddess; the priests of Cybele did the same (Schubart 1944, 43). And these were not ascetic performances where one felt guilty, where one had some kind of vulva envy in the face of the goddess of fertility. They were inner reflections of the vital/maternal attraction: The dissolution of any singular function was a convergence into and a spreading of strength across all living process.

What is peculiar about these and similar depictions is that the sacral was not only erotic, but also more fundamentally vital and anti-singular. Even the erotic was not privatized or attributed to a singular personality. The orgiastic reverie is, after all, a choiceless intermixture of anonymous personalities interacting at random—prepersonal, but not problematic. There is no search for individuality or individual salvation. The individual is only a reflective mode, which, in its orgiastic engagement, comprises a way of communicating without distance. Thus, a sin in the reverie is the *aeskesis,* the loyalty to one person and a lack of vitality and fruitfulness. The holy appears as the *urwhore,* which was rejected by Lutheran asceticism without being properly understood. The rule of this reflection is a nonpossessive call for self-abandonment: "Surrender yourselves to one another, with as many as possible, as often as possible." Woman should not belong to one and dry up; eroticism, here, is not love or libido, but a breakdown of limits of singularization and exclusivity. Every woman is hetaric, and so is every man, when he serves sacral life, the power of Shakti. Her beauty is bewitching and pervaded with the deepest wisdom. The bewitching beauty that cannot be resisted, and into which the singular dissolves, is not feared, not yet terrible, but most welcome and desired. Only when the individuating consciousness appears, cloaked in masculine signs, does beauty become both irresistible and terrible.

The dissolution of personal individuation is visible in the Persian celebration of Anaitis, where for five days all civic services and duties are suspended and each person is free to be with any person without restrictions. During the nocturnal tumult, each woman is Anaitis, and every man is her servant. At the end of the festival, man is sacrificed symbolically; it is not his person, but his power of fruition that is sacrificed. In certain races between naked men and women, particularly when one caught the other, the act of consummation was immediate. Customs such as giving up virginity to the entire public and not to one person reflect the vital participation and inner reflection of life. It could be said with justification that marriage, which singularizes, is against the vital sacrality. In numerous places, the bride had to atone for marriage by sleeping with every guest before she could consummate her relationship with the bridegroom. This turn is the source of hetarism, where the maidens at the temples signaled the dissolution of all rules, individuality and inhibition. Indeed, after years of temple service, they were sought as brides by kings and princes; they were regarded as most worthy. Even the daughters of kings vied to be part of hetarism. Their beauty appears precisely with the erotic power, reflecting an exuberant turn of the singular toward a dissolution into the all-pervasive pulse of mother life (Schubart 1944, 60).

Striving for a release from selfhood is reflected in melting reverie, and various functions are regarded as a means for the attainment of dissolution: wine, dance, song. It is no accident that Dionysos is a divinity of wine, eroticism and orgiastic reverie. The excitement brought about by wine and dance has a disruptive effect that leads to dissolution. All such means relate to the region of vitality. The characteristic state in this sacrality is intoxication, a loss of sense and a shifting of consciousness away from self-awareness. In the grip of *ekstasis,* the word rises to chant and the step to dance. The eros of Dionysos originates with dance, music and reverie and has the power to cause a dissolution of personality and a breakdown of cohesion. At the erotic level, every singular act, every effort to maintain individuality, flows, breaks up and dissolves singularity. The very movement of dissolution is the terrible, encompassing both an inescapable beauty and power of attraction and the inability to assume an individuated consciousness. At this vital juncture is found a total positivity, a persistence, a sacral origination, a presence, an insistence (Levinas 1981, 85).

Although the post-modern tradition uses eroticism as a sign of differentiation and deconstruction, eroticism is not viewed as a background of positivity without distance. This rescending reflection opens eroticism not as frustration, sublimation, lack of fulfillment or a cry signifying negativity as a difference from the signified; rather, it reflects a presence of positivity where fulfillment is not a calculated gratification of singular desires to be savored and verbalized, but a yielding to a pull that pervades the erotic. Such calculations would be a transcending reflection that opens a moment of negativity and an effort to deconstruct the feminine erotic. Yet this effort is a constant failure in the face of the pull of vital positivity. One may well suspect that the deconstructive practice is a last effort by patriarchy to purify the terrible beauty of the maternal domain. This transcending reflection allows eroticism to be posited as a force of differentiation in the post-modern West (Durante 1968, 271). The rescending reflection derails the transcending movement of negativity through music, rhythm and dance, thereby eliciting the madness of pulsating powers. There is pervasive evidence that suggests Indian music, appearing to the Western ear as monotonous, is in fact monotonic and manifests rescending reflection, thus demonstrating a monism of immersion, melting and depersonalization. Essentially speaking, erotic reflectivity, sacral ritual, music and intoxication reveal the melting presence of positivity and vitality. Shamanism is perhaps one of the more salient modes of this intimacy with the secrets of the origin. At times, it is expressed in terms of the classical Greek meaning of *poiesis,* as an active production, but not as a leisurely occupation (Durante 1968, 271).

Poiesis includes various activities, specifically those of feminine shamanism. The feminine is exceptional in healing, mastering natural forces, and providing visionary advice to the community. These functions are not simply medical, but also catharic and sacral. Even if the practices of these seers parallel medical magic, they are more inclusive. Medicine is protective. On the other hand, the female shaman not only is a goddess of battle, but also protects the hero in the future by a forward vision. Thus, heroic and shamanic literatures cannot be separated in any strict sense. Without the protectress, he cannot return to life. Facing nether enemies, evil spirits and the powers pervading the singular life, the hero depends on her shamanic activity. Her powers are both vital and erotic and cannot be conquered from the outside. But she knows how to establish working agreements between the sources of energy. She senses the environment to be more than what appears directly and acts on this insight. She recognizes that there are forces that are beyond human ken, yet she also senses that these forces are not just out there, but pulsate through the all. These forces are sensed to be intimately feminine and dangerous. The feminine is seen to be closely attuned to such forces and indeed is a disguised manifestation of them (Muehlmann 1984, 139). The name *shaman* stems from the San skrit word *shamana,* a non-Brahmanic ascetic. This immediately splits into a "house-holder" (*grihasta*) and a homeless wanderer (*sramana*) (Muehlmann 1984, 64). Homelessness as a condition for salvation later became a Buddhist canon. Despite this, the feminine is primordial in all shamanism. Indeed, in places such as Siberia, a woman is believed to be a shaman by nature and hardly needs any instruction. This is to say, a woman is directly rooted in the *arche.* The feminine is a sign of periodicity and the cosmological cycles; being a source of rebirth through the endurance of pain and in face of death, she reflects intimately the silent presence of the origin and can protect everything with her healing presence. Matram, matrix and materia are personified by the feminine and her vital and erotic beauty.

Her other side is the blood lust, the gruesome rituals and demands for heads, for torn flesh and fierce dissolution. One example is the death mask, in which an important female demands to be adorned with someone's head. In Iban, the feast of the war god (Singalang Burong) is postponed because his daughter demands to be adorned with a head for the feast. The head then is "honored" in numerous rituals; the females dance around the head and honor the fallen hero, and demand more heads. This phenomenon appears in numerous guises and places. The Dionysian ladies were not too averse in their blood lust and head hunt. In India, Nepal, Tibet and even Southeast Asia, the divinities are adorned with death heads. Thus, shamanism embodies not only the dissolution into the vitality of strength, into the enduring presence, but also into the vitality of the terrible. Indian goddesses, such as Ilbis Kysa, who were also initiatrixes, are ambiguous. They dance not only on the defeated demons, but also on the defeated husbands. Even love is regarded as a battle and is revealed in a dance that is an intricate play of Maya. Here the Great Kali, the Mahakali, has created the world in a love play and thus is a world player, Lalita. The Mahakali is protectress/destructress in one; she rules over time, Kala, and specifically over the destructive period of time, Kali-Yuga. She is the power of Maya and ties everything to her desires. Here one finds the extensively used metaphor of the spinning and weaving together of life and death (Durante 1968, 286).

The above-suggested modes of reflection on the vital element are given in the form of poetics, which encompasses all rituals, songs, music and sayings. Thus, the lady shamans are songstresses or are accompanied by a songstress whose enchanting songs (canto, cantado, carmen, charmer, charm) make visible and audible the vital source through direct experience. Here is found the Great Vulva as a sage (sayer and seer) who can call up the spirits with the invocation "Know ye more?" and then announce this knowledge. The accompanying song is not yet quite poetry, nor is it literature, but, as part of the shamanic rite, it is a way of revealing the origin and drawing the participants into its core (Muehlmann 1984, 81).

This intimacy is conveyed by poetic sayings; the latter are depictions of the *way* from within the intricacies of the origin. The way metaphor is one of the most pervasive means of rescending reflection. The great songstresses, the feminine sages, know the appropriate sayings that reveal the way (Durante 1968, 281). Such sayings are not directions, but encompass every activity and attitude. Indeed, the source of poiesis and the sayings is feminine. The feminine knows the way and in one manner or another is present as a guide. Every great hero has his guiding and cunning counterpart, exemplified by Odysseus and Athene and by Tristan and Isolde, among others. The greatest protection is needed to return home to the pulsating security of the living. The way is a mode of reflection most suited for deciphering the interconnections between the origin and the female shaman, and how she assumes the function of a protectress.

But the protectress must know the word of the way, and the word does not work in isolation; the word works only in the context of shamanic poiesis. The latter is a unity of rhythm and melos, a singsong recitation with its own vital power. The sound, the toning, is regarded to be the origin of the universe. Thus, Kali, as the great mother Mahasakti, dressed only by space, carries a wreath of death masks around her neck that are "toning signs." In another way, the *aum,* as the first tone, is the creative toning of the cosmos. Indeed, this kind of musical toning is understood all the way to Tristan and Isolde: Her siren, like music, is disruptive, yet her unity with Tristan is consonance, which becomes morality. Even a "rationalist" such as Boethius still spoke of morality as musical, thus requiring practice. Kali extends to Sarasvati, and the latter is a counterpart of Sophia. She is prior to all creation. Her creative instrument is the vina, which is able to resound all tones (*sabda*). Her name also means "a river," similar to a streaming of song. She is wisdom and learning and knows the flow of words. The toning rhythm is the way of the attractive and terrible beauty, which possesses both erotic allurement and bewitching dissolvement.

There is yet another form of reflexivity in shamanism: the ability to change into other life forms. At times, the form of transformation is theatrical, that is, masked dances, mimicry and stylized comportment; at others, it is regarded as taking place in the life of the shaman, as when she takes flight as a bird or attacks as a tigress. In this case, what occurs is a reflection of the vital upon itself: Every event is vitally interconnected in the origin that reflects all other events and can pervade everything (Gebser 1985, 45). The source, the mother, can yield every form and yet is not exhausted by any of them. Of course, to be drawn into the origin, the protecting and encompassing pulse, is to be abolished and only then to become invincible. Behind everyone is the mother, the protectress. Even metaphysicians such as Schopenhauer knew this: The dissolution of the will makes a person invincible.

This invincibility does not rest with an application of proper rules to a specific event in order to master it, but belongs to a precise ritual. In case of dis-ease, the attack is not frontal, but "insinuating." Mastery requires entry into and complicity with the event, becoming the event and outdoing it in accordance with its own ways. This again requires poiesis. Such a way is a reflection on the "hidden will," which is recounted not in choices, but in melodies and dances. The history of such a will should be written not along choices, ends/means, but in terms of excitements, cunning, insinuation, entrapment, tensions, charms, music, implorings, explosivity and indeed the "material" side or "maternal" substance. Modern psychology, apart from a few daring souls such as Nietzsche and Dostoevski, has obscured this history of the will and has made it into prose or an aesketic transcendence of the force of life. Yet the ritualistic, self-dissolving and cathartic will is also willing and forming. This is the reflective immediacy prior to prose. Indeed, the latter is a mere shadow of the alluring beauty of the former.

Vital power comes from her, and, thus, she is superior to him; she courts him and stands next to him in battle. This is regarded not as physical power, but as *sakti,* an intimate power that insinuates and defeats by an inner reflection. In erotic images, this power takes two paths: the banning, tabu, the ascetic, and the demand for erotic encounter and surrender. In Burma, Nat-Shamanism has become an alternative to Buddhistic asceticism. The Nats and their female shamans are seen as having a wild marriage without any respect for the rules of matrimony. They not only teach the young to be erotic, but also teach the art of war. Thus, the she-shaman is the initiatrix of the young and assumes the highest status as Sophia, Prajnaparamita or Tara. Even Parmenides, guided by the sun maiden, is moving toward the goddess to receive instruction about truth and deception. One should be cognizant that Parmenides is a *mystes* and is engaged in a shamanic journey. His Proomion, as poesis, is a journey within shamanic tradition. Thus, his *ennoia* (thought, knowledge) is also *pronoia,* a pre-vision; both originate in shamanic experience. In Hebrew, there is Chokma; she is there by his side before the world and during its creation. Without these ladies, the world would not be what it is. Since the Greek, Buddhist, Hebraic and other wisdom ladies are not dry twigs of impotent logic, their episteme is an adventure, a psycho-physiological trip from which one does not return unshorn and fearful of its dangers. One must learn that wisdom and courage are in love with one another. This Sophia motif is expressed in the Mahayana Buddhism; it is related to the cosmology where Buddha is the father and Prajnaparmita the mother; yet it is she who has "complete wisdom" and is depicted both grammatically and pictorially in feminine gender (Muehlmann 1984, 22). This is Shaktistic gnosis. The male must open up to the feminine without restrictions in order to abolish the transcending and impotent reflection and to become pervaded by the patience, vitality and healing of the feminine. Her beauty is not some pious look, an image of innocence, but a self-rejuvenating and indefatigable vitality.

The protectress and the initiatrix have their counterpart in their blood-lusting carnage. Thus, the shamans are more feared than loved. They are simultaneously foreboding, intriguing and dangerous: *What is the hottest fire? The sense of a woman between two men. What is faster than wind? The thought of a woman between two men.* In a Tantric text, the following is asked: Which man knows the heart of a woman?" The answer is offered to us: "Only Shiva knows the heart of a yogin; but who, after all, is Shiva?" The blood lust appears in such figures as Ilbis among the Jakuts. *Ilbis* means bewitchment, magic, deceit, lust to kill—in brief, "carnage." Most figures depicted in shamanic literature that are capable of initiating maladies are feminine. The unholy and its harbingers are her signs. Yet, peculiarly, the feminine can also counteract this carnage. The female shaman can bring about revenge for suppression during her lifetime. The revenge is understandable in light of the suppression of matriarcha by patriarchy and its hierarchy. The misdeeds of Medea are not just her doing; Jason is equally guilty. Thus, she can drive one to madness and revenge, but can also neutralize such drives and bring about peace. In turn, the blood lust can be transferred to the male and can lead to wars and carnage. This reflective rescendence wreaks havoc with the male effort at reflective transcendence. Among numerous examples would be the efforts of Shiva to perform *tapas,* to transcend and become detached from the "terrestrial enticements" only to find *kama,* or the force that troubles him and brings about a return to the feminine embrace.

Female shamans are regarded as young and unwilting, as vital and irresistible, yet revengeful. Thus, the efforts to abolish them have been drastic, as witnessed in medieval Christianity. But even burning could not abolish their vitality and return for revenge (Daly 1978, 292). What is equally interesting is that even wars are associated with the feminine. The magnetic Helena, Gullveig and Mayana are the reasons for war. Here the feminine is idealized as holy, bright and adored, and yet she causes and sanctions war. Sophocles' Aphrodite is not only Kypris, but also an incessant power and strife without end, a maddening storm (Lyssa Manias) and forceful demand. She is also Hades. More fearsome is Dojoji, who appears in a Noh play. She is pursuing nymphomaniacally a Buddhist monk who runs and hides under a sacred bell. The bell, as a sign of pure manly teaching, should protect him. Yet the bell sinks on top of him, and she, turning into a python, coils around it and melts it with her heat and cooks the monk.

Obviously, there is a continuous struggle between rescendence and transcendence. The rescendent reflection is concerned with immersion and surrender to the "logic" of life with all of its storms and vicissitudes, a beauty that is equally soothing/inviting and terrifying/dissolving. This reflectivity appears in figures that teach not a logic of analysis, but a logic of participatory experience with nothing guaranteed except being sullied by life. The Buddhists and the Hindus have fascinating and graphic depictions of this domain, with all of its entrapments, rewards and punishments. The signs of feminine beauty point to such a life.

TRANSCENDING REFLECTION

One of the first signs of this reflection is a specific kind of sacrifice that is distinguishable from the fructification ritual. The transcending sacrifice has at least two moments: placation and the surrender of something to which one is extremely attached. Such forms comprise a movement away from dissolution and submersion into the immediacy of life. In placation, one does not aim at atonement for guilt; rather, it represents powerlessness in the face of some inescapable force or attraction. Here tabu is beyond good and evil; yet, at the same time, it is an all-pervasive dimension, which reflects across everything that is to be avoided. Sacrifice is a defense against being submerged or drawn in and incorporated into the irresistible beauty. In some cases, this form of sacrifice can turn to radical virulence and a call for the sacrifice of those who manifest beauty, although the latter is considered to be demonic, decadent, and evil (Daly 1978, 180). The purification signs enhance and maintain transcending reflection bent on providing a way of becoming detached from the allurements of the erotic and vital beauty and its threats. Such efforts appear mainly in prophetic and patristic mythologies. This may include sacral secularisms such as Marxism, technocratism and historicism, all of which proclaim that the immediacy of life must be sacrificed for some future vision of the good, the true and the valuable.

Transcending immediacy reflects various facets, including the inadequacy of the world and society and the need to succumb to the transcending movement. Such rituals reveal the fascination and attachment to the dissolution by rescendence. To establish edicts, laws, prohibitions and rules is to establish an extremely strong attachment to, and recognition of, what one attempts to transcend. Every detail of the rescending danger is reflected in the laws and prohibitions. The laws offer an opposite movement to the "ways" that comprise the reflective understanding of the shamanic domain. Thus, she allows transcendence insofar as there is a way back to life. The transcending reflection reveals an escape from the dimension of dissolution and thus reflects all the traps by positing prohibitions and edicts. The prohibitions reveal what is there as dangerous and inaccessible. Thus, the escape demands, as mentioned above, the sacrifice of the very traps that are enticing. The violent mortifications of the flesh of Middle Eastern religions, and the Eastern Orthodox extensions, provide examples of this movement. This model embodies reflective immediacy; the law or prohibition is written in the flesh and directly excises the enticements. A peculiar limit is imposed on this reflective immediacy: Only one side of dissolving rituals is allowed—the painful. While in such rituals both pain and pleasure, joy and suffering, are intermingled at an ultimate level of intensity and fire, in the transcending edicts only the pain of excising is appreciated (Lingis 1989, 168). Here joy is found in release from, and in the face of, obedience to the law.

A milder form of transcendence is an ascetic sacrifice. In this form, the human does not relinquish what he has or has power over, but rather foregoes possessions, desires, and passions that he or she has or might want to possess. Examples are fasting and celibacy, monasticism and isolation. Tensions arise between the being that transcends the sensuous life and calls for ascetic practice and the dimension that contains the plenum of solicitations to be surrendered. The logic of this tension pervades various reversals of a precarious balance that can topple at any moment. The attractions that one must surrender have to be designated negatively as "evil, low, hateful." The transcendent being, accordingly, must then be regarded as "lovable, good, high" and, at the same time, reveal the hateful negativity of the dissolving domain of maternal bewitchment.

This designation can become virulent and destroy the solicitous domain in order to become totally free from it. Also, reflective transcendence may be endangered by turning it into an object of hate and deprecation. Thus, one lives ambiguously. She, the erotic fiend, wants to devour me, to dissolve my uprightness, my self; she must be resisted, and any surrender, a most desirable way out, becomes attached to an ambivalence: wanting and rejecting and hating simultaneously the very attraction to reject rescendence and transcendence. This experience is painful, yet in the transcendence of it, a sacrifice is made that is worthy because it represents a denial of the attraction. Accordingly, she will be seen and will have to see herself as ugly and sinful. This is the juncture at which morality emerges, thereby teaching only the feminine the virtues and prohibitions that man has already inscribed in his flesh in order to demonstrate his worth. Now she must become beautiful and pure in terms of his designation.

One such inscription afflicting the feminine is a settled marriage, a monogamy in which she is coded with prohibitions for herself and for others. This has two reflective moments: first, a rejection of the all-pervasive dissolution, the earthy pull; and, second, its control and transcendence. This comprises a shift that leads to a reversal of reflection. What once reflected reverence, reverie, holiness and wholesome beauty is now being restricted and sacrificed not as something that enhances fruitfulness, but as something decrepit. Patriarchy is this limiting and lowering force. The maternal/feminine origin is no longer celebrated, and her wisdom is defaced by a transcending reflection: The once terrible beauty of the hetare becomes an ugly, polluting prostitute, selling herself in order to obtain a dowry.

This shift is expressed in mythologies where the change is away from the stress on origin and toward an emphasis on salvation. Salvific transcendence is the reflective moment that not only rejects, but also demonizes the origin, the maternal and the vital. The she-fiend holds him down, back and entrapped in a sway of dissolution and playful reverie without a name. Her terrible beauty is demonized. Was it not James Bakker who proclaimed that the lady entrapped him by being a servant of the demonic? The aesketic salvation is a movement from mythos to logos, from immersion in the cosmic sway to the metaphysical logocentrism of univocity, restriction and limitation.

Contemplation, as one mode of reflection, practiced by such mythological figures as Shiva, is most revealing. In masculine depiction, Shiva is striving to liberate himself by transcending the immersion in the maternal dissolution. The guiding signposts along the way of this move are detachment, nonparticipation, purity and science. Yet one must recognize that the signposts signify two structures: (1) a singularization, centering on univocal signs such as soul, mind and spirit, all being substantial, yet pure and untainted, by the dissolving flesh; and (2) a convergence with, metaphysically speaking, purity itself—pure light, pure bliss and purity that is beyond description. One encounters here the entire Platonic tradition of pure beauty, ranging from monasticism to scientific rationality. The dissolving eros, the beauty of the sensuous and vital is mastered, subdued and dismissed. And yet eros returns in the rituals of rebirth, the deadly sacrifices for salvation, the rites of rejuvenation, the resurrection of the dead and the ejection from the earth's womb.

In some cases, the salvific reflection requires degradation. The ejected son is not what gives rebirth; the earth, the dark tomb, allows him to emerge into the light. And he represents a transcending detachment of the soul from the dirt of the earth. Here, in the cases of such sons as Jesus, Gilgamesh, and others, the very birth is ascetic, untainted by the soil of passion; the father did not even touch the mother. It may be said in all fairness that he was equally afraid to be drawn into the sway of dissolution and experience the loss of the transcending aeskesis. And the son? He, too, is pure and lives ascetically. Indeed, he is the sign of transcending reflection and demands aeskesis of everyone. The son is not the one who gives rebirth or lends attractiveness to erotic reverie. Reborn by ejection, by extraction from mother earth, he is a transcending reflection destined for a world of aeskesis. This salvific move abandons the rescending reflectivity to its nether demons of kama, eros, passion and libido. All that is voluptuous, passionate, tempted and tempting, wild, luscious and growing is signified with a stigma of foreboding and forbidding.

The patristic/prophetic conceptions, reflecting on a life of salvific release, were also signs of the feminine dominating the masculine. The pagans, such as the Greeks, mixed the two reflectivities for a long time. What is of note is the appearance of signs that restrict the maternal principle. Hetarism is replaced by the cult of marriage: Demeter slowly turns into a goddess who directs the feminine eros along the paths of marriage. Indeed, her cult turns into a state holiday where married women must "abstain" for nine days. This asceticism is foreign to the mother cults. Coextensive with such restrictions, one discovers the disruption of Dyonisian reveries by orphic mysteries, where the birth from corporeity is degraded and the soul is divine and imprisoned within the body. The body is a "grave" of the soul, and the latter can be "liberated" from the prison only through aeskesis. It has been documented that the orphic tradition extends all the way to romanticism, thus revealing these two moments of reflectivity to be in constant tension (Rehm 1972). Be that as it may, there emerges a striving to reflect upon and transcend the reverie, the erotic corporeity. The creative origin is shifted toward salvific purity. The cultic orgiastic reverie is transformed from erotic dissolution into a sort of decadent pastime of a Roman hero. Regarding the erotic reverie, he is biologically cynical. By transcendent reflection, yielding pure episteme and practical sophistication, knowledge is acquired about how things work. Although the female might show up at spring/Easter rites, Mary is already regarded as a "natural creature" who is mortal and fallible. Christostomus was no longer held back from calling her "despicable as all women," while Epiphanus and Nestor are firmly set against any mother/Mary cult. In this context, the verdict of Luther against some of the papal rites is completely understandable. How can one make Mary divine: a most gruesome superstition. Calvin concurred. Here is a turn to Paulinism and the prophetic/salvific reflectivity of transcendence. The erotic flesh is dirty, although biologically unavoidable. Consequently, all reverie is replaced by barren walls and a stern mien. Punishment without warmth, boring and dull, extends the medieval monasticism across entire populations.

This is the consequence of the transcending reflection in its salvific form: Everything is denigrated in the face of a presumed "higher unity." This salvific transcendence has two forms, one religious and the other secular. Both seem to converge in the effort to be extricated from the origin, the source and the material and to attain a salvation in a future "higher state."

INTERREFLECTIVITY

Supplication is a religious conception, while melting into unity is an erotic one. This eroticism appears in religion when one wants to melt either into an origin or into a transcendent unity. Conversely, in order to achieve a distance, and retain an identity, in the face of the object of attraction, one engages in supplication that elevates and lowers the supplicant. This is a dual reflectivity that involves both the transcending and the rescending movements. The love of the supplicant mixes love and fear, and even hate, attraction and rejection. It might take on a strong ascetic form, which, while attractive, requires distance in order to avoid being engulfed by the "flames."

The eroticism of supplication in the West appears in a very intense form in the twelfth century. As far as can be determined, it emerged at the papal palace of Avignon. Spreading throughout Europe, it led to the mannerisms of gallantry and reached its banal state in Rococo. In historical annals, this cultural form of mixed reflection was designated as *mine* (courtly love). Seen for so long with disgust, the feminine is suddenly elevated to become an object of supplication—indeed to such an extent that the male saw his value as stemming only from this elevated person. She became a goddess after centuries of being a demon. In their love lyrics, men addressed their "beloved" in terms that regarded the male as a slave and vassal of a lady. Even emperors and kings were no exception. This seems to be a reflective compensation, which always required an origin from which transcending reflection would acquire its impetus.

But what type of origin? What form did it assume in order to be accepted? She does not embody force, dissolving creativity, reverie and a rebirth of life. She is untouchable. Some examples can be offered. Jaufre, an aristocrat in love with a baroness of Tripoli, has, in fact, never seen her. This is regarded as the "true love" of detachment, where the woman is loved more the farther she is removed from the lover. Thus, the priest Andreas wrote about this kind of love by differentiating between *amor* and *drudaria* and thus detached "genuine love" from the "love of melting." One does not love if one is shaken by passion (Devereux 1972). According to the Leys d'Amors (laws of love), stemming from the fourteenth century, it is inappropriate for the supplicant to ask for a kiss from his lady. After all, a kiss requires an embrace, and the latter is erotic and leads not only to the rescending reflectivity, but also to a "loss of genuine love." As Peirol suggests, one should doubt that in such an embrace the lover still loves genuinely. Of course, marriage must also be rejected as a place of love. There cannot be genuine love between marital partners. As Fauriel points out, if a man were to behave toward his wife like a knight toward his lady, he would be acting counter to marriage. This is to say, marriage was rejected not because one advocated free love, but because one rejected immediacy and unity. The greater the distance, the greater her pure and elevated beauty. The terrible beauty is made impotent. In fact, the *mine* love was usually a love for a lady who was married, thus maintaining the distance required for purity.

Although one finds here a "salvific" and "pure" motive that would characterize the transcending reflection, one also discovers a movement toward erotic beauty that is held safely in the distance. This safety is seen in the elevation of Mary, who, until then, was still regarded as Theotokos (mother of god). But now she becomes madonna and thus loses her erotic attraction. From maternal, birthing feminine, she is transformed into a point that shines with "purity." She is no longer a force of nature and nurture, but a counterpoint of salvific reflectivity. What is found is a movement where there appears a divinization of eroticism, albeit in the form of safe religiosity and even metaphysics. The madonna cult, with erotic supplication coupled with a separation from the feminine, reveals the duality of being saved from and enticed by the pure beauty of the feminine. This, of course, is very different from the reverence for Mary of earlier periods, where maternity, birth and rebirth were more influential. After all, the maternal goddess is approached by women as an equal and a natural force, while the supplicant relates to the madonna as a man to the untouchable. Indeed, no woman painted the madonna, and no woman invented the convent.

The melting contains both forms of the salvific principle: In the cultic eroticism, it reflects the terrible beauty of the maternal attraction and resistance, feminine encompassment and the fear of loss of the self, while throughout supplication, attachment is sought from a distance. Although the latter seems to be safer, it nonetheless constitutes a positive negation and a source of demonization of the feminine. One expression of this attraction to feminine encompassment, and yet maintenance of a safe distance, is mysticism. One seeks salvation not by supplication of a divinity, but by an effort to melt into it. Such an ekstatic melting is an expression of a deflected and yet a safe mode of attachment to the maternal origin. Thus, the Mystical salvation is a search from a hidden place for the origin. Transcendent reflection of mystical unity becomes the obverse of unity with the origin. This is the ambivalent logic that allows the divinization and demonization of feminine beauty. She can become a purified object of adoration or a polluted object of debasement.

The mystical melting motive appears quite obviously in mass reveries, where the so-called religious fervor reaches such an exalted pitch of unity with the one that it turns into an erotic orgy with the feminine origin. Thus, mystical religiosity, with its salvific unity, fulfills itself in the erotic unity of the origin. One reflects the other. This mode of experience appears among the Indian sects of Shakti and Cainonya, in the Judeo-Christian Sarabaists (fourth through ninth centuries), the Nikolaists, the Adamites, the Valesianists, the Kinites, the Koeningsberger Pietists (eighteenth century), the Foxians of Hydesville, England (1901) and the Theocratic Unists in the United States.

POSTSCRIPT

The reflective interplay supplies various parameters within whose confines feminine beauty, both as a force of dissolving attraction and as a purified repulsion, plays out its destiny. The Western patriarchical tradition has a tendency toward transcending reflection, thereby deflecting the terrible beauty of the feminine by nonparticipation, ideality of law, purification, individuation, monasticism and celibacy. While there are rescending movements in some Western mythologies, such as mysticism, materialism and, above all, psychoanalysis, such movements tend toward purification that has the characteristics of transcendence. In this sense, one can understand the appearance, in this century, of various countermovements that are "speechless," although they represent the rescending domain: cynicism, flaunting of the flesh, negative dialectics and even consumerism, with its submersion into the sea of materialism, that is, maternity (the terms *mother* and *matter* have the same origin). Every materialist is seeking a dissolution into the maternal rhythm, pulse and security. This is not a wish to return to the womb, but a broader design of rescendence toward dissolution. The appearance of rescendence in numerous guises is a sign that transcendence nowadays might, too, become a reflection on rescendence, a reflection whose shape is yet to be deciphered.

Some discussions in semiotics have indeed confirmed the two reflective moments and their variants. Following Merleau-Ponty, for example, one has located a pivot that constitutes a shift from sense to non-sense and from non-sense to sense. The signs that function as sense deploy structures with coordinates, thus maintaining objects at a distance, transcendent in appropriate places and times: in front/future, behind/past, up/good, down/bad, left/right, peopled by formal codes of appropriate attunement, attire, deference and hierarchical status. Yet these signs are constantly haunted by an overdetermination, a superfluity that disrupts the intentional univocity of signs. This superfluity is a source of metaphorical deviation that never succeeds in reasserting univocity, which deconstructs and postpones a signifying function and leads to the dissolution of such a function. The signifying distance, the transcending intentionality, collapses under the weight of imagery that does not represent or stand for deployed objects, but becomes immediate, obsessive and insistent and fires images and phantasms that constitute a melting body without a world, without significance. A French example is eroticism. Within a semiotics of signs, eros signifies and has intentions: an aim at an object, another human, a divinity, even the reproduction of the species. Yet eros also functions to dissolve distances and becomes whispers, breaths, gropings and the spreading of images that are erotic. These images chase one after another and decompose any signifying posture, thus melting the unitary being into a swamp of breath and moisture and insinuating into all crevices that abolish hierarchies, good and evil, and gods and demons. This is a carnalization that haunts the precincts of signs and exposes them to immediacy and bodiness, which is obsessed with firing and dissolving a flood of phantasms. The result is a melting and vivifying presence.

WORKS CITED

Daly, M. 1978. *Gyn/Ecology.* Boston: Beacon Press.
Devereux, G. 1972. *Ethnopsychanalyse Complementaristes.* Paris: Flammarion.
Durante, M. 1968. Untersuchungen zur Vorgeschichte der Indogermanischen Dichtersprache. In R. Schmitt (ed.), *Indogermanische Dichtersprache* (pp. 261–291). Darmstadt, Germany: Wissenschaftliche Buchgesellschaft.
Gebser, J. 1985. *The Ever-present Origin.* Trans. N. Barstadt and A. Mickunas. Athens: Ohio University Press.
Gimbutas, M. 1991. *The Civilization of the Goddess: The World of Old Europe.* New York: HarperCollins.
Levinas, E. 1981. *Otherwise than Being.* Trans. A. Lingis. The Hague: Martinus Nijoff.
Lingis, A. 1989. *Deathbound Subjectivity.* Bloomington: Indiana University Press.
Muehlmann, W. E. 1984. *Die Metamorphose der Frau.* Berlin: Reimer Verlag.
Rehm, W. 1972. *Orpheus: Der Dichter und Die Toten.* Darmstadt, Germany: Wissenschaftliche Buchgesellschaft.
Schubart, W. 1944. *Religion und Eros.* Munich: C. H. Beck'sche.
Sloterdijk, P. 1983. *Kritik der Zynischen Vernunft.* Frankfurt: Suhrkamp.
Smith, D. E. 1987. Woman's Perspective as a Radical Critique of Sociology. In S. Harding (ed.), *Feminism and Methodology* (pp. 84–97). Bloomington: Indiana University Press.

2

Body Images and the Politics of Beauty: Formation of the Feminine Ideal in Medieval and Early Modern Europe

Ben Lowe

I opened another book, and this seemed of the Hispanic school. The colors were violent, the reds suggested blood or fire. . . . Here the artist had dwelled at greater length on the woman's form. I compared her face, her bosom, her curving thighs with the statue of the Virgin I had seen. . . . The line was different, but this mulier also seemed very beautiful to me. I thought I should not dwell on these notions, and I turned several more pages. I found another woman, but this time it was the whore of Babylon. I was not so much struck by her form as by the thought that she, too, was a woman like the other, and yet this one was the vessel of every vice, whereas the other was the receptacle of every virtue. But the forms were womanly in both cases, and at a certain point I could no longer understand what distinguished them. Again I felt an inner agitation; the image of the Virgin in the church became superimposed on that of the beautiful Margaret. "I am damned!" I said to myself. Or, "I am mad."

—Umberto Eco, *The Name of the Rose* (1983, 241)

In this chapter, gender is assumed to be a social construct. For a historian with formative training in traditional historiography, a nuanced understanding of this fact has been immensely difficult, and yet, for that reason, all the more compelling once realized. History has too often helped reify patriarchical categories of analysis, which accept the Rankean postulate that there is an ultimate truth to be discovered. Only recently has gender as an interpretive framework been theorized sufficiently to permit a small, but growing, number of historians to reconceptualize the past and make it less teleological and centered (Scott 1988; Novick 1988, 491–510).

If there are no definitive explanations for female behavior in the past—

of either biological or ontological foundation—it can become part of the historian's job to "deconstruct" the images of women by unmasking the social and sexual power relationships that created them. As women were most commonly the recipients of cultural norms imposed by patriarchical superstructures, beauty served as a convenient trait that could be strictly defined and monitored and as a means of coercion in Western history that could perpetuate the power relationship that found such controls necessary. But what constitutes beauty in this tradition, and how is it differentiated from the female identity in and of itself? If beauty is an acculturated value based on a temporal, socially created notion of gender, how did it come to be so, and in what manner has it been transformed into more modern images of the feminine?

The following chapter is simply an exploration into some of these crucial questions. By focusing on the classical and medieval constructs that informed, and to a certain degree idealized, specific female behaviors, we can begin to fathom better the metanarrative(s) and discourses that have sought to encapsulate and define feminine beauty in absolutist terms and that, to use Levi-Strauss's phrase, have helped lead to the "reification of women." The integration of these beliefs into a particular European social, political and cultural milieu suggests that they could become so accepted by women and men that frequent recourse to overt, violent coercion became unnecessary.

Certain conditions in medieval and Renaissance Europe mitigated the more extreme forms of misogyny, which adherence to traditional beliefs in female beauty would have produced had they been taken to their "natural" conclusion. Once Europeans invaded other lands previously unknown to them, however, and brought these ideas into preexisting cultures, which possessed no bulwarks against their insistent enthnocentrism, the more unadulterated versions of what female beauty constituted and legitimized in intersexual relations were allowed to flourish unbounded (except for a few religious caveats). It is argued that in these new environments part of the "civilizing process" included denoting impositions of male-directed beautification on women as axiomatic and totally justificatory, the logical and necessary refinements of mature, even progressive, society.

The means for internalizing modern Western concepts of female beauty appear to have remained relatively constant since the Middle Ages, despite the permutations of metanarrative. This assertion can be substantiated in almost any examination of colonialism from the fifteenth century on that analyzes carefully both imperialist policies and the receptions given to them by resistant foreign cultures.

The passage from Eco, whose specialty is medieval aesthetics, demonstrates that images of feminine beauty in early Western thought are complex, sometimes ambivalent and often contradictory; but beneath them lie a few premises and presuppositions about the female body that have remained relatively consistent over time. As the agent of beauty and at the same time the corporeal essence of woman, "exalted by poets, painters, and sculptors, the female body, often reduced to its isolated parts, has been mankind's most popular subject for adoration and myth, and also for judgment, ridicule, esthetic alteration and violent abuse" (Brownmiller 1984, 27).

There is always something imperfect about the female body, which probably originates to a large extent in the biblical portrayal of Eve, the first woman, who represents the sensual, carnal and temptress-like nature of her sex, leading men to sin and unholy sexual relations. Eve's allure is her enticing beauty, which has lust as its basis. With God's curse that she would experience pain in childbirth as a result of eating from the tree of the knowledge of good and evil, right from the start the Judeo-Christian concept for woman is one that inferiorizes and consequently deprives her of control over her own body, including reproductive control. Eve's sin was moral, but it affected her physically. Her naked body was now shameful and needed to be covered, since its exposure would surely lead to unholy sexual relations and provide further means for ensnaring men into sinful ways. Thus, the more rational Adam/man had to restrain her and exercise authority over her.

Ancient Mesopotamian traditions mirror these biblical injunctions in their use of fashion (the now necessarily clothed woman) to sustain patriarchical systems that serve male appropriation of female sexuality. Slaves and harlots should not be veiled because they are not "under one man's protection" and hence are not "respectable." If a slave girl is caught wearing a veil, her clothes are taken away and her ears cut off. As her shame is revealed, she is exposed for what she really is, corrupted flesh. Any latitude women had, therefore, in controlling their lives existed within the parameters of being "sexually and reproductively controlled by men," and this was most obviously demonstrated through such public determinations of the feminine worth (Lerner 1986, 135, 213–15).

This commodification of women's bodies, based on distrust and the assumption that women were in dire need of control because of their greater bent for sinning, formed another basis for the soul/body dualism that dominates the early Christian era. Physical beauty was evil if its attraction was sexual and to the external self (body); it was good if its appeal was spiritual and internal. The former, then, must be subdued, which meant control over all the accoutrements that contributed to its allure. Yet the latter was the product of an inner goodness and a rejection of all vanity. As such, the feminine body became like a piece of clay to be formed, shaped and manipulated in an effort to save the weak female soul.

Early Christian writers believed that the female body must be mortified and asceticized in order to control those wiles that would cause men to desire sex for reasons other than procreation. For this reason, Jerome warned widows and women who can remain pure not to eat meat (which indicates carnal desire) or lie in soft beds. Instead, "let paleness and squalor be henceforth your jewels." He assumed that all women dressed in ways to attract men and that they constantly fantasized about having sex, even with their confessors. Augustine was, of course, even more adamant in this regard, developing fully the notion that the Fall brought lust into the world and profaned the sex act, thereby relegating women to being sex objects for either good (procreative) or bad (carnal) use. Theologians following in his footsteps further depersonalized women, treating them as an "extension of the male body," sometimes even justifying their subordination to men's sexual desires simply because they were responsible for creating those desires in the first place (Ruether 1974, 162–63, 171–72).[1]

The canonists employed the functional construction of female sexuality in a number of self-satisfying ways, finding new, more intricate means for making this dualism seem real and natural in a post-lapsarian world. Hostiensis claimed that women were often ignorant of their flirtatiousness because they were constantly preoccupied with sex. Husbands were necessary to keep women from being whores, and prostitution was tolerated in large measure to keep "those types of women" from profaning the marriage bed (Brundage 1982, 152–53, 156). Hence, beauty subdues what is natural/sexual (soul) and yet is a component of the desire for sexual license (body). True beauty was spiritual and more than the skin-deep type that appealed to men's most base desires.

Of course, gender systems took their cue from these prescriptive formulas regarding the feminine character. By the fourteenth century, women's bodies were construed as inferior versions of men's bodies, or at least in opposition to the primary trait. Following the lead of Aristotle and Gratian, male/female dyads such as reason/emotion, limited/unlimited, square/oblong, straight/curved, and light/darkness helped legitimize and regularize the inferior status of women that found expression in physical appearance (Stuard 1987, 164–68). As the Alexandrian Jewish philosopher Philos proclaimed, therefore, women could only begin to approach male rationality if they denied their sexual nature and remained virgins, leaving that other Christian female prototype, the Virgin Mary, as the great example for all to follow (Bullough 1982, 44–45).

Since women were excluded from the legal discourse that constructed these types, they could not comment on this new, emerging system of gender in which they were inferiorized and subordinated (Stuard 1987, 164–68). As for the men who were building these theories, they believed a woman should find it easier to be virtuous because, as Philip of Navarre stated in the thirteenth century, "if she be a worthy woman of her body, all her other faults are covered, and she can go with a high head" (Travitsky 1981, 4).

Control of the body is, therefore, a fundamental means for enacting social power. But the ideal body that has been dictated from time immemorial can, once realized, begin to attack the basis of power itself and the "moral norms of sexuality" that accompany it. When this occurs, existing power arrangements are not so much delegitimized or transcended as they are likely to retreat for re-creative purposes (Foucault 1980, 55–56). As a result, women and men may feel great ambivalence over the uses of the body and the nature of beauty itself.

Since women are to be passively respondent, Western patriarchies had to develop structures and systems that prevented the physical body from challenging traditional, biblically ordained sex relationships, meaning that there must be manageable outlets for both acceptable and unacceptable beauty images. As a result, representations of the harlot and the virgin are both grafted onto a utilitarian matrix that prevented men from being threatened and subverted by female beauty every time. The dualism is reified and "naturalized" even as it serves primarily as a cognitive expedient. This is what makes Western images of female beauty so difficult to access and elucidate, since the imposition of dominance over the body is often unconscious and unexplainable, if only because it is approached in theoretical terms that emphasize timeless and consistent norms of social power.

To offer a useful paradigm for making these assumptions a bit clearer, it might help to examine more closely the medieval concept of beauty within its wider context, removed from a strict consideration of body images. In the Middle Ages, beauty was seen, above all, as a unified aesthetic that combined both the active and the passive elements of perceived reality. Internal and external beauty were inseparable and yet intelligible in their unity.

Influenced by Plato, Cicero, Augustine and Aristotle's *Rhetoric,* scholastic literature made no distinctions "between beauty (*pulchrum, decorum*) and utility or goodness (*aptum, honestum*)." John of la Rochelle and others found *honestum* (honor or nobility) the essential ingredient in true beauty, for "truth and beauty were . . . both defined in terms of form: truth was the disposition of form in relation to the internal character of a thing; beauty was the disposition of form in relation to its external character." Alexander of Hales insisted that "the good is distinguished from the beautiful by intention. . . . The nature of the beautiful consists in general in a resplendence of form, whether in the duly-ordered parts of material objects, or in men, or in actions" (Eco 1986, 5, 9, 22–26). In this Platonic stance, the form is, therefore, a moral expression of reality, with the most beautiful being the most real.

Returning to the body image as form, Matthew of Vendôme also subscribed to this holistic definition and formulated rules for describing beautiful women in *Ars Versificatoria*. He and Gilbert of Hoyt emphasized moderation and equipoise. The latter specified that "the breasts are most pleasing when they are of moderate size and eminence.... They should be bound but not flattened, restrained with gentleness but not given too much licence" (Eco 1986, 11–16).

Moderation in physical appearance for both men and women has survived as a valued norm in many societies over the centuries, but in the Middle Ages, it was clearly the product of an aesthetic that idealized beauty, while defining it in behavioral terms that were unattainable. If, like Eve, women were considered temptresses by nature, it would only stand to reason that they had an almost uncontrollable power over men through their appearances, which, if unrestrained, could draw men into deep sin. This external beauty, however, was hardest to control and could be regulated only by getting women to attack and punish (or at least sublimate) those physical attributes that led men to sin, and there was no better way to do this than by exacting preferred behaviors from the former. Thus, patriarchical power could be maintained through the idealization of the female body and be given a still firmer basis by always making the ideal unreachable. A strong sense of self-affirmation, therefore, is never permitted to become established enough so as to challenge the ethos that would encourage such.

At this point, by bringing together the elements of early Western beauty images already discussed, significant interrelationships emerge. Beauty as an aesthetic has its idealized forms, but these forms are transformed and utilized (although not devalued) within a Stoico-Judeo-Christian tradition that exalts the weak and imperfect nature of women, so that the forms become ideals that are rigorously applied to women despite their great inability to achieve them.

Within the prevalent gender system of the later Middle Ages, the journey toward a greater mystical correspondence with these forms comes only through the submission to men of the attribute of women that above all others would separate them farther from truth and morality—their beauty. Men must, therefore, possess the female body so completely that physical beauty becomes little more than an imposed affectation—the signifier for legitimate appropriation of the woman (including reproductive control) through an enforced body image. By the fourteenth century, a number of women mystics turned to the ascetic lifestyle, denounced the worldliness and vanity of their physical existence and passionately submitted to the control of religious men. Margery Kempe was almost pathological in her self-abasement and insisted that she could even wear white because God had made her a virgin once again (after having given birth to fourteen children) (Kempe 1985).

If external beauty was to mirror internal beauty, and if men could properly channel female sexuality into so-called productive purposes, then it was incumbent upon men to encourage women to look pleasant and moral, even if in actuality this affected aspect of physical beauty was utilized by men to serve a myriad of other purposes as well. By the time of the Renaissance, women were strongly encouraged to be decorous in their relations with husbands, in spite of their seductive inclinations. Since wives were little more than married harlots whose husbands were saving them from themselves, they should reflect modesty and even chastity outwardly.

Surgical treatises included chapters on "methods of beautification," exhorting women to use cosmetics, creams and depilatories so as to become smooth and agreeable to their husbands. Hair removal was often painful, but this was the price women had to pay for their vanity. It was a fine line often crossed, for when did the obsessive need to "look right" ever become a nonprurient form of vanity? Margery Kempe's spiritually based metamorphosis became available to all women as hair ointments made of ground glass; astringents and dyes now "enabled a woman to simulate virginity" (Braunstein 1988, 599–600). It is that paragon of refined Renaissance taste, Castiglione, who perhaps draws most clearly this connection between outward form and inner self-abasement when he equates feminine beauty and decorum with the responsibility of men to protect women's reputations and to inculcate self-discipline, for

> a loose life does not defame them as it does women, who, due to the frailty of their sex, give in to their appetites much more than men; and if they sometimes refrain from satisfying their desires, they do so out of shame and not because they lack a ready will in that regard. Therefore men have instilled in women the fear of infamy as a bridle to bind them as by force to this virtue, without which they would truly be little esteemed; for the world finds no usefulness in women except the bearing of children. (Castiglione 1959, 241)

Those women who had to work least at being outwardly beautiful, therefore, were assumed to be the most moral and godly. For example, in *Roman de la Rose,* the lady named Beauty, as bright as the moon, outshines all of the other stars because she is neither "painted nor made up." Other women, however, must embellish their appearances, whether it be by sticking hot needles into follicles to remove hair, by using magic powders to bring color to the face or by eating a good breakfast to improve the complexion (Régnier-Bohler 1988, 358–61). Above all, for women it was always propriety and never seduction that should determine appearance. Such a norm led to a certain amount of fetishism, as large breasts were to be bound, thinness hidden by extra clothing, décolletage used appropriately and so on. Echoing a standard theme, Robert of Blois remarked that the essence of female beauty is moral, rather than physical: "A lady acquires a bad reputation if she does not carry herself properly. A careful and agreeable bearing is better than neglected beauty" (Régnier-Bohler 1988, 362–63).

If anything, this formulation of the ideal beauty image found greater expression during the Renaissance and the Reformation. It became a common theme of early modern European popular culture, as exhibited in contemporary German woodcuts such as the 1533 Nuremberg broadsheet *There Is No Greater Treasure Here on Earth Than an Obedient Wife Who Covets Honor* by Albrecht Glockendon, which portrays a victimized husband falling prey to an angry or troublesome wife. These prints, which depicted angry wives, gossips and skinflints as very ugly (with skin that feels like codfish) and encouraged beatings that would further disfigure, gained widespread circulation due to the development of printing (Moxey 1989, 101–15).

English humanist Thomas Elyot wrote at about the same time, in his *The Defence of Good Women,* that truly beautiful women were temperate, gracious and moderate. They were by nature softer and more delicate than men, which made them less perfect (Elyot 1940, 21–22, 32–34, 57). Even though Elyot wrote his treatise against those who would disparage the character of all women, a bit of that disparaging attitude had been prevalent since the tenth century, when the monastic reformer Odo of Cluny remarked:

> The beauty of a woman is only skin-deep. If men could see beneath the flesh and penetrate below the surface with eyes like the Beotian lynx, they would be nauseated just to look at women, for all this feminine charm is nothing but phlegm, blood, humours, gall.... We are all repelled to touch vomit and ordure even with our fingertips. How then can we want to embrace what is merely a sack of rottenness? (Warner 1985, 251)

For women of medieval and early modern Europe, beauty was, therefore, not so much a physical trait as a behavioral one, tied to the twin notions of morality and moderation. The truest beauty was found in the ideal life of the virgin, with the wife who let her husband control her sexuality also finding begrudged acceptance. [This did change somewhat with the Reformation. Both Martin Luther and John Calvin tended to disparage the holy ideal of virginity and found greater virtue in the moral, obedient Christian wife (Davis 1975, 81; Wiesner 1988).]

All the same, outward appearance was a reflection of the inner self and, as such, needed to be maintained properly through behavior modification, as it was more readily controllable and then likely to be reflected externally. Those women who were incorrigible (prostitutes, adulterers, etc.) were left to their moral and physical ugliness and legitimately abused for their depravity. Not under the protection of men, they could be stripped, reviled and shamed, even to the point of being sexually violated. Yet in Renaissance Europe, forms of social coercion were so deeply embedded in the culture that patriarchical power and submission of body images to that power were recognized with little overt resistance. For most women, the body stayed clothed, and the overall feminine appearance remained morally pleasing.

There were ways also for women to manipulate contemporary beauty images somewhat by accepting outwardly the patriarchical determinations of what constituted beauty and then fashioning individual identities within these parameters.[2] This was especially true for middle- and upper-class women. Yet, as stated, certain aspects of physical beauty were beyond the control of men. Because Christian theology provided a protective dignity for women, which worked against unrestrained violence to them due to features that were beyond their control, and from which God provided redemption (although a harsh one at that), it is often difficult to fathom the extent to which prevailing beauty images penetrated and affected Western culture. The steady movement from the flesh to an emphasis on behavior, which during the Counter Reformation found its greatest expression in the confessional's growing control over that behavior, also muted the more outward forms of misogyny, as gradually a more inward control was being developed (Foucault 1990, 18–19). In addition, women were being encouraged all the time to display such virtues as chastity and modesty, which, when exhibited, might afford situations where they could be treated relatively well. For these reasons, it would be instructive to conclude this discussion with a look at how attitudes about feminine beauty were imposed on women who were not Christian, who were not cognizant of or in conformity with European paradigms and who were even more powerless and unprotected in their ability to withstand not only a superimposed alien gender system, but also a rampant cultural imperialism. It is in the conquest of the Americas that we can find such an "uncluttered" milieu.

From the time of Columbus's first voyage to the New World, when the admiral noticed the Amerindian women's "very pretty bodies," the most commented upon attribute of the new people was their nakedness (Morison 1963, 128). As the body is the agent of beauty, whether one wears clothes or not was the clearest manifestation of either acceptable or unacceptable body images in the Western world at the time overseas explorations were undertaken. We have already seen the degradation associated with female nakedness, a condition that resulted from women's uncontrollable lust and attachment to the body. Contemporary European views on nudity connected clothes with civilization; the absence of clothing was a sign of anarchy. A naked man in public was seen as a destroyer of order, while a naked woman was always associated with "nascent or confirmed desire." Once again, it was the male prerogative to contain the depraved nature of the female, and so "female nudity was explicitly linked to the affirmation of manly power." If clothing was a metaphor for civilization, men, being more rational by nature, could violently strip women to expose their beastliness, and if, in so doing, the men give in to their desires, they are not really at fault, for the women are undeserving of any better treatment (Régnier-Bohler 1988, 367–72).

Stories proliferated in Renaissance Europe of men and emperors who did just that, ordering women to be unclothed before them so the women would suffer humiliation for their lechery. European artists used female nudity to teach Christians the evils of carnality. In many Gothic church sculptures, lust is signified by a naked woman who suffers for her sin by having snakes devour her genitals and breasts. According to the *Malleus Maleficarum,* the late medieval guidebook on witches, as Eve used her naked body to tempt man to sin, women's bodies were "beautiful to look upon, contaminating to touch, and deadly to keep." But nudity can also display imperfections of the body more readily, and representations of old hags with poison dripping from their breasts and sixteenth-century tombstones depicting the body victimized by worms were quite common (Warner 1985, 295–99).

It is understandable, then, why the first European men to notice the naked Amerindian women considered them beastly and in need of domestication, while at the same time they feared them for their supposedly uncontrollable urges and egalitarian customs. The most famous and thorough of the early reports of Amerindian women (gaining much greater circulation than Columbus's descriptions of his discoveries) came from Amerigo Vespucci's *Mundus Novus,* published first around 1504–05. Vespucci's account fixates on the nudity of the natives, especially the women. The writer clearly ties together European notions of cultural superiority and the prevalent perceptions about the disorderliness of naked beauty, so that while Amerindian customs appear harmless on the outside, they lead inevitably to a multitude of heinous sins. A lengthy quotation from this work is thus warranted:

> All of both sexes go about naked, covering no part of their bodies; and just as they spring from their mothers' wombs so they go until death.... They are comely, too, of countenance which nevertheless themselves destroy; for they bore their cheeks, lips, noses and ears. Nor think those holes small or that they have one only.... For women do not bore their faces, but their ears only. They have another custom, very shameful and beyond all human belief. For their women, being very lustful, cause the private parts of their husbands to swell up to such a huge size that they appear deformed and disgusting....

> ... They live together without king, without government, and each is his
> own master. They marry as many wives as they please and son cohabits with
> mother, brother with sister, male cousin with female, and any man with the
> first woman he meets.... They live according to nature. (Berkhofer 1978,
> 7–8)

Here the explorer draws a clear link between the nudity of the natives
and a society that knows no bounds of sexual depravity, all of which causes
them to live in a lawless, anarchic way, bestial in their inability to over-
fjcome animalistic behavior as civilized Europeans did long ago. But such
a view, while castigating this immediately obvious trait of Amerindian
culture, is laid alongside the natural beauty of the women, which the writer
declares was deformed through pagan practices, all to enhance their bodies
for carnal pleasures, since they are without doubt "very lustful" and sod-
omites (Crosby 1972, 10). Vespucci goes on to recount the ineffective attempts "to dissuade them to desist from these depraved customs," yet
"when they had the opportunity of copulating with Christians, urged by
excessive lust, they defiled and prostituted themselves" (Berkhofer 1978,
9).

Throughout his description, the explorer develops what would become
a justification for all sorts of ill treatments of Amerindian women by European men. Their beauty is obviously of the carnal type and finds its fullest
expression in nakedness, since only women of unusual lust would live their
lives unclothed. Their world was so disorderly and without restraint that
they were not under the consistent supervision of Amerindian men, who
were themselves unequipped to contain properly their own lust (Scammell
1989, 187–88). When sin entered the world, God forced Eve to cover her
nakedness and shame, but these pagans were instead flaunting their depravity, proving that they were by nature nothing more than prostitutes.
As in Europe, such women became fair game, as if rape or other abuse
was their just reward.

For the early explorers, who had been separated from women for quite
some time, the ability to indulge their sexual urges with native women
proved almost too much to handle. For example, one of Columbus's ship-
mates, Michele de Cuneo, gave this astounding account, in the earliest
existing evidence of sexual relations between the two cultures:

> While I was in the boat I captured a very beautiful Carib woman whom the
> said Lord Admiral gave to me, and with whom, having taken her into my
> cabin, she being naked according to their custom, I conceived desire to take
> pleasure. I wanted to put my desire into execution but she did not want it
> and treated me with her finger nails in such a manner that I wished I had
> never begun. But seeing that (to tell you the end of it all), I took a rope
> and thrashed her well, for which she raised such unheard of screams that
> you would not have believed your ears. Finally we came to an agreement

in such manner that I can tell you that she seemed to have been brought up in a school of harlots. (Morison 1963, 212; see also Sale 1990, 140)

Amerindian women could be subjugated in the most violent and cruel manner, since they had not been socialized to conform to European ideals about beauty images and the submissive behaviorial norms that such represent.

While nudity was the essence and source of much comment about the physical appearance of native women, the descriptions betray an overall feeling that the bodies of pagans are so corrupt that the body itself is completely desacrilized, for these men and women have no basis for believing that the body is God's holy temple. Inevitably, nakedness must, therefore, lead to other forms of deviance and bodily profanity, most notably cannibalism. This is the natural consequence of their sexual license according a Dutch pamphlet from 1511–12, which was also published in English:

> But all thinges is comune/this people goeth all naked. But the men and women have on theyr heed/necke/Armes/knees/and fete all with feders bounden for there bewtynes [beautiness]. . . . These folke lyven lyke bestes without any resonablenes and the wymen be also as comon. And the men hath conversacyon with the wymen/who that they ben or who they fyrst mete/is she his syster/his mother/his daughter/or another kyndred. And the wymen be very hoote and dysposed to lecherdnes. And they ete also on[e] another[.] The men eteth his wyfe[,] his chylderne/as we also have seen and they hange also the bodyes or persons fleeshe in the smoke/as men do with swynes fleshe. (Berkhofer 1978, 9–10)

With this sort of propaganda being spread and enhanced more with each telling, it is no wonder the European explorers believed that any treatment of native women would be preferable to that which they were already receiving. A number of woodcuts, accompanying Vespucci's works and those of others like him, offered in horrifying detail the nonchalant cannibalism of these depraved beings. Between 1503 and 1515, the illustrated *Mundus Novus* was published in France, Germany, England, Italy, the Netherlands and Portugal. The powerful naked women who were ready to strike Europeans with heavy clubs were in sharp contrast to the domesticated, modest women of the Old World (Honour 1975, 10–11).

One other aspect of feminine appearance was also interpreted in Eurocentric fashion. For the English colonists in North America, the practice of Amerindian women painting their bodies was particularly abhorrent. Preachers often censured women either for doing this or for engaging in other forms of "excessive adornment." The belief that these customs were clearly inspired by the devil and associated with the magic arts found expression in Thomas Tuke's *Treatise Against Painting and Tincturing of*

Men and Women (1616). Tuke claimed that the natives were obviously bestial for continuing to practice body painting, suggesting that all cosmetics "doe ill become the *bodies of Saints,* which are *Temples* of the Holy Ghost" (Sheehan 1980, 48–50). According to the unitary aesthetic, which had developed in Europe and was based on a transcendant body/soul dualism, such ostentation was immodest and prurient and revealed a soul given over to evil. The external form clearly matched the internal self, and the more unusual, grotesque and repulsive the "adornment," the more reviled and dehumanized its wearer. Other European commentators found these corrupted female bodies responsible for a virtual panorama of ills, from the introduction of syphilis into Europe (also due to the sin of European men who had sexual relations with them) to the lack of resistance to other diseases such as the pox (Kupperman 1980, 59–62; Foa 1990, 33).

Yet there was much about Amerindian society and culture that simply angered Europeans, who were looking to establish their institutions, religion, norms, mores and customs in a land they had to find "legitimate" means (of course, within European parameters) for appropriating. Amerindian women did not fit into their perceptions of what the female figure should be, and as emphasized throughout this discussion, that centered largely on behavior; true beauty had a submissive character to it. In fact, Englishmen were surprised and put out to find that native women were assuming what they believed to be male duties, such as carrying heavy packs of household items on journeys. Also, there seemed to be too much equality and too little deference on their part to class distinctions, which existed everywhere in Europe and were assumed to be part of the natural order of civilization (Axtell 1985, 138). Amerindian women also appeared more modest than traditional European females, and most men found this hard to incorporate into their sex-beauty images, which stressed congruence between prescriptive outward appearance and inward behavior. The cultural tension that resulted challenged attempts at fashioning a normative discourse with respect to gender and has become a specter "haunting" Western colonialism ever since. The cognitive dissonance these uncomfortable dichotomies created should not be understated. As was true in the case of Cuneo's rape, for the most part the "lustful" native women resisted with all of their might unwanted sexual advances by European men (Salisbury 1982, 40, 121).

European men were often frustrated in their inability to control either the inner or the outer expressions of beauty, which had become such an integral part of patriarchical sex relationships in Europe. In one classic example, the attempt by the Spanish conquerors to implant the cult of the Virgin in the New World, along with the panoply of sex/body images that accompanied it, met with both fierce opposition and indifference from many Amerindian women. The response to this disinterest was one of shock and disorientation, and the words spoken in 1590 by one of the disappointed missionaries, José de Acosta, say it all: "How great and al-most divine is the honour which all other peoples pay to virginity, these beasts consider it to be all the more dispicable and ignominious." He goes on to recount all kinds of sexual license among the hard-hearted Peruvi-ans, whose women have sex with men for "many days and months" before bothering to get married (Boxer 1975, 108).

This discussion has shown how beauty images in medieval and early modern Europe were the products of a longstanding patriarchical gender system, how the body and its deportment were the most obvious and con-trollable manifestations of that system and how such power arrangements were maintained and strengthened through contact with an uncooperative culture that did not have the technological means to resist effectively. Of course, the tremendous social, economic, political, intellectual and cultural changes in Europe after 1100 provided much of the context for why beauty images became more concrete and socialization became so much more important. For that first generation of contact with Amerindian women, such internalization of gender subjection was nearly impossible, but for European imperialists, their ability to enforce this code eventually, either through acculturation or through violence (removing the nonconformists), helped to create an even greater sense of their correctness. As Joan Kelly demonstrated in her seminal essay, women really did not have a Renais-sance, but we can add that in being increasingly controlled by a gender system that included appropriation of the body and its appearance, they lost not just their public voices, but much of their private voices, too (Kelly-Gadol 1987; Ferrante 1988).

NOTES

The author would like to thank Catharine Randall Coats for reading a draft of this chapter and offering a number of helpful suggestions.

1. Because Eve was created out of Adam's rib, most theologians regarded women, after the Fall, as further removed from God than men were.

2. Recently some historians have sought to identify patterns of resistance among European women at this time, proving that exclusion from political and social discourse did not mean the complete absence of female "voice" or autonomy. See, for example, C. W. Bynum, 1987, *Holy Feast, Holy Fast: The Religious Significance of Food to Medieval Women* (Berkeley: University of California Press); J. C. Brown, 1986, *Immodest Acts: The Life of a Lesbian Nun in Renaissance Italy* (New York: Oxford University Press).

WORKS CITED

Axtell, J. 1985. *The Invasion Within: The Contest of Cultures in Colonial North America.* New York: Oxford University Press.

Berkhofer, R. F. 1978. *The White Man's Indian: Images of the American Indian from Columbus to the Victorians.* New York: Alfred A. Knopf.

Boxer, C. R. 1975. *Mary and Misogyny: Women in Iberian Expansion Overseas, 1415–1815.* London: Duckworth.

Braunstein, P. 1988. Toward Intimacy: The Fourteenth and Fifteenth Centuries. In G. Duby (ed.), *A History of Private Life.* Vol. 2, *Revelation of the Medieval World.* Trans. A. Goldhammer (pp. 535–630). Cambridge Mass.: Belknap.

Brown, J. C. 1986. *Immodest Acts: The Life of a Lesbian Nun in Renaissance Italy.* New York: Oxford University Press.

Brownmiller, S. 1984. *Femininity.* New York: Fawcett Columbine.

Brundage, J. A. 1982. Prostitution in the Medieval Canon Law. In V. L. Bullough and J. A. Brundage (eds.), *Sexual Practices and the Medieval Church* (pp. 149–60). Buffalo: Prometheus.

Bullough, V. L. 1982. Transvestitism in the Middle Ages. In V. L. Bullough and J. A. Brundage (eds.), *Sexual Practices and the Medieval Church* (pp. 43–54). Buffalo: Prometheus.

Bynum, C. W. 1987. *Holy Feast, Holy Fast: The Religious Significance of Food to Medieval Women.* Berkeley: University of California Press.

Castiglione, B. 1959. *The Book of the Courtier.* Trans. C. S. Singleton. New York: Anchor.

Crosby, A. W. 1972. *The Columbian Exchange: Biological and Cultural Consequences of 1492.* Westport, Conn.: Greenwood Press.

Davis, N. Z. 1975. *Society and Culture in Early Modern France.* Stanford, Calif.: Stanford University Press.

Eco, U. 1983. *The Name of the Rose.* New York: Harcourt.

———. 1986. *Art and Beauty in the Middle Ages.* New Haven, Conn.: Yale University Press.

Elyot, T. 1940. *The Defense of Good Women (1540).* Ed. E. J. Howard. Oxford, Ohio: Anchor.

Ferrante, J. 1988. Public Postures and Private Maneuvers: Roles Medieval Women Play. In M. Erler and M. Kowalski (eds.), *Women and Power in the Middle Ages* (pp. 213–29). Athens: University of Georgia Press.

Foa, A. 1990. The New and the Old: The Spread of Syphilis (1494–1530). In A. Foa (ed.), *Sex and Gender in Historical Perspective* (pp. 26–45). Baltimore: Johns Hopkins University Press.

Foucault, M. 1980. *Power/Knowledge: Selected Interviews and Other Writings 1972–1977.* Trans. C. Gordon, L. Marshall, J. Mepham and K. Soper. New York: Pantheon.

———. 1990. *The History of Sexuality.* Vol. 1. Trans. R. Hurley. New York: Vintage.

Honour, H. 1975. *The New Golden Land: European Images of America from the Discoveries to the Present Time.* New York: Pantheon.

Kelly-Gadol, J. 1987. Did Women Have a Renaissance? In R. Bridenthal, C. Kroonz and S. Stuard (eds.), *Becoming Visible: Women in European History.* 2d ed. (pp. 175–201). Boston: Houghton Mifflin.

Kempe, Margery. 1985. *The Book of Margery Kempe.* Ed. B. A. Windeatt. New York: Viking Penguin.

Kupperman, K. O. 1980. *Settling with the Indians: The Meeting of English and Indian Cultures in America, 1580–1640.* Totowa, New Jersey: Rowman and Littlefield.

Lerner, G. 1986. *The Creation of Patriarchy.* New York: Oxford University Press.

Morison, S. E. (ed.). 1963. *Journals and Other Documents on the Life and Voyages of Christopher Columbus.* New York: Heritage.

Moxey, K. 1989. *Peasants, Warriors and Wives: Popular Imagery in the Reformation.* Chicago: University of Chicago Press.

Novick, P. 1988. *That Noble Dream: The "Objectivity Question" and the American Historical Profession.* Cambridge: Cambridge University Press.

Régnier-Bohler, D. 1988. Imagining the Self. In G. Duby (ed.), *A History of Private Life.* Vol. 2, *Revelation of the Medieval World.* Trans. A. Goldhammer (pp. 311–93). Cambridge, Mass.: Belknap.

Ruether, R. R. 1974. Misogynism and Virginal Feminism in the Fathers of the Church. In R. R. Ruether (ed.), *Religion and Sexism: Images of Woman in the Jewish and Christian Traditions* (pp. 150–83). New York: Simon and Schuster.

Sale, K. 1990. *The Conquest of Paradise: Christopher Columbus and the Columbian Legacy.* New York: Plume.

Salisbury, N. 1982. *Manitou and Providence: Indians, Europeans, and the Making of New England, 1500–1643.* New York: Oxford University Press.

Scammell, G. V. 1989. *The First Imperial Age: European Overseas Expansion c. 1400–1715.* London: Unwin Hyman.

Scott, J. 1988. *Gender and the Politics of History.* New York: Columbia University Press.

Sheehan, B. W. 1980. *Savagism and Civility: Indians and Englishmen in Colonial Virginia.* Cambridge: Cambridge University Press.

Stuard, S. 1987. The Dominion of Gender: Women's Fortunes in the High Middle Ages. In R. Bridenthal, C. Kroonz and S. Stuard (eds.), *Becoming Visible: Women in European History.* 2d ed. (pp. 153–72). Boston: Houghton Mifflin.

Travitsky, B. 1981. *The Paradise of Women: Writings by Englishwomen of the Renaissance.* New York: Columbia University Press.

Warner, M. 1985. *Monuments and Maidens: The Allegory of the Female Form.* New York: Atheneum.

Wiesner, M. 1988. Women's Response to the Reformation. In R. Po-chia Hsia (ed.), *The German People and the Reformation* (pp. 148–70). Ithaca, N.Y.: Cornell University Press.

3

The Sita Myth and Hindu Fundamentalism: Masculine Signs of Feminine Beauty

Usha Zacharias

This chapter considers feminine beauty both as an interpellative sign and as a sign of dissolution[1] with regard to the masculine moral order defined within contemporary Hindu fundamentalist[2] politics in India. Feminine beauty is erotic insofar as the experience of beauty is sensual. Even with the *Kamasutra,* the 3rd–4th-century A.D. Indian text on the erotic, it is clear that *kama*[3]—"the consciousness of pleasure" arising from "the enjoyment of appropriate objects by the five senses . . . assisted by the mind together with the soul"—is culturally and materially constructed and morally/religiously regulated[4] (*Kamasutra* 1.2).

In this context, I attempt to selectively analyze some aspects of the 1987–88 television version of the *Ramayana*[5] epic, produced and directed by Ramanand Sagar, focusing on its heroine Sita as the interpellative, moral paradigm of Hindu womanhood. Sita's chaste beauty and the *kama* or erotic desire she invokes are central to the widely popular myth of the *Ramayana.* The erotic is bound up with *dharma,* righteous conduct, and Hindu religio-cultural morality.

The *Ramayan* on television was not purely mythology; as Rajagopal contends, it was also a narrative that implodes tradition and modernity—a "parable of the modern national security state," which India is today (1993, 3). As several writers point out, it is impossible to dissociate the *Ramayan* telecast from the phenomenal growth of Hindu nationalism in India in the late 1980s and early 1990s (Thapar 1989; Surendran 1989; Bhattacharji 1990; Krishnan 1990; Rajagopal 1993). While there is no necessarily causal link between the telecast and the rise of Hindu fundamentalism, the television *Ramayan* has a strong intertextual link with Hindu politics, a "dialogic interrelation" on a semantic plane (Bakhtin 1986, 105–

17). Politicians of various shades relied on intertextual connections with the epic telecasts in the 1989 national election campaign. The late Indian Prime Minister Rajiv Gandhi promised the electorate *Ram rajya* (the kingdom of Ram or the ideal state); several leaders traveled in ornate *raths* (chariots) for election campaigning, and Hindu symbolism was widely prevalent in political discourse (Surendran 1989).

More significantly, Ram, the hero of the *Ramayana,* was presented similarily to what Eco calls a "cultural unit" for "the defense or destruction" of which "men are ready to go to their death" (1976, 66). (Surprisingly, so were women, as will be discussed later.) Ram becomes the powerful metasignifier of fundamentalist politics. The rhetoric of fundamentalism creates a mythic glorious history (symbolized in Ram's hypothetical temple) supposedly destroyed by the Muslims (by building a mosque at the sacral site), which has to be recovered by the assertion of an aggressive Hindu masculinity (Bhattacharya 1990). The need to overcome Hindu male effeminacy in order to assert an aggressive masculinity is central to militant Hindu rhetoric (Bhattacharya 1990; Pandey 1991). Building a temple for Ram at the alleged *Ramjanmabhumi* (Ram's birthplace) in Ayodhya, the town named after his mythical birthplace, precisely at the same site where the sixteenth-century Muslim mosque Babri Masjid stands becomes the national Hindu mission. This reached its logical culmination in the Hindu militants' December 1992 frenzied demolition of the Babri Masjid and the subsequent bloodbath in India (Gupta & Thapa 1992).

The *Ramayan* telecast constitutes part of the conditions of signification of the politics of religious nationalism. I contend that it does so not only in its reassertion of Hindu symbolism, but also in its very narrative, which metaphorically enacts the mythical structure of lost glory and the heroic mission of recovering the past for the future, which in turn constitutes the imaginary consciousness of fundamentalist politics. Ravan, overpowered by *kama* or erotic desire for beautiful Sita, carries her away from Ram, her rightful husband. Ram, a true Kshatriya (the militant warrior caste), fights a battle to avenge this violation. He kills Ravan and regains Sita, thus establishing his manhood and ascending the throne to rule the ideal state. In this sense, the television *Ramayan* enacts the narrative of threatened Hindu masculinity coming into its own in the battle for lost (feminine) territory, interchangeable with the nation, which is the narrative posited within fundamentalist rhetoric. What is involved, therefore, in the serial is not so much the past as the present and the future. The familiar myth of the *Ramayana* not only evokes a normatively glorious past and an intertextual political present, but also carries both over into the construction of the future—specifically, the fundamentalist proposition of the Hindu state.

This chapter focuses on Sita as the womanhood of Hindu political fundamentalism and feminine beauty (or eroticism) in this particular political context as both interpellative[6] and dissolutionary. I make the semiotic distinction drawing on Mickunas's differentiation between the signs of submersion and the signs of transcendence (1986).

THE *RAMAYANA* METAPHOR

Socialist feminists express two differing views on womanhood within Hindu fundamentalism—one of the woman as passive victim caught in a masculine battle, exemplified by Sita (Chhachhi 1989); and the other of the woman as militantly empowered, resembling the warrior goddess Durga (Sarkar 1991).

Chhachhi (1989) argues that fundamentalism chooses the ideal of Sita as the epitome of female virtue: the chaste, suffering wife who worships her husband. The family's honor resides in the woman, and manliness is proved through the possession or violation of women. Many riots are set off by "alleged acts of harassment of women of one community by men of the other community. Threats to or the loss of their women . . . is seen as a direct threat to their manhood" (Chhachhi 1989, 575). The myth of uncontrollable Muslim lust (Chakravarti 1986; Chhachhi 1989; Sarkar 1991) is contrasted with the weakness of "docile, emasculated" Hindus (Chhachhi 1989).

Actual violation of women or the possibility of violation recurs in the imagery of communal tension: "They captured beautiful Hindu women, forcibly converted them and used them as temporary partners of life" (Chandra in Chhachhi 1989, 575) or "the harijans do not really want reservations, they want our women" (Jhabvala in Chhachhi 1989, 575). Speeches by local political leaders exhort men to take revenge for the "violation of our mothers and sisters" and "prove that men of that particular community are still men" (Chhachhi 1989, 575).

The *Ramayana* narrative is a striking metaphor for this political imagery, with its central narrative pattern of the lustful, demoniac Ravan abducting the beautiful Sita, thereby forcing her divine, rightful husband, Ram, into an epic battle to win back his wife. The *Ramayan,* in the context of contemporary India, thus becomes uniquely expressive of the religio-nationalist sexual equation, with its theme of the masculine battle for the recovery of the lost (feminine) territory/nation.

However, this version of the *Ramayana* would appear to leave no room for the dramatic foregrounding of women in Hindu fundamentalist politics since the mid-1980s. Fundamentalist politics, curiously enough, enables the "self-constitution of women as active political subjects" (Sarkar 1991, 2057). Women in the movement, Sarkar observes, are notable not only because they are increasing in number, but also because they are exploding the myth of passivity—they are vocal and participative, and often violently so. While the majority of leaders are male, the voices of women leaders Sadhvi Rittambara and Uma Bharti are the ones heard most frequently over loudspeakers on street corners, rousing people with unprecedented effect.[7]

Sarkar also points out that the *Ramjanmabhumi* struggle to recover Ram's holy birthplace inverts the earlier symbolization of the "fetishized sacred object" as feminine—"the cow, the abducted Hindu woman, the motherland" (Sarkar 1991, 2057). In the struggle to found/build a temple for Ram at his birthplace (the alleged *Ramjanmabhumi* occupied by the controversial mosque, Babri Masjid), "Sita's sex is coming to the rescue of Ram," to save his honor (Sarkar 1991, 2058). The appeal of Ram, Sarkar points out, is at three levels: as the chubby infant of Hindu imagery; as the vulnerable man who loses his kingdom, his father, and Sita; and as the warrior Ram who "arouses a response to an aggressive male sexuality" (Sarkar 1991, 2058). As child and man, then, she argues, Ram invites human sympathy, while being particularly appealing to the powerful mother in the woman, so that the icon of the fundamentalist movement is the warrior goddess Durga.

We could construct, then, from Chhachhi's and Sarkar's accounts, two different narratives, both embedded within the political context. In one, the male asserts his virility to possess or to save the female. Here it appears that feminine beauty, with its erotic power, endangers the masculine moral order and signifies dissolution by threatening the masculine moral order of monogamy and racial/religious purity. In the other, the powerful female gathers her partly maternal strength to save a vulnerable male. This necessitates an interpellative asceticism in the woman, a rejection of her own erotic self—an ideology within which the dissolutionary power of beauty is transcended. My contention is that the two images are not dichotomous, but dialectical, and that both are politically necessary to the proposed Hindu patriarchical state. In the television *Ramayan,* Sita does not fit neatly into the traditional passive, suffering image with which she is frequently associated. Neither is she an embodiment of the militant Durga. Instead, she breaks out of the active/passive dichotomy to enact a more complex field of relations, which I will now explore.

THE SPLIT FEMININE

Sita, originally the "Corn Mother of the vedas," is born of the earth (Bhattacharyya 1977, 22). She is found by King Janaka in a furrow as he ploughs the earth for a sacrifice (*Ramayana* 1.66). Her name itself means "furrow," an indication of the agricultural myth that relates to the personification of the furrow (*sita*) as a goddess (Singaravelu 1982, 235). The earthly dimension is cast off with her adoption by King Janaka and with her marriage to Ram—she becomes a princess. Sita is identified with Lakshmi (*Ramayana* 1.1), the radiant goddess of wealth, victory, fame, luck, riches, virtue and cleanliness (Olson 1983; Kinsley 1986). Lakshmi is also the model, devoted, dutiful wife, completely subservient to her divine lord, Vishnu. The dark counterpart of Lakshmi is Alakshmi, who symbolizes the opposing qualities: poverty, hunger and ill-fortune (Olson 1983).

Though initially an independent fertility goddess, Lakshmi changes into a tame symbol of wifely devotion and material prosperity (Olson 1983), with the shift from matristic to patriarchical semiosis described by Gimbutas (1991). Lakshmi, symbolically abstracted from her darker self, Alakshmi, and deified, now constitutes the morally and socially appropriate feminine. Like several other goddesses, Lakshmi becomes a legitimizing force for the male gods through divine marriage to Vishnu (Kosambi 1965). In contemporary wall calendars, she is often seated at her divine husband Vishnu's feet, and she embodies the auspicious half of the binary code within the feminine.

Sita and Ram are the earthly manifestation of the divine Vishnu-Lakshmi couple. Sita's status as princess and her identification with Lakshmi serve to obliterate her identity as the daughter of the earth. With Sita, the fertility goddess is purified of her "signs of submersion" (Mickunas 1986, 2–16), a semiotic process perhaps traceable back to the splitting of goddesses along the binary codes of the divine and the demoniac (Wadley 1977; Olson 1983; Ganesh 1990).

The epics, particularly the less morally ambivalent *Ramayana*, also have a normative role: They set the ideals for moral conduct—Sita as the ideal woman and Ram as the ideal, semidivine man (Bhattacharji 1980; Chakravarti 1983; Krishnan 1990). In the epic, Ram symbolizes "masculine heroism, valor and honor" and Sita, "feminine self-sacrifice, virtue, fidelity and chastity" (Chakravarti 1983, 71). The same ideals are reasserted in militant Hindu writing on the teleserial (Gupta 1987; Bhatia 1987). On television, Ram and Sita, the ideal couple with their combination of royal status, semidivinity and all too human tragedy, are already established deities. Eroticism, as far as the semidivine couple is concerned, is contained and channeled within a regulated monogamous marriage and the interpellative ideology of the *pativrata—pativrata* being the ideal wife who is dedicated to the service of her husband. Television episodes are punctuated with deifying songs to both Ram and Sita, with Sita often referred to as "mother Sita" (despite the fact that the serial does not cover the period of her motherhood), signifying her exalted sexual status as well as the auspicious half of the split feminine she embodies.

BHAKTI AND THE EROTIC

Watching the *Ramayan* was a national Sunday ritual in the religious and performative sense, as Lutgendorf points out (1990). Narrative strategies created the mood of *bhakti,* reverence and devotion (Rajagopal 1993). The television set itself was "garlanded, decorated with sandalwood paste and vermillion, and conch shells are blown. Grandparents admonish youngsters to bathe before the show and housewives put off serving meals" (Melwani in Lutgendorf 1990, 137). Business was suspended, and ritualized public viewings were common.

The television *Ramayan* simulated the folk performances of the epic to some extent, where the actor cannot escape the magnetic field of the divine. The space in which the television epic was enacted was, therefore, the magical space of complete presence and lack of distance in which the distinctions of signifier, signified and subject do not hold (Mickunas 1992). The television Sita *is* the Sita of all or any of the *Ramayanas,* the Sita created in the orality that calls her into existence. In this context, beauty is not a subjective/objective category. Insofar as the deity and the actress are identified, insofar as the narrative demands it, Sita has to be beautiful, and, therefore, she is beautiful. It is one of her virtues. In the magical space of the epic, physicality is insignificant, much like the short, dark Hitler evoking the image of the tall, blond Aryan (Mickunas 1992).

Sita's deified status in the *bhakti* or devotional mode necessitates the subduing of her erotic expressivity and the redefining of the very nature of her beauty, quite unlike, for instance, Valmiki's *Ramayana.*[8] In Valmiki's text, Sita's beauty is the beauty of a woman whose bodily presence is outward, as is evident from Ravan's description when he first sees Sita:

On seeing the Princess of Videha [Sita] . . . whose eyes resembled lotus petals, the titan [Ravana] struck by Kama's [Eros's] arrow, joyfully accosted her. Praising her beauty, unequalled in the three worlds . . . he said, "O Thou, possessed of the brilliance of gold and silver . . . clad in a yellow silken sari . . . art thou Lakshmi bereft of her lotus . . . ? How even, sharp and white are thy teeth, how large thy slightly reddened eyes with their dark pupils, how well-proportioned and rounded are thy thighs and how charming thy legs, resembling the tapering trunk of an elephant! . . . How round and plump are thy cheeks like the polished fruit of the Tala trees . . . how enchanting thy bosom, decorated with pearls! . . . O Lady of sweet smiles, lovely teeth and expressive eyes, as a river sweeps away its banks with its swift current so dost thou steal away my heart, O Graceful One! Slender is thy waist, glossy thine hair, thy breasts touching each other enhance thy loveliness . . . I have never seen any [one] on earth so perfect. (*Ramayana* 3.46)

After Ravan, under the spell of Kama (the god of desire and eroticism), abducts Sita, Ram looks in vain for his beloved, and imagines her heavy thighs resemble those of the creature most tied to the earth—the elephant. In her absence, Sita's beauty to Ram *is* nature in all the fullness of its presence, as evinced in Ram's lament to the trees of the forest. Sita, he tells the forest, is as fair as the "young green shoots"; her breasts resemble the fruit of the tala tree, her eyes those of a gazelle, her countenance that of the moon and her skin the winter jasmine (*Ramayana* 3.66). Sita's body here is the earth-bound, "blossoming, fruitful body of the goddess of the life-force," part of the north Indian ideal of feminine beauty in the fertility goddess tradition (Zimmer 1964, 116). In its rich, sensual abundance, Sita's body overflows into the earth; it metaphorically dissolves back into an essentially feminine, fruitful nature. In keeping with her identity as the daughter of the earth, Sita's body is inseparable from nature; she is vitally a part of its lush sensuality.

I called up the image not to insist on its re-creation, but to make the semiotic displacement apparent. This is the body that is missing in the moral idiom of Hindu womanhood created on national television. Sita has to be divorced from the materiality of earth/body to be merged with the ideality of masculine morality. This is the mode of *bhakti,* in which the spiritual must transcend the erotic (Sangari 1990). Sita appears in the forest clad not in the yellow robes of Valmiki's description, but in the saffron robes synonymous with contemporary Hindu fundamentalist parties and worn by women leaders in these parties. Sita, sari draped around her head in a sign of sexual reticence and moral propriety where upper-class Hindu women are concerned, appears without a body, so to speak, completely shrouded in a light saffron sari. Her face is the primary vehicle of expressivity. The expression on Sita's face is the same as that on Ram's, a beatific piety well in keeping with a mechanical interpretation of *bhakti.* This is the expression they maintain even while looking at each other, so that the erotic is constantly sublimated into the pious.

With the negation of bodily expressivity, together with overcoded *bhakti* and spurious spirituality, the room left for the erotic is the surreptitious (including rape or abduction). On television, Ravan occupies the classic position of the unseen male voyeur before directly addressing Sita. Ravan draws on the "unconscious," and therefore virginal, erogeneity of Sita to empower his own sexuality. Sita herself is seen gathering flowers, since erotic expression and virginal assertion of the gesturally limited feminine are possible only through the medium of caressing flowers, trees, rain and grass.

WOMAN AS MAGICAL PROPERTY

The only erotic desire Sita expresses in the *Ramayan* is her desire to possess the alluring *maya mrg* (magical animal)—the golden-skinned, silver-speckled deer. Sita is fascinated by the jewel-like beauty of the animal, which she glimpses while she, Ram and his loyal brother Lakshman are living in exile in the forest. The deer is a supernatural ploy, wrought in

Ravan's plot to isolate Sita by the demon Maricha's magic (*maya*)—*maya* being the perceived, possibly deceptive, appearance of the sensual world. Sita's desire is expressed as a desire for others and not for herself: She says the deer, alive, would please her mothers-in-law, and, dead, it could serve as skin for Ram to sit on. Driven by Sita's wish and enraptured himself by the deer, Ram sets off after the illusory animal, being lured farther and farther from their forest dwelling by the cunning Maricha. Having led him sufficiently astray, the deer falls to Ram's arrow, turns into its real form of Maricha and falsely cries out for help in Ram's voice.

Hearing the cry, Sita forcefully provokes a reluctant Lakshman, accusing him of lack of manhood, into leaving her and going to Ram's help. She refuses to listen to Lakshman's plea that Ram had commanded him to stay with her at any cost and to his assurance that Ram was divine and no one could harm him. Before unwillingly leaving Sita alone in their forest dwelling, Lakshman draws the *lakshmanarekha*[9] or the line of Lakshman, warning Sita that she should, on no account, step outside the line. Inside the line—called *maryada ka seema,* the line of rectitude and propriety—Sita would be safe, protected. With the male guardians out of the picture, Ravan arrives in the guise of a weary mendicant seeking alms. Lulled into security by his disguise and fearful of his threats to cause her husband's death if she does not bring food to him, Sita hesitantly steps outside the line. Once outside the line, Sita is unprotected, powerless, thereby creating the opportunity for Ravan to abduct her.

Metaphorically, the *lakshmanarekha* indicates the peculiar, magical property relationship—both moral and material—the man has over the woman in religious patriarchy. The ownership of the woman that the husband enjoys becomes magical by virtue of the masculine religious order. That the *lakshmanarekha* is a metaphor for the masculine edict, moral and material, on the woman's body is obvious from the words used—*maryada ka seema,* the line of propriety and rectitude, the crossing of which, however well intentioned, is dangerous for the woman. Once outside the line, the woman is prey to the lurking danger of *kama* and thereby in danger of falling irretrievably into social disrepute and moral chaos.

The permanence of her fall on violation of the line is borne out by Ravan's words when he reminds a frightened Sita, now outside the line, that once a woman steps outside the line of *maryada,* she cannot seek refuge within it again; she is at his mercy. There is no redemption, since the line is ruled by a magical law—once violated, it no longer has its protective power with all the fatal irrevocability of fairy tales. (Unfortunately, the line is all too real for women, even in contemporary India.) In the television version of the epic, Sita's violation of the line is what finally enables Ravan to carry her off. Feminine sexuality is safe only within the magical, moral stasis of territorialization of the *lakshmanarekha.* The *lakshmanarekha* defines the feminine as magical territory, in the contemporary context, a moral/economic property defined by and relational to the male. The line circumscribes not only the woman's body, but also the space surrounding her, which is now defined as a space relational to and drawn by the male, a space she may violate only on pain of eternal condemnation.

The violation of the *lakshmanarekha* is implicit in the drawing of the line; the existence of the line opens up the possibility of its violation. This violation or the possibility of violation is in turn a slur on Sita's virtue. Ravan's desire for Sita's beauty and his attempted violation of Sita comprise a power struggle between males, which for Sita results in a never-ending trial of her virtue. With the *lakshmanarekha*, feminine beauty becomes the erotic stage for male battles of *dharma/adharma.* The male earns his masculinity through protecting or violating the feminine, the key theme of the fundamentalist narrative, as pointed out earlier.

The *lakshmanarekha* indicates that Sita's beauty is its dissolutionary power; it upsets a masculine order, pulling it into a depth in which it mistrusts itself. It is to guard against this power that the line has to be drawn; to protect not the female, but the masculine, which can prove itself only through the moral validation of the line. The violation of the line is a crime for which Sita can never atone, whatever the suffering she undergoes, because the danger in violating the line is not for the female alone, but also for the masculine order. Sita proves that within the monastic walls of purification and transcendence, feminine beauty signifies dissolution (Mickunas 1986). Feminine beauty is the dissolutionary pull of *kama,*[10] which patriarchical morality transcends (Mickunas 1986). If one collapses the characters, as is done in metaphysical readings, the *Ramayana* battle is over *dharma,* righteous conduct, so that a particular moral order is preserved/projected (Bhattacharji 1980). *Kama,* undifferentiated eroticism, remains regulatable within this order.

In the context of the threat masculinity faces, any woman is beautiful because within the magical property relationship of religious patriarchy, she symbolizes masculinity in all its vulnerability. Beauty is invested in Sita as a political property marker, which magically gains importance with its violation/possession. This is borne out by the earlier cited communal metaphor—that beautiful women are raped during communal hostilities or stand in danger of violation. Here feminine beauty could be termed a circular signifier—Sita is abducted because she is beautiful, and it is because she is abducted that she is beautiful. The temple for Ram has to be built at precisely the same site as the Babri Masjid for no other reason than that is where the Babri Masjid stands. This is the internal logic of fundamentalism.

THE MILITANT *PATIVRATA*

The essential argument with which the abducted television Sita confronts Ravan is the power of the *pativrata.* This emerges in Ravan's declaration of love to Sita, once he has brought her by force to his kingdom, Lanka. Ravan's words arouse a passion of negation in Sita that is never expressed in her relations with Ram, her godly husband. Ironically, the righteous denial of sexuality seems far more forceful than the affirmation. In response to Ravan, who says that Sita's beauty has made him a slave to her, she says that in touching her body once while forcibly carrying her off, he has violated a *pativrata,* and, therefore, the future holds only doom for him. When Ravan offers her the material inducement of a life of luxury in his kingdom, she scornfully rejects it, saying that a *pativrata* will not forget her *dharma,* or righteous conduct. Sita has been true to her husband in mind, speech and action—a real *pativrata*—and, therefore, Ravan cannot violate her.

The *pativrata* worships her husband as god and renders dedicated service to him (Chakravarti 1986). Chastity and fidelity to a single male are essential to the *pativrata.* The Sita ideal has, over time, crystallized the *pativrata* concept into a model for Indian womanhood (Chakravarti 1986). The true *pativrata* channels her sexual desire and "surrenders body, heart and mind to the husband" (Sangari 1990, 1543). In Sita, this sacrifice is so deeply inscribed that it is her primary expression of herself: Her first instinct is to deny her own instincts and to affirm the male's. The devotion of the wife to the husband is ascetic, since it requires sacrifice or subordination of the woman's own primary instincts or interests. Being a *pativrata,* therefore, is asceticism for the woman because it entails a renunciatory exercise of the will. Like male asceticism, it carries its own ascetic powers. In its total compliance to, or rather enactment of, the male order, *pativrata*hood *is* masculine asceticism and masculine morality.

Indeed, Sita gains her moral power by excessive enactment of the masculine order, so that she is, in a way, *more masculine than the masculine.* The masculine Ravan is defeated by Sita's complete submission to the masculine order itself, with the excess of masculine asceticism that Sita can generate in comparison to him. The *pativrata* ideology redeems masculinity. This is evident when Sita affirms the power of her asceticism over her beauty and her sensuality, is not prone to the adoration of her beauty and asserts the doom of *kama* or unbridled lust, which Ravan embodies. In fact, in order to be beautiful, one has to be a *pativrata*—"women who are not obedient *pativratas* will be unable to win their husband's love, are dogs and pigs and unworthy of being called beautiful" (Sangari 1990, 1543). Beauty is here a moral category. The female demon who guards Sita and Ravan's wife are both shown to be moved and led to revere Sita for her demonstration of her power as *pativrata.* The *pativrata* ideology makes Sita the political, interpellative womanhood of Hindu fundamentalism.

The affirmation of masculine morality is sometimes violent enough that Sita herself appears empowered by the assertion, as in her forceful countering of Ravan's advances and in her taunting of Lakshman's lack of manhood in order to compel him to go in search of Ram against his brother's own command. On both counts, Sita's assertion is based on loyalty to her husband. In the articulate Sita, we see the violent and hysterically assertive side of fascist morality with its curiously ascetic sexuality. The righteous womanhood gains its strength from rigorous refusal of *kama*, the realm of eroticism, while affirming masculine morality within a hysterical sexuality of negation. Although not directly evoked in the epic or in the teleserial, the assertive feminine (as redefined in neo-Hinduism)—invoking her power as embodiment of masculine morality—alludes to a reworked myth of *shakti*.

Shakti is the female energy, which is at once terrible and beautiful, divine and demoniac, of the *Devi-Mahatmyam* (1.78–81). The powerful goddess of the *Devi-Mahatmyam* is created by the gods to save themselves when the demons have usurped their place. In her warlike manifestations, the Lakshmi/Ambika/Durga of the *Devi-Mahatmyam* wears the masculine symbols of the sword, spear, club, bow and arrows and executes the masculine mission of slaying the buffalo demon, thereby saving the gods from the overpowering demoniac threat.[11] There is an erotic element between the goddess and the demons, and in one version, the goddess even takes on a surpassingly beautiful form to lure the demons before killing them and thus restoring heaven to the male gods. It is no wonder that Durga, the militant goddess, appears as the "destroyer of demoniac forces" in right-wing Hindu writing (see, for example, Chatterjee 1987).

Without stretching the parallel too far, one could point out the similarity in the lustful Ravan, who is lured by Sita's beauty into a battle that ends in his death. Feminine beauty in both cases could be an illusory lure, an instrument of the gods, promising eroticism, while actually ensuring the triumph of *dharma*. While Sita does not physically take to arms, her very presence as ideal of purity and her staunch assertion of her status as *pativrata* create and demand the masculine retribution that ends in the victory of *dharma*. This is the ascetic power that Ravan is warned of when he is told that Sita would be like "hot coal" in his hands.

THE MASCULINE BURDEN

The television *Ramayan*, while deifying Sita and making her the spokeswoman for Hindu womanhood, excludes her earthly trials after the victorious Ram ascends the throne of Ayodhya. The serial, following the Tulsidas version, stopped with the killing of Ravan, but public pressure forced the telecast of the sequel to the epic, the *Uttararamayan* (Lutgendorf 1990). The sequel's omission of both Ram's controversial killing of a Shudra ascetic in order to save a Brahmin child (*Ramayana* 7.76) and his decision to abandon a pregnant Sita (*Ramayana* 7.45) was not accidental.

The political Ram had to be portrayed without the poetic ambiguity of the epic in good/evil, black/white dichotomy (Krishnan 1990). Court cases and demonstrations for and against (Krishnan 1990; Lutgendorf 1990) resulted in questions of what would be the "proper" version of the controversial aspects to present on government-owned, government-censored television. The textual sacrifice made was Sita's suffering at Ram's hands—Ram's rejection of Sita after he wins her back from Ravan and his suspicion regarding her chastity because she had spent a year in Lanka as Ravan's captive. In most versions, this public scandal leads Ram to decide, *without Sita's knowledge,* to abandon her in the forest during her pregnancy (Bhattacharji 1990).

However, in a new twist for the benefit of contemporary Hindu morality, the television serial depicts *Sita herself* arguing with and finally convincing Ram to abandon her in the forest, since he should not be tainted with scandal, a variation absent from all existing versions of the *Ramayana* narrative (Bhattacharji 1990). Sita forcefully reminds Ram that she had spent a year in the kingdom of Ravan, who was notorious for his lasciviousness. She argues, as a true *pativrata* would, that she has to guard the reputation of her husband. Ram must, therefore, banish her in order to satisfy his subjects and to save the reputation of his glorious family (Bhattacharji 1990).

Once again, we see a Sita who is not passive or docile, but passionately articulate—on this occasion, to save Ram's honor and the ideological self-consciousness of the *Ram rajya* (the kingdom of Ram) through her self-sacrifice. Sita becomes the vocal citizen of the projected Hindu state, protecting a Ram vulnerable in his lack of masculinity. Indeed, Ram's strength as a political symbol as far as the serial goes lies in his feeble masculinity, in the fact that he is never phallic. Once again, the feminine of Hindu fundamentalism has to redeem masculinity in its lack by professing a masculinity more masculine than the masculine, as pointed out earlier.

CONCLUSION

Thapar points out that Hinduism, unlike Christianity, is not a linear, homogeneous religion. The currently propagated "syndicated Hinduism," she contends, is an attempt to "restructure the indigenous religions as a monolithic, uniform religion" (Thapar 1985, 14–15). The government-approved television *Ramayan* is part of the attempt to redefine Hinduism as an ideology for modernization (Thapar 1990), an ideology that is the ideology of the modern Indian state (Rajagopal 1993).

The television *Ramayan's* critical significance for Hindu politics also lies, as noted earlier, in the fact that it enacts the narrative of the revival of threatened Hindu masculinity. The political narrative thus provides room for both the lack of masculinity and its fulfillment. In its movement to conquer its own femininity, this "masculinity" contains both the feminine and the phallic. In the process, a complementary discursive space is created for Hindu womanhood, a womanhood that has to be fought for and protected/violated within the morality of the *lakshmanarekha* and one that is directly or indirectly, through the ideology of the militant *pativrata*, empowered to save the fe/male symbol of Ram. When both these levels are combined, the male/female subject distinction collapses for all political purposes.

On one level, feminine eroticism (beauty) is the dissolutionary power of *kama*, constituting a standing threat to the masculine moral order and indicating a vulnerable masculinity. It evokes the magical property relationship of possession/violation in religious patriarchy, where beauty is implicated in circular signification. On another plane, the dissolutionary power of beauty is transcended by perceiving it as illusory or by disguising it in morality. Masculinity is redeemed by the feminine herself, who generates an excess of masculinity with the interpellative ideology of the *pativrata* and accompanying asceticism. There is no real contradiction here— in both narratives, it is the masculine that is threatened, and it is the masculine that has to be saved. In the fundamentalist semiosis, both Sita and Durga are one, dialectical aspects of the womanhood essential for the masculine order. This womanhood may violate the rules only to resurrect the threatened masculinity of the metaphoric Ram and the sacral site of Ayodhya.

NOTES

I wish to thank Martin S. Carter of the New School for Social Research, New York, for his disturbing criticism of an earlier draft of this chapter and Karen Callaghan of Barry University for her infinite patience and encouragement.

1. The central idea for this chapter is derived from the distinction between the signs of submersion and the signs of transcendence drawn by Mickunas (1986).
2. I use "fundamentalism" to indicate the inflexible political assertion of religious identity. It is practically interchangeable with "communalism," the word commonly used in India to designate the same phenomenon. Since fundamentalism has emerged in and through Hindu religious nationalism, I use the terms as correlatives.
3. I use the word *kama* frequently, since there is no real English equivalent. Zimmer (1967) gives a good account of the philosophical dimensions of the word.
4. In the *Kamasutra*, the erotic is not composed of two bodies alone; it also includes the socioeconomic-caste context, emotions, surroundings, skills (ranging from the mathematical to the verbal) and objects, natural and humanmade. It seems obvious that the sensual here is not limited to so-called physical experience, but also encompasses consciousness as a whole.
5. I use *Ramayan* when referring to the television serial, in keeping with its

title, and *Ramayana* for the ancient myth itself with all its different variations. These terms are not mutually exclusive, since the television serial is part of the *Ramayana* tradition. I use "Ram" and "Ravan," rather than "Rama" and "Ravana," for the sake of consistency.

6. Althusser (1971) defines interpellation or "hailing" as the way subjects are constituted/recognized/identified within the dominant ideology in the name of an Absolute Subject. Within the religious ideology of Christianity, the Absolute Subject would be God, who interpellates or hails individuals so that they recognize themselves in Him and feel that they are recognized by Him. Interpellation is the process that ensures our complicity with the ideology of our own "free" will.

7. I am here basically concerned with imagery and symbols. The feminine presence does not imply that the Hindu political parties are different from any other male-dominated parties in terms of power structure.

8. I use Valmiki's *Ramayana* not as the "original" or "real" text, but as a useful context or vantage point from which to view the television serial. Taking India's cultural plurality as well as multiple versions and performances of the *Ramayana* extant in culturally diverse parts of India into account, neither the "original" myths nor the television version can be said to necessarily have any kind of performative priority (Lutgendorf 1990). However, in India, television is a government-owned, government-censored medium with a built-in normative sense of national morality and the consciousness of statehood. Therefore, the question arises as to why one version seems more legitimate and politically apt for national television than the others.

9. The *lakshmanarekha* incident is absent in Valmiki's version. It is introduced by Tulsidas, as Bhattacharji points out (1990).

10. *Kama,* on one level, could be the central theme of the *Ramayana.* Ram's father, Dasaratha, yields to his weakness for his youngest queen and gives in to her demand to banish Ram; Lakshman and Ram reject Ravan's sister, Shurpanakha, who desires them; and Sita herself is abducted by Ravan in the metaphoric forest of demoniac threats and moral wilderness. *Kama* thus appears to constitute the most important causal link in the narrative up to Ram's victory over Ravan.

11. Interestingly, in one version of the *Ramayana,* the *Adbhutha Ramayana,* when Ram is helpless on the battlefield, Sita appears as Kali, the goddess of time/death, and single-handedly vanquishes Ravan (Thapar 1990).

WORKS CITED

Althusser, L. 1971. *Lenin and Philosophy.* Trans. B. Brewster. New York: Monthly Review Press.

Bakhtin, M. M. 1986. *Speech Genres and Other Late Essays.* Trans. V. W. McGee. Austin: University of Texas Press.

Bhatia, V. P. 1987. *Ramayana* as a "Destabilising Force." *Organiser,* July 26.

Bhattacharji, S. 1980. Validity of the *Ramayana* Values. In V. Raghavan (ed.), *The Ramayana Tradition in Asia.* New Delhi: Sahitya Akademi.

———. 1990. Sita on Television: Cunning Distortions. *Telegraph,* May 4.

Bhattacharya, N. 1990. Myth, History and the Politics of *Ramjanmabhumi.* In S.

Gopal (ed.), *Anatomy of a Confrontation: The Babri Masjid Ramjanmabhumi Issue.* New Delhi: Penguin Books India.

Bhattacharyya, N. N. 1977. *The Indian Mother Goddess.* New Delhi: Manohar Book Service.

Chakravarti, U. 1983. The Development of the Sita Myth: A Case Study of Women in Myth and Literature. *Samya Shakti* 1: 68–75.

———. 1986. Pativrata. *Seminar* 318: 17–21.

Chatterjee, K. R. 1987. Durga—The Destroyer of Demoniac Forces. *Organiser,* October 18.

Chhachhi, A. 1989. The State, Religious Fundamentalism and Women: Trends in South Asia. *Economic and Political Weekly* 24: 567–78.

Devi-Mahatmyam: The Glorification of the Great Goddess. 1963. Trans. V. S. Agrawala. Varanasi, India: All-India Kashiraj Trust.

Eco, U. 1976. *A Theory of Semiotics.* Bloomington: Indiana University Press.

Ganesh, K. 1990. Mother Who Is Not a Mother: In Search of the Great Indian Goddess. *Economic and Political Weekly* 25: 58–64.

Gimbutas, M. 1991. *The Civilization of the Goddess: The World of Old Europe.* New York: HarperCollins.

Gupta, M. M., and V. J. Thapa. 1992. Kar Sevaks Destroy Babri Masjid. *The Times of India,* December 7 (Bombay ed.).

Gupta, R. R. 1987. Rama Is the Heart-beat and the *Ramayana,* the Song of the Soul of Crores of Hundus. *Organiser,* July 19.

Kamasutra of Vatsyayana. 1962. Trans. R. Burton. New York: Medical Press.

Kinsley, D. 1986. *Hindu Goddesses: Visions of the Divine Feminine in Hindu Religious Tradition.* Berkeley: University of California Press.

Kosambi, D. D. 1965. *The Culture and the Civilization of Ancient India.* London: Routledge & Kegan Paul.

Krishnan, P. 1990. In the Idiom of Loss: Ideology of Motherhood in Television Serials. *Economic and Political Weekly* 25: 103–16.

Lutgendorf, P. 1990. Ramayana: The Video. *TDR: The Drama Review* 34: 127–76.

Mickunas, A. 1986. Cultural Modes of Reflection. Paper presented to the International Society for the Comparative Study of Civilization, Santa Fe College, Santa Fe, New Mexico, May 23.

———. 1992. Semiotics in Communication. Lectures presented at the Department of Philosophy, Ohio University.

Olson, C. 1983. Sri-Laksi and Radha: The Obsequious Wife and the Lustful Lover. In C. Olson (ed.), *The Book of the Goddess: Past and Present.* New York: Crossroad.

Pandey, G. 1991. Hindus and Others: The Militant Hindu Construction. *Economic and Political Weekly* 26: 2997–3009.

Rajagopal, A. 1993. From Inversion to Implosion: Postcolonial Improvisations on Orientalism. Unpublished paper.

The Ramayana of Valmiki. 1952–59. 3 vols. Trans. H. P. Shastri. Bristol, England: Burleigh Press.

Sangari, K. 1990. Mirabai and the Spiritual Economy of Bhakti-II. *Economic and Political Weekly* 25: 1464–1552.

Sarkar, T. 1991. The Woman as Communal Subject: *Rashtrasevika Samiti* and the

Ram *Janmabhoomi* Movement. *Economic and Political Weekly* 26: 2057–62.

Singaravelu, S. 1982. Sita's Birth and Parentage in the Rama Story. *Asian Folklore Studies* 41: 235–43.

Surendran, C. P. 1989. *He* Ram (and Sagar). *The Sunday Mid-Day,* December 10.

Thapar, R. 1985. Syndicated *Moksha? Seminar* 313: 14–22.

———. 1989. The *Ramayana* Syndrome. *Seminar* 353: 71–75.

———. 1990. A Historical Perspective on the Story of Rama. In S. Gopal (ed.), *Anatomy of a Confrontation: The Babri Masjid Ramjanmabhumi Dispute.* New Delhi: Penguin Books India.

Wadley, S. S. 1977. Women and the Hindu Tradition. *Signs* 3: 113–15.

Zimmer, H. 1964. *The Art of Indian Asia.* Vol. 1. New York: Pantheon Books.

———. 1967. *Philosophies of India.* Princeton, N.J.: Princeton University Press.

4

Changing Perceptions of Feminine Beauty in Islamic Society

Amira Sonbol

Is there a connection between ideals of feminine beauty and particular roles played by women in Islamic society? Do connections between such ideals and patriarchical attitudes correlate with the socioeconomic structures of the particular era? Finally, how useful are such microstructural studies for understanding social relations and hence Islamic history? These questions are central to this chapter, which deals with a subject that, on examination, proved to be quite new for Middle East studies, notwithstanding its popularity in the West. The connection between sociocultural perceptions of beauty and other gender issues, such as marriage and sexuality, has yet to become a focus for Middle East historians. Hence, this chapter raises many questions and attempts to lay a framework for further research.

Generally speaking, studies drawing connections between ideals of beauty and social hierarchization reflect contemporary feminist ideology's attempt to make women aware of the "relationship between female liberation and female beauty" (Wolf 1991, 9) and hence to encourage them to work toward their liberation. In this political feminist discourse, the "enslavement" of women is a function of family, while standards of beauty are "determined by politics" and are established by patriarchical society as a "belief system that keeps male dominance intact" (Wolf 1991, 12). Nawal Sa'dawi has been the most vocal Arab feminist, espousing the view that Middle Eastern women are the chattel of husbands or male family members. Leila Ahmed projects the modern feminist paradigm to the past, tying the appropriation of women as property to the establishment of the nuclear family: Whereas in pre-Islamic Arabia (*jahiliya*) women had lived relatively unfettered under conditions that included both polygamy and polyandry and widely held matrilineal practices (Ahmed 1992, 4), Islam, with its merchant economy, gave preeminence to "paternity and the vesting in the male of proprietary rights to female sexuality and its issue." It did so by establishing a patriarchical order in which allegiance was determined by blood and a moral code intended to ensure lineage and hence inheritance through the father's bloodline. For Germaine Tillion, by making inheritance by women obligatory, the Quran forced tribes converting to Islam to find ways to keep this inheritance within the tribe. The seclusion of women, the use of the veil, cousin marriage, and the domination of women became the answer (Tillion 1983, 73).

A number of points provide premises for this chapter: (1) There is no question that women stand on a lower step in the Islamic world's patriarchical order, but it is also too simple to view women as the victims of a male-dominated structure. In this study, women are considered not as objects of subjugation, but as subjects and participants, and sexuality represents an important factor in power relations. (2) Studies underscoring the enslavement of women depend largely on prophetic *hadiths* (traditions) and *fiqh* (theological interpretations), which they consider as representing actual social relations, when such sources actually constituted the ideal with which the dominant discourse wished to shape society. The "social" discourse exists elsewhere, particularly in archival and literary sources. (3) Islamic society has always been patriarchical, notwithstanding specific incidents from pre-Islamic Arabia. But there is not a single unchanging form for this patriarchy; rather, each age and place presents its own form of patriarchy.

ISLAMIC AND MEDIEVAL DISCOURSES ON FEMININITY

Islam appeared in the Arabian Hijaz at a time when merchant capital was becoming the established system of exchange and tribal society was experiencing deep transformations. The new "order" proposed by Islam represented a continuation of the tribal structure, but within a framework that integrated these new transformations. Thus, while Quranic laws introduced a patriarchical order fitting with the new conditions brought about by merchant capitalism, the clan continued to be central to the Quranic discourse. Historical continuity between pre-Islamic and Islamic cultural practices should not be undermined, even with the introduction of new economic practices.

Purity of the *'asab* (central nerve) and hence the *nasab* (relation by blood) on which inheritance depended was clearly defined by the Quran (4:7); the emphasis on *nasab,* however, was an elaboration on pre-Islamic tribal practices. The Quran associated children with their natural father and established mechanisms to assure legal inheritance, but *nasab* went beyond the nuclear family to include uncles, aunts, and cousins of varying degrees, all of whom could have rights to inherit (Anas 1990, 76). The Quran also admonished that an inheritance should be left to companions, slaves and wards (4:33).

Quranic marriage laws and moral codes are consistent with the organization that the Prophet was building, a new allegiance in which Islam was to play the paramount role in cementing society together. Marriages were not to be based on love or physical attraction as much as on religious, social and economic comparableness (*kafa'a*). Arguably *kafa'a* was a form of protection for a woman after marriage, but it also reflected the pre-Islamic stress on *kafa'a* that cemented groups and clan alliances. Sex was confined to legitimate relationships, particularly marriage (24:30–32). While women were expected to remain monogamous, legitimate relationships outside of marriage were recognized by the Quran, severe penalties being prescribed for those who go outside "legitimacy" (24:3).

The demand for sexual "purity" from women was not new to Arabia; pre-Islamic Arabian poetry has illustrated that the hegemonic discourse supported a moral code that allowed gender mixing, but made this mixing "legal" by idealizing certain standards of gender relationships and equating personal and tribal honor with upholding these standards. Thus, models of gender relations presented by pre-Islamic love poetry were as important as the standards of chivalry (*muruwa*) and courage constructed by the poetic epics of tribal warfare. The purer and more unattainable the love, the greater the glory of the tribe and its women: An untouchable (*'afifa*) and hard to get (*muhsina, sa'bat al-manal*) woman was the ideal (Al-Sioufi 1991, 25). Thus, Hakam al-Wadi sang the praises of his beloved who on her wedding night to another proved through her purity that she was the "noblest of her race" (Ibn Abi Rabi'a 1987, 61), and Buthaina's *'uthri* (platonic-poetry) love for Jamil reached a point where he decided to test her integrity by proposing that they consummate their love. When she turned him down, he informed her that had she agreed, he would have killed her (Al-Jahiz 1980, 61).

"Legal" mixing seemed to have continued in Arabia during the early Islamic period. The Islamic moral code presented by the Quran was probably meant to set a religious discourse allowing for such mixing, while cementing allegiance to the Islamic community. Thus, the moral code was supposed to apply equally to men and women: "Say to the believing men that they should lower their gaze and guard their modesty. . . . And say to the believing women that they should lower their gaze and guard their modesty" (14:30–31). Terms like *muhsinat* (chaste) and *ghayr musfihat* (not lustful), reminiscent of the Jahili period, are used often to describe desirable women, that is, women that the Quran informs men would make desirable wives (4:25). Men were encouraged to marry women of faith in preference to beautiful ones (2:221), and marriage is described as a most intimate communion in which "the mystery of sex finds its highest fulfill-

ment when intimate spiritual harmony is combined with the physical link"
(Ali 1934, 86).

The moral code for women in the Quran, when taken literally, emphasizes gender hierarchization. This is further emphasized by the Quran,
which considers women to be in need of a man's protection and economic
support for which men are given precedence (2:228–29). However, when
the female code is understood within the context of the equal spiritual
and religious duties expected of both genders, social hierarchization could
have been structured differently. The patriarchical order, however, has
constantly confirmed a patriarchical interpretation of the Quran based on
Prophetic *hadith* (traditions), the transmission of which over the ages
helped in shaping gender relations. According to Mernissi, Abu Huraira,
an important transmitter of *hadith* who "helped out" in the Prophet's
household, was a misogynist who disliked the Prophet's wives, and whose
relationship with the Prophet constituted a model for Islamic traditions
regarding women (Mernissi 1987, 71–74).

Hadith interpretation became central to the patriarchical discourse of
the Islamic empire, which presented a different superstructure than Arabia
had. Whereas Arabia was largely desert where clans and their members
were identifiable and tribal honor acted to cement the social fabric, the
cities of medieval Islam were crowded centers where strangers interacted
together. The medieval Islamic patriarchical order was based on the extended family, with a male head of the household rather than the clan or
tribe that predominated in Arabia. The lands into which Islam expanded
were peasant communities with highly urbanized centers. No matter how
much medieval "Islamic ideals" are assumed by Muslims to reflect the
Quran or the early Islamic period, they are more typical of urban patriarchical orders whose roots are to be found in the pre-Islamic territories
of the Middle East.

Veiling and seclusion for the upper and middle classes already existed in
many Middle Eastern cities before Islam, and the practice continued after.
The fabrication of *hadith,* which was largely practiced during the early Ab-
basid period, may have been the result of the separation of the sexes and the
ensuing lack of understanding, suspicion and misogyny that were legitimated by *hadiths* traced back to the Prophet or his companions, but that
were probably later fabrications. Thus, if in the Quran there is no concept of
"original sin" and the moral code was applied equally to the two genders,
hadith literature has laid sin and shame on the shoulders of women, who,
therefore, must be secluded lest they cause evil: According to the Hanbali
jurist Ibn al-Jawzi, "Women are an *'awra,"* that, is sexual weakness, nakedness or imperfection; "when she goes out she is accompanied by the devil"
(Al-Jabri 1983, 92), and even if she intended no evil, "people would still not
be safe from her" (cited in Al-Jabri 1983, 4). The image of women built by
medieval *fuqaha'* was one of sinfulness, ignorance, emotionality and inherent meanness and dishonesty (Al-Jawzi 1984, 4).

How do standards of beauty illustrate the great differences experienced by Islam in its expansion and contact with other cultural traditions in the Middle East? In the tribal society of pre-Islamic Arabia, protection of the tribe was paramount. Battles fought against attackers and attacks undertaken against other tribes for defensive or raiding purposes were part of one's daily existence. Ideal characteristics for men and women of a tribe included chivalry, courage, generosity, character, physical strength, endurance, agility, loyalty and functionality. Ideals of feminine beauty presented by pre-Islamic poetry reflect tribal standards of the ideal "man." "There she is tilting with the knights, her face glowing with determination, riding her horse, taming the [men] with her charm, and intoxicating their souls with her beauty" ('Amru b. Kulthum in Al-Sioufi 1991, 22–23).

Beauty is not given physical attributes in the Quran; rather, ideals of womanhood are given moral, religious, social and spiritual standards. This does not mean that this was the mold followed in gender relations; instead, the social discourse incorporated gender mixing. The poetry of 'Umar b. Abi Rabi'a, a rich Qurayshite seventh-century Muslim, is reminiscent of the sensuous poetry of pre-Islamic Arabia. His poems portrayed the sweetness of a woman's breath and her "sultry" walk, which communicated her "availability" as a sexual partner (Shusha 1991, 25). In *Nu'am,* he described a night he spent with a "femme fatale" who played hard to get before admitting him into her tent. The following morning, her sisters smuggled him out of the tent dressed like a woman. Leaving him far from their camp, they asked him not to recognize them if they met in public (Shusha 1991, 30–39).

In Arabia, physical desires were explicitly voiced through such expressions as the "hotness" of the woman leading to "extreme heat and arousal" (*"shidat al-harara wa'l-tawahug"*) in the male: "I have love (*shawq*) messages waiting to be delivered—directly to your mouth" (Al-Sharif al-Tadhiy in Algosaibi 1986, 31). Sexual pleasure was expected by women as much as men; for example, 'Abid b. al-Abras's sixth-century poem, entitled "An Arab Chieftain to His Young Wife," describes a husband's frustration with his wife's continuous demand for sex. "Enough complaining more can wait till dawn, I may be worn in age, need you tell me so?" (Pound 1986, 35).

The Quran spoke of sex quite directly, admonishing men not to approach their wives unless they were ready for them. Early Islamic society seemed to follow the same pattern. Thus, 'Abdal-Rahman b. Abi Bakr had fallen in love with a Syrian princess and asked that she be captured and given to him after the Arab invasion of Syria. However, once she was his, she did not find him sexually appealing—"I do not desire him" (*"la ashtahih"*)—and he had no choice but to let her go (Karim 1991, 48).

Certain symbols of beauty remained constant in the social discourse. For example, women are likened to a full moon from pre-Islamic times until today. Common flirtations such as *"ya qamar"* point to the continuity of the moon as a symbol that is always female, representing beauty, purity and brightness: "She is formed complete, and beauty is complete in her face; beauty which lies not in her face lacks beauty's total. Once a month people see a new moon in the sky. Every dawn I hold a new moon in her face" (Ibn al-Ahnaf 1975, 37).

A tenth-century work cataloged descriptions of various parts of a woman's body as described by poets in order of importance: hair, temple, in praise and criticism of virgins, cheeks, brows, eyes (blueness, softness, cross-eyedness, eye diseases), nose, teeth, scent, saliva (al-rayq), conversation ability, voice, complexion, face, skin color, the effect of the small-pox, physique, neck, neck ornaments, breasts, hips, thighs (fullness, leanness and firmness), how women walk, clothing and its colors and embracing and its pleasures. Beauty was also measured according to elegance of manners, mannerisms, symmetry, proportionality of build (i'tidal al-tarkib) and roundness of the body. Contrast of colors seemed to be in demand: a dark beauty spot in a fair face, a fair face framed by long dark hair, marked contrast between the white of the eyes and the color of the iris, dark black kohl and pink "blushing" cheeks—"Does the red [dress] reflect the color of your cheeks, or did you dye it with the blood of the hearts [who love you]" (Al-Rraffa' 1990, 297). Eyes were particularly important, each part of the eye being described in detail: lively, large and "liquid" eyes "as though water could fall from them"; dark, long, curved and precise eyebrows ending in a curve; eyelids hesitant between coyness and aloofness; eyes recalling those of deer or wild buffaloes (Al-Rraffa' 1990, 6).

Focusing on face and eyes and the drama of contrast should be expected of a society where women show the face, rather than other parts of the body. The walk was also important in revealing femininity and sensuality. Metaphors used to describe a sensuous woman included "gliding gracefully like a cloud, moving neither fast nor slow" (Al-Rraffa' 1990, 284). Walking behind a woman with a lingering walk was a favorite pastime, since her pace allowed for the appreciation of her figure and flirtation (Al-Rraffa' 1990, 511). Ibn Miyada likened a woman's walk to a horse skip-dancing in mud, the hips swaying, the neck extended and the body trim (Al-Rraffa' 1990, 294).

The proliferation of medieval literature on brothels, slave women, drinking, gambling and general dissipation belies the medieval official discourse's strict moral code and, if anything, indicates that the looser the social habits, the stricter the fuqaha' in regard to moral scrutiny (Al-Ghazali 1990, 7). For example, Al-Ghazali chose "Making Marriage Desirable" as the title for his discussion of marriage in Marriage Etiquette and Defeating Passions. If the jurists spent their efforts trying to integrate love and sex into marriage, that was hardly the norm for medieval Islamic society, where marriage, love and sex represented different forms of relationships. "Love and infatuation may both be present, and the combination still not qualify to be termed passion" (Al-Jahiz 1980, 29).

MODERN DISCOURSES ON FEMALE BEAUTY

The modern period witnessed the introduction of a new patriarchical order suited to the new Western-style nation-state structures on which imperially dominated Islamic countries were being modeled. This new "modernizing" state-patriarchy was in contrast to earlier forms of patriarchy in which the family head was the arbiter of power relations within the family and tradition (*'urf*) determined the extent of patriarchical powers. In the modern discourse, the state became an actual "creator" of culture and the giver of laws that were enforced directly from the center. This meant that its legal jurisdiction was extended into social intercourse through which it became a direct determinant of patriarchical relations. In this "modern" discourse, modernization was never meant to be a total system; rather, it was applied selectively and became an instrument of the new order, confirming its powers and not undermining it. Thus, while the state applied Western legal codes based on individual or human rights as the basis for property, criminal and commercial laws, personal and family laws continued to be judged according to the *shari'a* (Islamic law) based on the communal good.

Translated into feminist issues, this meant that while women were given access to education and jobs, gender relations were structured on stricter principles than ever before, principles that reflected the contradictions of the state-patriarchical order. Qasim Amin (1865–1908) exemplified these contradictions. Hailed as the "emancipator of Egyptian women," Amin at first called for the necessity of female seclusion "because our religion . . . demands that men gather without the presence of a single woman, and that women gather without the presence of a single man" ('Imara 1989, 56). Later, Amin attacked the veil and called for the education of women, but he disapproved of the freedoms practiced by Western women ('Imara 1989, 59). As a middle way, he suggested the "legal veil" as dictated by the *shari'a,* actually a head cover adopted by westernizing middle-class women early in the twentieth century in Egypt. Such a cover, he argued, allowed women to participate in public life, but still made a symbolic seclusion possible. The family laws he proposed for reforming Islamic society are actually a confirmation of the new patriarchical order, which continued to allow the man full rights in regard to marriage and divorce, but which made the state a participant in these decisions. "Putting divorce under the control of a [government] judge would reduce the number of divorces and provide better supervision over the institution of marriage" ('Imara 1989, 63).

In most major old cities of the Islamic world in the twentieth century, ideals of beauty could be divided between the modern and the traditional, with great variations in between. Bayram al-Tunsi has represented these two ideals in his *zajals* about a thirty-five-year-old *sheikh* without previous experience with women. On his first visit to Cairo's modern center, he compared modernized foreign-looking (*khawagat*) ladies (*hawanim*), from whom he felt alienated, to women of older areas of the city, who interested and excited him: haunches of "pyramidical size" worthy of being followed, beautiful legs with flashy anklets (*khulkhal*), large heavy bosom, towering height, taut ripe body, small waist, fair color and a coy and sassy walk (*tata'awad wa tatabakhtar*) (Al-Tunsi 1985, 38–42, 153–54). The "popular" woman, covered with a *milaya laff,* a long, silky black cloth that is wound tightly around the body, showing its contours and leaving the arm, neck and face naked, excited Al-Tunsi. As for women lying on the beaches in swimsuits, he found them intriguing, but not exciting (Al-Tunsi 1985, 92–96).

In the modern moral discourse, marriage, love and sex are integrated, all other relationships being relegated to a "shady" area not recognized publicly. Prostitution was included in that shady area, as was common *'urfi* marriage, which is legal. The sanctity of marriage was emphasized by both the "official" and the social discourses during the modern period. While the official Islamic discourse stressed the unity of sex and marriage, with love occurring after marriage, rather than before, the social discourse discussed love in its pure form as a feeling occurring before marriage that could be associated with sex after marriage.

The Quran was used to confirm the vision of love as the loftiest of all bonds, particularly within the confines of marriage (Qutb 1984, 8). Love was romanticized, experienced, an attraction in itself not necessarily connected with a beloved's physical characteristics: "You who lives in my mind and being, yet far from my vision and my eyes. You are my soul which I cannot behold. Near to me. The closest" (Qutb 1984, 13). Thus, marrying for love became the theme of the modern Islamic world; marriage without love was no more than a shell: "Love is the loftiest of all human emotions . . . marriage is but a frame created by society for the relationship between a man and a woman . . . it could be a frame of love or of duplicity" (Qutb 1984, 38).

For bourgeois writers such as 'Abdal-Qudus (1980), elegance and intelligence were very important ideals for a woman; being "chic" was a sign of belonging to westernizing classes and acquiring Western tastes. Smoking cigarettes, wearing high heels, having one's hair dressed at a beauty salon, manicuring one's fingernails and affecting a cultured speech were all superimposed on the traditional picture of an exciting, coy woman. As in the medieval period, the eyes continued to be a focus of attention even among westernizing classes, which indicates separation of the sexes and the need for the language of the eyes to communicate between them. The art of hushed flirtation became even more important in a society that allowed women out of the home and permitted them to mingle, but frowned upon any real communications with the opposite sex, a real distinction from pre-Islamic and early Islamic Arabia, when conversing (*musamara*) and "legal" mixing were usual. Love at first sight was quite popular, and the "meeting of the souls," rather than physical beauty, was the reason for sexual attraction. The carnal possibilities—femaleness, sultriness or suggestiveness—hinted at in a woman's eyes formed the basis of the attraction. Very often in love relationships, the *'uthri* love, which the woman expected to lead into marriage, was reciprocated by a more carnal love on his side, which could also lead into marriage ('Abdal-Hamid 1986, 13–17).

It should be added that notwithstanding the romanticism attached to love, marriage remained very much under the control of the family, and compatibility continued to be a method of controlling marriage and class by patriarchical society. A woman was expected to be untouched (*'Afifa*), and a love relationship often ended when the woman allowed it to turn physical. Films and novels are full of stories where a woman who squandered herself (*faratat fi nafsiha*) pays a severe price, quite often death and at least the contempt of the very man she allowed to touch her ('Abdal-Hamid 1986, 26–27). The hypocrisy of the moral discourse is well described by 'Abdal-Qudus:

> A man has the vanity, selfishness, and innocence of a child. He likes to think that he was the first at everything, and that he married a woman untouched by any man before him, and that she has never found a man to love before he came along . . . we do not allow our wives to confess their past to their husbands even if this past contained no more than an innocent relationship because old meaningless traditions insist on considering any relationship between a boy and a girl as a great sin. . . . And yet even though we claim to hold on to these traditions we still commit this sin, we commit it because the realities of life compel us to commit it, propelling and pushing us. (1980, 46–48)

These confusing contradictions must be seen as one cause for the return of women to veiling. Sherifa Zuhur looks at the return to the veil today as the creation of a new female self-image that is being structured by women themselves; that is, it is a form of empowerment (Zuhur 1992, 4). In an autobiographical study of the process of becoming veiled, Kariman Hamza stated that her decision resulted from a personal crisis and peer pressure, but that it was ultimately a process of self-worth, of "liberation" in the contemporary situation where women wanted a return to the ideals of purity and respectability. This ideal was one that she felt she was opting for herself, even though she noted the pressure of *sheikhs* whose approval she needed to be successful in a career as a hostess of religious programs on Egyptian television (Hamza, 1986).

Two discourses can be identified in regard to conceptions of female beauty in the Islamic world today. They correlate with the modern and traditional and the variations in between. Within each of the two categories, there are differences in style and taste. The modern conceptualizes women as striving for liberation and gender equality; conscious of the importance of political and economic power, they work toward achieving both. Women espousing this discourse model their looks according to Western fashions; they include women of the wealthy elite classes and wives and daughters of high government dignitaries or businessmen with foreign affiliations. To belong to the elite, women almost have to accept this elite's picture of formal female sophistication: a wife who is a good hostess, who dresses impeccably, as close to Western styles as her own tastes and traditions allow. Since many of these women in fact originated from the 'ama (powerless masses), their tastes may continue to exhibit more "popular" characteristics, a fact that women of this class work very hard to hide; otherwise, it becomes a handicap in their families' social climbing.

Middle-class women tend to emulate women of the upper classes. Since money is not as available to them, they tend to depend on local, rather than imported, goods. Most women in this category are educated and are professionals, married to professionals or the children of professionals. Western garb is common among them; however, today, traditional garb is also making an appearance. Western garb can also be found among members of the urban lower classes, particularly younger women who work in offices, shops and homes.

As for traditional wear, that remains very close to the countryside where the dress of peasant women continues to be the same as it was at least since the nineteenth century. In the cities, traditional wear has changed greatly during the last century. Thus, the alluring popular figure of a woman wound up tightly in the silky black *milaya laff* admired by Al-Tunsi and worn by Nagib Mahfouz's characters in popular quarters of Cairo has been replaced today by the "Islamic garb," which is considered to have been prescribed by the Quran and *hadith*. The Islamic garb appears in different forms according to class; thus, whereas all believe the head, arms, and legs have to be covered, the covering differs. Wealthier middle-class women are stricter in their observance of the requirements, usually wearing a long, loose, dresslike *jalabiya* and a head cover reaching the waist and covering the shoulders and arms. When women go out, they sometimes wear a black *habarah* (women's garment covering from head to toe), which is similar to those worn in early nineteenth-century Egypt (Lane 1986, 53).

Is wearing Islamic garb a sign of less education or less wealth? Not really, since increasingly college students and graduates have opted to wear Islamic garb even if they come from a social class that was at one time "becoming westernized." At the same time, women of once poorer families that have become enriched through trade, services or manufacturing (e.g., families of butchers, grocers, electricians and mechanics) have as often opted to wear Islamic garb as to wear Western clothes. Some middle-class women who consider themselves modern and socially mobile have opted for the veil because it represents a more affordable form of beauty or reflects growing Islamization within their societies.

However different the modern and the traditional discourses seem to be, the two may be seen as actually one discourse that allows for the continuation of a patriarchical structure. Wearing Islamic garb is not in itself an acceptance of male dominance any more than wearing Western clothes is an acceptance of Western-style feminism. Both groups advocate the state-patriarchy's approach to the integration of marriage, love and sex into one legally recognized relationship. Women wearing Islamic garb are as insistent on husband loyalty, fidelity and monogamy as are modernized women. Furthermore, the servility of women is no more a matter of the clothes worn or the ideals of beauty espoused than is the issue of liberation. One woman may be forced into covering herself by a dominating husband, while another may be expected to wear the latest fashions, undertake regular physical exercise and live a lifestyle dictated by the needs of her husband's or father's business.

One dramatic change taking place today that pertains to the subject of ideals of feminine beauty has to do with skin color. During the Mamlukid and Ottoman periods, the ruling elite purchased slaves of different ethnic and racial origins (Croutier 1989, 30). A slave's price depended on her intellectual and artistic abilities, rather than on her ethnic origin. However, when it came to marriage, the elite preferred to marry women of their own race and ethnic group (Mahmud 1988, 29–32). Ethnicity and physical attributes formed one of the bases for the exclusivity of the Mamluk caste; hence, they preferred to marry women from their own tribes in Central Asia. The Ottomans preferred Turkish women or women from European countries over women from other parts of the Islamic world (Croutier 1989, 103). Because of the association of fairness of skin color with the ruling elite, fairness became a predominant ideal for female beauty from the medieval period and into the modern.

At the end of the Ottoman period, the national upper and middle classes, who were forming new, indigenous, mobile social forces, looked upon fairness of skin as symbolic of a relationship to an old Turkish "aristocracy." Such standards continued into the twentieth century, but, today, we do not see the differentiation between races in conceptions of beauty or marriage choices. This is a result of the growing homogeneity of classes within Islamic society and is a reflection of the moving forces to whom "alien" standards of beauty do not represent an ideal. It is not a reaction to the West as much as it is a part of a discourse by which people are taking off their "white" masks and accepting their "black" skins, to paraphrase Franz Fanon.

CONCLUSIONS

In modernization paradigms, what is traditional is considered backward and oppressive, and any manifestations that do not constitute modern images, including modern ideals of beauty, become part of the perpetuation of the patriarchical domination of women. This chapter on ideals of feminine beauty in Islamic society has touched upon many questions pertinent to gender relations, class relations, cultural patterns and the historical process in general.

First, notwithstanding the clear break between pre-Islamic and Islamic religious and political patterns, there are important areas of continuity, particularly at the sociocultural level. The importance of this type of focused study is that it takes culture as the substructure in contradistinction to political-economic concerns. By doing so, a different image of gender relations became evident in which women appear as participants and "enslavement" becomes rather more complex. Feminist studies need to begin with the cultural base of each specific society and undertake a methodology in which culture is seen in process, as the realm of historical continuities and discontinuities. Political agendas have directed feminist studies; an approach focusing on the state has only obfuscated the realities of society.

Second, the ideals of beauty in Islamic society seem to differ according to the nature of the gender relationship; thus, beauty standards differed depending on whether the gender relationship was based on marriage, love or sex. There seems to be a consistent image of female beauty in the traditional or Islamic discourse, this image of beauty being based more on female allure than on particular features.

Finally, in this research I could find no definitive correlation between the veil and seclusion and sexual inhibitions. Questions should be raised about the historical nature of sex relations with the intent of discovering when particular patterns of gender control became established. Moral codes undermining female sexuality in the Middle East may have accompanied modernization and westernization with the establishment of a "Victorian" moral discourse, which was spread among upper- and middle-class women through European schools, missionaries and a state hegemonic culture. To reflect this approach to sexuality back into Islamic history, however, only distorts both the past and the present, since it obfuscates the patterns of paternalism in the premodern period as well as the real reasons for the male-dominant societies of the Islamic world today. If a "liberation" of Muslim women is to be achieved, as is the goal of feminists, then the origins, history and nature of the contemporary patriarchical order must be understood.

WORKS CITED

'Abdal-Hamid, 'A. 1986. *Ishtaqt Ilayka.* Tunis: Matba'at al-Qawmiya l'il-Nashr.
'Abdal-Qudus, I. 1980. *Ayyam Shababi.* Cairo: Al-Maktab al-Misri al-Hadith.
Ahmed, L. 1992. *Women and Gender in Islam: Historical Roots of a Modern Debate.* New Haven, Conn.: Yale University Press.
Ibn al-Ahnaf, A. 1975. *Birds Through a Ceiling of Alabaster.* Ed. G. Wightman and A. Al-Udkri. London: Penguin Books.
Algosaibi, G. 1986. *Lyrics from Arabia.* Washington, D.C.: Three Continents Press.
Ali, Y. 1934. *The Holy Quran.* Baltimore: Amana Press.
Anas, M. 1990. *Al-Muwwata'.* Al-Muhammadiya, Morocco: Manshurat dar al-Afaq al-Jadida.
Croutier, A. 1989. *Harem: The World Behind the Veil.* New York: Abbeville Press.
Al-Ghazali, A. 1990. *Adab al-Nikah wa Kasr al-Shahwatayn.* Susa, Tunisia: Manshurat Dar al-Ma'arif l'il-Tiba'a wa'l-Nashr.
Hamza, K. 1986. *Rihlati min al-Sufur ila al-Hijab.* Cairo: Dar al-Fath.
'Imara, M. 1989. *Qasim Amin: Al-A'mal al-Kamila.* Cairo: Dar al-Shuruq.
Al-Jabri, 'A. 1983. *Al-Mara fi'l-Tasawwur al-Islami.* Cairo: Maktabat Wahba.
Al-Jahiz, A. 1980. *The Epistle on Singing-Girls of Jahiz.* Trans. A. Beeston. Warminster, England: Aris & Phillips.
Al-Jawzi, A. 1984. *Ahkam al-Nisa'.* Cairo: Maktabat al-Turath al-Islami.
Karim, I. 1991. *Tara'if al-Nisa' min al-Turath al-'Arabi.* Cairo: Dar al-Nadim.
Al-Khamash, S. 1973. *Al-Mar'a al-'Arabiya wa'l-Mujtama' al-Taqlidi al-Mutakhalif.* Beirut: Dar al-Haqiqa.
Lane, E. 1986. *Manners and Customs of the Modern Egyptians.* Cairo: East-West Publications.
Mahmud, 'A. 1988. *Al-Jawari fi Mujtama' al-Qahira al-Mamlukiya.* Cairo: Al-Hay'a al-Misriya al-'Ama l'il-Kitab.
Mernissi, F. 1987. *The Veil and the Male Elite.* New York: Addison-Wesley.
Pound, O. (ed.). 1986. *Arabic and Persian Poems in English.* Washington, D.C.: Three Continents Press.
Qutb, 'A. 1984. *Al-Hubb wa'l-Gins min Manzur Islami.* Cairo: Maktabat al-Quran.
Ibn Abi Rabi'a, 'U. 1987. *Al-'Iqd al-Farid.* Askaloosa, Iowa: William Penn College.
Al-Rraffa', A. 1990. *Al-Muhib wa'l-Mahbub wa'l-Mashmum wa'l-Mashrub.* Damascus.
Shusha, F. 1991. *Ahla 'Ishrin Qasidat Hubb f'il-Shir'r al-'Arabi.* Cairo: Dar al-Shuruq.
Al-Sioufi, 'I. 1991. *Al-Mar'a fi'l-Adab al-Jahili.* Beirut: Dar al-Fikr al-Libnani.
Tillion, G. 1983. *The Republic of Cousins.* London: Alsaqi Books.
Al-Tunsi, B. 1985. *Maqamat Bayram.* Cairo: Madbuli Bookshop.
Wolf, N. 1991. *The Beauty Myth: How Images of Beauty Are Used Against Women.* New York: William Morrow.
Zuhur, S. 1992. *Revealing Reveiling.* Albany: State University of New York Press.

PART II

WOMEN, BEAUTY AND SELF-IMAGE/CONTROL

5

Symbolic Violence and the Disembodiment of Identity

John W. Murphy

A new mode of social control is now operative in almost every institution. This strategy is consistent with the "market psychology" that became prevalent during the 1980s. Due to the emphasis that has been placed on individualism and freedom, control should not be ostensibly overt. Therefore, an unobtrusive means of control had to be invented. Most important, this method had to appear to be apolitical because politics is understood to be anathema to the market.

Writers such as Say, von Mises, and Hayek have had enormous impact on neo-conservative thought (Winchell 1991, 1–8). Assumed by their justification of laissez-faire economics is that no one has complete knowledge. Accordingly, any attempt to construct politically, through government intervention or some other means, a thoroughly integrated society is considered to be both futile and disruptive. Simply put, because no person has the all-encompassing knowledge required to accomplish this feat, manipulation and oppression are likely to occur. Because of the personal character of every knowledge base, whose insights should be trusted to organize society?

But without violating the implied pluralism, social order has to be enforced. Key to the success of this endeavor is to discover a means of social control that is divorced from opinions, personal values and the whims of political figures. The source of control, in short, has to transcend the exigencies of everyday life. For if this is not the case, personal idiosyncrasies will eventually undermine social order.

Typically, conservatives refer to this base of order as tradition. Accordingly, persons are not entirely free when they are trading or engaged in any other endeavor. Sustaining these activities are what post-modernists call "metanarratives" (Lyotard 1984, xxiv). As defined by Lyotard, these universal principles are not subject to interpretation and are recognized by all rational persons and societies. In this way, order is preserved because human action is not guided by opinion (*doxa*) or other personal elements.

Nonetheless, this belief in universals has spawned a very effective means of controlling behavior. A kind of dualism is invoked that allows order to appear absolute and any opposition to the dominant norms of a society to be effectively undermined. Especially ingenious about this tactic is the fact that control is made to appear rational and even necessary. In point of fact, persons often begin to join voluntary programs that are designed to extinguish eccentric or abnormal demeanor. Exposure to certain messages and images, in other words, results in persons seeking "normalization" and becoming accomplices in their repression. And due to the apparent absence of force, this style of socialization is called symbolic control or, as some modern critics say, "symbolic violence" (Thompson 1984, 42–72).

THE THEORY OF SYMBOLIC CONTROL

For the most part, physical beatings and other brutal methods of social control have been outlawed. According to Foucault, corporal punishment is inconsistent with the modern desire to be refined and enlightened (1977). Physical coercion is deemed to be invasive, haphazard and thus barbaric. Yet almost daily, increasing numbers of persons consult psychiatrists, psychologists and plastic surgeons in order to better cope with reality. More than ever before, persons are trying to achieve normalcy through therapy and a host of other interventions.

Central to this process of remediation is symbolic, rather than physical, control. As is suggested, compliance is gained through the exercise of language. In this case, language should be understood in the broadest sense to include speech, logic and images. Most important is the fact that so-called "dominant significations" are able to subvert alternative ways of speaking, thinking and acting. "Symbolic violence . . . is a violence exercised . . . in formal terms." Formal in this context means that the "force of the universal" is united with the "force of the official" (Bourdieu 1990, 84–85). Accordingly, an apparently neutral means of control is substantiated by an equally neutral source of legitimacy. And because of the exalted status that is given to a particular conception of knowledge and human action, a monolithic version of social reality is easily enforced. Indeed, this reality has almost magical power to entice persons and gain their support. As a result, certain bodily images, for example, are considered to be indicative of perfection and sought at all cost.

What is the source of this ability of select images to monopolize reality? This hypostatization of reality is achieved through a dubious theoretical démarche. Specifically, dualism, particularly the distinction that is made between fact and value, is recognized as valid. What this means is that a hierarchy is established between knowledge bases. Those that appear to be unencumbered by interpretation and other human foibles are thought to be objective and most valid. Bourdieu describes the assignment of this status as taking place according to the "law of price formation." As a result, knowledge that is scientific and objective is simply presumed to depict reality accurately, while other forms of information do not.

In the case of social imagery, primacy is given to structural approaches to describing normativeness. By the term *structural* is meant that speech is stripped of the human element and made to appear neutral. Several arguments have been adopted to justify this practice. Most popular is the claim that as language becomes more scientific and formalized, an unmediated picture of reality is easier to obtain (Newmeyer 1986, 31–62). And because these pure descriptions most closely reflect reality, all others pale by comparison. Hence, the stage is set for symbolic control to be exerted over persons.

Especially important is that the "reality *sui generis*" extolled by Durkheim can be imposed with little difficulty, thereby establishing an unfettered standard of normalcy (1983, 86–88). The rationale for this conclusion is quite simple. Because scientific or formalized images are unbiased, the norms they convey are assumed to be universal and demand serious attention. As indicated by Durkheim, this transcendent ideal embodies a standard that every rational or normal person should strive to emulate. A base of reality that is untarnished by politics or other quotidian concerns is thus accessible, and norms that would otherwise seem arbitrary are given the patina of respectability.

The result of this dualism is that scientific significations are allowed to mask all others. Actually, the gradual inferiorization of other languages, concepts, definitions and images is soon expected because these alternatives are affected by interpretive considerations and presumed to be unreliable. Furthermore, and essential to social control, all oppositional knowledge bases, ideas and proposals are undermined. Clearly, why would any reasonable person choose an option that is by definition irrational? Establishing such asymmetry between versions of knowledge serves to reinforce a specific rendition of reality and subtly suppress rebellion.

Also noteworthy is that pluralism is not believed to be violated by this symbolic protection of reality, for economic and similar class-based motives do not seem to be involved in this process. After all, science does not represent a particular social or political viewpoint; science, according to the usual claim, is universal. Consequently, rules that are sustained by scientific objectivity cannot be treated as intrusive, prejudicial or otherwise socially disruptive. Standards that are legitimized by science, or other neutral languages, are surely natural and reflect the commonweal.

Could there be a more efficient means of social control? A single reality is justified in such a way that all challenges to it are discredited. Moreover, this winnowing process is undertaken in a manner that appears to be apolitical. After this activity is under way, persons are left with what Marcuse calls a "one dimensional" world. This is a realm where everything is classified in a binary manner, and acceptance of this scheme is assumed to be a measure of rationality. Volatility is removed from reality because norms appear to be sequestered from interpretation.

MANIFESTATIONS OF SYMBOLIC CONTROL

Nowadays, symbolic control is commonly enacted through images of the body. Particular conceptions of beauty and fitness, for example, are extolled as desirable. However, specific styles of thinking, speaking and behaving are also regularly idealized. As was suggested earlier in this discussion, the hallmark of this activity is that persons gradually become dominated by specific symbols. Certain images, in other words, gain the autonomy necessary to differentiate reality from illusion; these images are considered to be objective and inviolable.

How is such authority attributed to symbolism? Simply put, a number of bodily or other images are given unquestioned legitimacy. Although the techniques for legitimation vary, they share a common theme. That is, the justification for key symbols is cited to be derived from so-called natural tendencies or laws, and thus the desirability of these images is thought to be innate and beyond question.

For example, genetic factors are regularly invoked to rationalize all sorts of policies, for various combinations of DNA molecules are assumed to determine how persons should be treated. These so-called building blocks of life, notes Barthes, are treated as if they constitute a primordial alphabet (1986, 45). Hence, many of the predictions that are made about a person's future performance in school or elsewhere are believed to have validity because the information used is presumed to be uninfluenced by interpretation. To those who praise the benefits of genetic explanations, literal portrayals of individual and group potential are possible.

While slightly different, other physiologically based scenarios have been used to reinforce specific bodily imagery. Quite common in current advertisements is the claim that makeup should be selected on the basis of biological factors. As a result, a woman supposedly will choose the proper colors. Moreover, so-called scientific tests have begun to proliferate that are assumed to be able to specify everything from a person's proper weight to cholesterol level. In this regard, a body image can be fostered that is balanced, proportionate and thus perfect.

But as persons begin to age, these images become harder to maintain. Nonetheless, the pursuit of an ideal body does not necessarily abate. What cannot be achieved through exercise and diet is gained through surgery. Elective surgery, which is often dangerous and may result in mutilation, has become commonplace. Both males and females seem to be so enthralled by promotional material that they will squander money and risk their health to acquire a particular bodily form.

Assumed by symbolic control is that a literal, not metaphorical, language depicts an acceptable human image. Usually, this language is couched in scientific or other terms that appear to be objective, neutral and natural. Most popular is to have bodily changes linked to physiology or descriptions derived from medical or psychological exams. Because the resulting images are ostensibly value-free, rational persons are expected to strive to fulfill, through any means and for as long as possible, these ideals.

But critics of this analysis charge that beauty has always existed and that persons have always used makeup or other adornments (Wilson 1990). Indeed, the aim of this discussion has not been to deny the existence of beauty or to argue that all images are identical. The idea is that certain standards are accepted to embody principles that are not culturally invented, interpretive, imposed by those in power or employed to curtail growth or spontaneity. Through slick portrayals, persons are encouraged to approximate a Platonic ideal, which, of course, is impossible. For mere mortals, the accompanying abstractions can be viewed only as universal, lawful, rational and good. In short, these images epitomize what is thought to be rational and acceptable.

Yet because no one occupies this ethereal realm, persons must labor intensely to create this identity. Often associated with this activity is self-denial, for every sign of contingency or imperfection must be concealed. In a manner of speaking, persons are terrorized by abstractions that are gradually venerated. For this reason, symbolic control is also referred to as symbolic violence. Specifically, personal desires and predilections are quashed by unadulterated images. Without overt coercion, persons abandon willingly their cultural heritage, ethnic identity and customary approaches to constructing reality because the flaws associated with a quotidian existence should be concealed.

SIGNIFICANCE OF SYMBOLIC VIOLENCE

The purpose of this discussion has not been to suggest that symbolic control is not violent or to diminish the presence of physical attacks. On the contrary, symbolic violence often culminates in serious psychological and physical wounds. Once a person's own definition of self has been undermined, for example, surgery, therapy and other masochistic interventions are often sought. Persons often begin to degrade themselves in a host of awful ways, following the evisceration of their *raison d'être* by an authority figure or another agent of social control.

Therefore, what is the significance of drawing attention to symbolic control? In order to answer this query properly, several issues need to be addressed.

First, social control is usually thought to be enacted through overt or covert force. Implied is a clash of viewpoints, whereby power determines which one will survive. The thrust of symbolic control, on the other hand, is to conceal the exercise of force because constraining persons through a forceful means is understood generally to be inefficient, unsophisticated and thus passé. A more effective method for restricting the ideas that circulate throughout a society, for example, is to convince the populace that a particular genre of knowledge—that is, scientifically produced input—is more valid than any other kind (Habermas 1973, 263–76). In this way, persons will often suppress their own views because of the advice of technical or professional experts. And while this adjustment is occurring, patients or clients may even begin to feel cured or enlightened. What is actually happening, however, is the gradual and systematic homogenization of thought.

Second, symbolic violence is far more serious than labeling. The point at this juncture is that critics may charge symbolic control has already been discussed by labeling theorists. But whereas behavior is classified through labeling, much more is involved in symbolic control. Most noteworthy about this difference is that knowledge bases are asymmetrically arranged, reason is differentiated clearly from irrationality, the dominant reality is assumed to be inviolable and opposition to norms is discredited in the case of symbolic violence. While several of these themes are sometimes associated with labeling, they are not regularly emphasized. Therefore, the process of labeling is expanded during symbolic control.

And, third, Bourdieu and Passeron (1977) introduced this notion as a critique of Marxism. Their intention was not to dismiss the role played by power, structural barriers and class interests in social control. On the contrary, they wanted to illustrate the new methods whereby the working class is managed. In the past, crude practices, such as the overt manipulation of the media, the installation of political officials in key institutions and the generation of propaganda, were emphasized. Nowadays, however, such ideological activities are deemed to be inefficient and possibly counterproductive. Accordingly, social control has been placed within the bailiwick of scientists, physicians and other technocrats, who are ostensibly not partisan. The lesson of symbolic violence is that control is not necessarily ideological.

New renditions of dualism have gained credence that makes social control almost unobtrusive. In order to assess rationally beauty and other aspects of society, this philosophical principle must be abandoned. Serious questions about social control, accordingly, may in the future be philosophical, rather than practical. This would be an odd twist, for rarely has this dimension of social life been viewed as a philosophical issue.

EMBODIED VISIONS

As a consequence of symbolic violence, persons are disembodied. Their identity becomes increasingly rarefied as they strive to covet idealized qualities. Many modern writers have noted correctly that this trend can be reversed only by undermining essentialism (Bordo 1990). Essentialists are dualists and thus believe that persons or events have inherent meaning. Hence, certain bodily images are thought to represent, without question, health or illness. Of course, as already suggested, questioning this typology would be indicative of a lack of proper understanding.

In order to refute essentialism, the ahistorical referent that sustains the differentiation between fundamental and accidental traits must be exposed as illusory. When this is accomplished, beauty can be pursued in an unslavish manner. "Nonrepressive Narcissism," according to Bartky, can serve as a proper justification for beauty (1990, 42). In other words, beauty can be seen as reflecting opinions, desires and personal or collective images that can be either accepted or rejected. Beauty can be treated as a "social construction," rather than a natural phenomenon.

What advocates of essentialism forget is that all knowledge is mediated by interpretation. Reminiscent of the work of Kuhn (1970), critics of essentialism write that even science is theory-laden. Concepts, facts and laws do not appear on the scene undefiled by perception, historical context and a commitment to a particular portrayal of nature or society. In point of fact, Mary Hesse argues that progress in science consists of a battle between competing metaphors, as opposed to the methodical selection of the most realistic descriptions of nature (1980, 111–24).

What this means is that the cornerstone of symbolic violence is subverted, thereby challenging the way in which novel or unique knowledge bases have been inferiorized in the past. Because no norms escape from the influence of interpretation, all renditions of beauty reside on the same ontological plane. And, to paraphrase Alfred Schutz, any one of these realities can become paramount through an act of volition (1964, 135–58). From a melange of definitions, one or more conceptions of beauty may be selected as valid until further notice.

Beauty is thus embedded within a "language game" (Lyotard 1984, 9–11). Rather than being eternal, beauty is a matter of convention, thereby restoring history to nature. Subsequent to this emancipation of criteria, persons can either define themselves or accept the monikers applied by others. Likewise, the so-called normal metaphors can be rejected without recrimination. Irrationality, simply put, does not automatically accompany the adoption of an idiosyncratic image of beauty.

This way of evaluating beauty is mature, in the manner intended by Horkheimer and his Frankfurt colleagues, because the legitimacy of a definition is not derived from a metaphysical source of authority (Jay 1973, 119–20). Although those who are in power may try for any number of reasons to impose a particular version of beauty, the outcome of this action is not irreversible because, as Marcuse contends, refusal is always possible. The moral of this story is that legitimacy granted by persons can be recalled at any time.

Due to this anti-dualistic position, persons are able to embody their identities. They can feel at home in their self-concepts, for achieving or maintaining normalcy does not require the removal of so-called human flaws. Persons can thus shape themselves in any way they desire, without having to be compared to a traditional, but irrelevant, standard. What could be more liberating?

TEXTUAL POLITICS

Not everyone is elated about the claim that the world is a linguistic text. This portrayal is presumed by some to be apolitical (Aronowitz & Giroux 1991, 57–86). The social world, these critics contend, is far more than a piece of literature. Derrida (1980) has tried to address this objection, but his rejoinder has been either misunderstood or not recognized as viable. From this discussion, however, politics should be seen as pervading a textual description of normalcy.

What could be more political than understanding reality to be subject to interpretation? Through dialogue, which at times may become internecine, order is formed and protected. That the outcome of dialogue may be unpredictable may bother opponents of this viewpoint. Moreover, the absence of a program for change may be disconcerting. Nonetheless, the use of the textual metaphor certainly invites interpretation and debate, which are not necessarily a part of other social ontologies.

Most discouraging is that the majority of persons do not accept their invitation to engage the polity. Clearly adopting the text as a way to envisioning reality does not solve the problem of alienation. But a text, at least in terms of modern theory, does not deter criticism. What more can be asked reasonably of a descriptive device? Making reality accessible to critique is clearly quite radical, according to the Western political tradition. Denied the status of a reality *sui generis,* the polity is believed to be very vulnerable to attack.

J. Hillis Miller is correct in his assessment of interpretive epistemologies

(1991, 359–84). In the face of unfettered interpretation, canons dissolve, and absolute authorities lose their appeal. The idolization of the word, according to Barthes, is challenged and reversed (1972, 149). Because texts are rendered open, the polity no longer rests on a pedestal. As a result, shaking the foundation of knowledge in this way allows persons to invent their own destiny. That they should somehow escape from this freedom does not signal that interpretation is apolitical.

WORKS CITED

Aronowitz, S., and H. A. Giroux. 1991. *Postmodern Education.* Minneapolis: University of Minnesota Press.

Barthes, R. 1986. *The Rustle of Language.* New York: Hill & Wang.

———. 1972. *Mythologies.* New York: Hill & Wang.

Bartky, S. L. 1990. *Femininity and Domination.* New York: Routledge, Chapman and Hall.

Bordo, S. R. 1990. Postmodernism and Gender-scepticism. In L. J. Nicholson (ed.), *Feminism/Postmodernism* (pp. 133–56). London: Routledge, Chapman and Hall.

Bourdieu, P. 1990. *In Other Words.* Stanford: Stanford University Press.

Bourdieu, P., and J-C. Passeron. 1977. *Reproduction: In Education, Society and Culture.* Beverly Hills, Calif.: Sage.

Derrida, J. 1980. The Law of Genre. *Critical Inquiry* 7(1): 58–81.

Durkheim, E. 1983. *Pragmatism and Sociology.* Cambridge: Cambridge University Press.

Foucault, M. 1977. *Discipline and Punish.* New York: Pantheon.

Habermas, J. 1973. *Theory and Practice.* Boston: Beacon Press.

Hesse, M. 1980. *Revolutions and Reconstructions in the Philosophy of Science.* Bloomington: Indiana University Press.

Jay, M. 1973. *The Dialectical Imagination.* Boston: Little, Brown.

Kuhn, T. S. 1970. *The Structure of Scientific Revolutions.* 2d ed. Chicago: University of Chicago Press.

Lyotard, J.-F. 1984. *The Postmodern Condition.* Minneapolis: University of Minnesota Press.

Miller, J. H. 1991. *Theory Now and Then.* Durham, N.C.: Duke University Press.

Newmeyer, F. J. 1986. *The Politics of Linguistics.* Chicago: University of Chicago Press.

Schutz, A. 1964. *Collected Papers.* Vol. 2. The Hague: Nijhoff.

Thompson, J. B. 1984. *Studies in the Theory of Ideology.* Berkeley: University of California Press.

Wilson, E. 1990. These New Components of the Spectacle: Fashion and Postmodernism. In R. Boyne and A. Rattansi (eds.), *Postmodernism and Society* (pp. 209–36). New York: St. Martin's Press.

Winchell, M. R. 1991. *Neo-conservative Criticism.* Boston: Twayne Publishers.

6

Making Love Alone: Videocentrism and the Case of Modern Pornography

Eric Mark Kramer

To understand pornography, one must understand the conflicting compulsions that create it. Pornography is a clue to more fundamental forces of modernity and their consequences. Civilizational expressions reveal the world of a people: what they value, how they think, what they conceive and perceive (Gebser 1985; Gadamer 1975; Giedion 1962; Kepes 1944; Kilpatrick 1961; Sapir 1949; Gibson 1950, 1962; Hall 1966, 1976; Geertz 1973; Kramer 1992a, 1992b). Transactional psychology demonstrates that experience changes how a person "sees," that humans learn how to perceive, as for instance when one learns to see/recognize camouflage and optical distortion, and adjust accordingly (Gibson 1962; Kilpatrick 1961; Berkeley 1708).[1] In this way, pornography is changing our world. Like other civilizational expressions such as architecture, clothing, proxemics, philosophies, sciences, arts and religions, pornography manifests the predominate mode of awareness, the phenomenological attitude of its creator(s) and the community that consumes and resonates with it (Wellek 1963; Barthes 1964; Dufrenne 1964; Poulet 1971; Ingarden 1965; Doubrovsky 1967; Husserl 1970; Heidegger 1971; Gadamer 1975).

There is no sense in claiming that something exists outside of direct, personal experience. Even a suspicion must be directly experienced to be meaningful. The fundamental attitude with which one turns toward a phenomenon will determine its sense. Sense or meaning is identical to perception. Sense perception is the result of orientation in accord with one's prejudices (limitations and abilities), metaphysical and otherwise. Thus, two people may undertake to present explicit sexuality. One may see/depict pornography, while the other sees/depicts erotica, or something else. The difference between the two modes of expression (and thus their identities) is only relevant via comparison, and their respective qualities are revealed by contrast.

The ground of communication is the hermeneutic field of shared meanings—world. Values, utilities, interests, aesthetics, modes of perceiving and ways of being are expressed artifactually. Even the medium of communication manifests ontological prejudices and interests (Habermas 1968; Apel 1972; Ong 1982; Mumford 1934; McLuhan 1964). Modern pornography, with its sharp focus, intimate sound, color and penetrating angles, is violent and violating. The pornographic revelation is immediate, clinical—robotic. It is an unmistakable expression of an urban(izing), modern(izing), perspectival world. Pornography is "obscene," violent and violating—overdetermination.

By comparison, erotica is a product of a preindustrial, preperspectival rural world. Erotica is an expression of a culture concerned with fructification (not efficient manufacturing with its temporal stress), fertility and cosmic harmony. Pornography shuns domesticity as evil and, as such, manifests a particularly virulent attack upon the maternal and mature. One could hardly imagine a porno film that followed sexuality through pregnancy, childbirth and the rigors of parenting.

Although pornography is a particularly vengeful rejection of domesticity, it is nonetheless an expression of a larger phallocentric bias in the modern world. Other cultural expressions of the modern masculine fear/ hate of the domestic are exemplified by marginal television and film characters (often the butt of jokes). These characters represent the domestic realm, such as Hop Sing on "Bonanza," Festus and Chester on "Gunsmoke," Uncle Charlie on "My Three Sons" (which also raises the issue of the trend of the happy widower),[2] Granny on "The Beverly Hillbillies," Barney Fife and Aunt Bea on "The Andy Griffith Show," Mrs. Livingston on "The Courtship of Eddie's Father," Mr. French on "Family Affair," and so forth.

Domestics are infirm, childish, foreign or otherwise marginal. They nurture and support heroes. While lovable and loyal, they cannot be trusted with great responsibility. The realm of the domestic is clearly marginalized on a culturewide basis. Housework is socially and economically invisible. Caretakers in American zoos earn an average of over $9 an hour with insurance, while child care and nursing home workers are paid little more than the legal minimum wage and often are permanent part-timers without insurance.

Domesticity is not sexy. Absolute freedom from domestic responsibility is portrayed in countless television series (including the most popular ones), films, novels and pornography as the most highly valued state of being. Such cultural icons range across several media, including pop and rap music; athletic, industrial and political stardom; and numerous film and television images. Examples include the cowboy drifter (any number of Clint Eastwood and John Wayne incarnations and numerous television "westerns"), the avenging vigilante (*Rambo,* "The Equalizer," "Quantum Leap," "Kung Fu," "Have Gun Will Travel," "The Incredible Hulk," *Aliens*), the mechanized nomad ("The Wild Wild West," "Knight Rider," "The Dukes of Hazzard," "Route 66," "The A-Team," "Star Trek," "The Man from U.N.C.L.E.," "The Six Million Dollar Man," "Run for Your Life," "Voyage to the Bottom of the Sea," "Blue Thunder"), and the grcat patriarch (Major Dad, Captain Stubing, Marshal Matt Dillon, Sheriff Andy Taylor, Dr. Welby, Captain Kirk, Jed Clampett, Hawkeye Pierce, Charlie on "Charlie's Angels," Jim Anderson on "Father Knows Best," and so forth).

The phallocentric bias is also evident on shows that have a master of ceremonies in the prime time and late night genres, such as Ed Sullivan on "The Ed Sullivan Show" and "The Tonight Show Starring Johnny Carson" (which included frequent allusions to ex-wives as a staple source of monologue material and ad-lib gags). A male is nearly always in charge, even in children's programming and advertising, such as Mister Rogers on "Mister Rogers' Neighborhood," Kermit (certainly not Miss Piggy) on "The Muppet Show" and "Sesame Street," Lee Iacocca in Chrysler ads and endless local and national ads staring the male owners of businesses. The patriarch dispenses wisdom, control, guidance. This extends to news anchoring, game and dance show hosting and religious programming as well.

To be a hero, free, wise and strong, is to not change diapers, buy groceries or wash dishes. The hero's very name often equates the character with a semantic correspondence between masculinity and the use of deadly force, as illustrated by Mannix, Peter Gunn, Remington Steele, Cannon, Baretta, Magnum, the Rifleman, Crockett, and so on. A hero's time is much too valuable for domestic concerns. Meanwhile, with very few exceptions, powerful independent women are usually portrayed as lovable freaks in utterly fantastic circumstances, including "I Dream of Jeannie," "Bewitched," "The Flying Nun," "The Girl with Something Extra," "Wonder Woman," "Beauty and the Beast," "Mork and Mindy" and "The Ghost and Mrs. Muir," or as ludicrous buffoons fumbling from one "zany antic" to another, as on "I Love Lucy," "Rhoda," and "Laverne and Shirley." Women are usually portrayed as rather dim, yet harmless, innocents who must band together for companionship, as on "Green Acres," "Petticoat Junction," "Designing Women," "Golden Girls" and so on. It must be noted that this phallocentric trend spans the entire history of American mass media and includes all genres. All of these (and many other) shows represent great commercial success, with some properly labeled "smash hits," generating the largest audiences in human history—audiences of both sexes and all ages. Furthermore, the practice of syndication maintains the circulation of this cultural bias for future generations, possibly retarding the social evolution of collective values.

Pornography, as perhaps the most extreme expression of phallocentrism, neglects the possible consequences of sexual relations. The isolated consumer of pornography represents the implosion of ego hypertrophy (idealism/perfectionism). Pornographic ejaculation via masturbation is efficiently convenient and utterly sterile—far removed from any sacral meaning or reciprocity. As a transcending act, the subject objectifies himself with reference to his penis as a "love tool," "screw," "ramrod," "joy stick," "gearshift," and so on. By stark contrast, erotica emphasizes a fruitful relationship with an authentic Other (subject), which is often expressed as magical spirituality (as in the *Kamasutra*). Romanticism has a spiritual dimension. Pornography is not romantic. Pornography expresses a patriarchical desire for power/domination and also an intense isolation that results from a drive for total control.

Pornography is part of a modern Western attempt to cope with eros, to manage it by materially reducing it to brute behavior. Such managerial mentality that marks the post-Renaissance West is, as Nietzsche, Baudelaire and Freud understood, doomed in its attempts to control the powerful forces of the feminine. Consequently, by demonizing and humiliating women, the modern/masculine manages only to suppress this force, so that it emerges as various pathologies, such as graphic pornography. The feminine becomes an enemy to be purged, segregated, beaten and exorcised. Pornography offers a female object that is completely powerless. Masturbatory interaction with a video or magazine image is not complicated by the presence of a potentially troublesome Other. Unlike the actual rape of an authentic Other (mind/subject), the image offers absolutely no resistance: potential, physical, legal or any other kind, such as guilt. Pornography completes the process of lobotomization or deminding. The pornographic image has no consciousness (is not a subject), which means that the image is not a "real" person. Therefore, the viewer's experience is not characterized by any sense of conscience or subjective/personal responsibility. Pornography is uniquely post-Cartesian (modern). The consumer and the content of pornography are simultaneously demonized (objectified). Video images are absolutely (mindlessly) obedient. Pornography is merely a technological expression of this more fundamental modern attitude that motivates the effort of masculine transcendence to overcome feminine rescendence (Mickunas 1990).

Pornography is an attempt to civilize (technologize) the wilderness—human *nature*—to grasp, possess and control it. As it is exported and copied around the globe, it manifests a form of cultural imperialism, for with it goes not only a technological imperative to enhance presence, but also a way of seeing the sexed self, sexual relationships, gender relationships, voyeurism and beauty. Pornography reorients fantasies and expectations. The drive for ever greater realism manifests the modern metaphysics of presence (logocentrism) expressed videocentrically (Kramer 1992a; 1992b; 1992c; 1988). Representing something gives control over it. Pornography exemplifies modern perspectivism manifested as visual spatialization/rationalization. Seeing is the new Truth (empiricism). The new Truth is immediate, graphic and powerful. Facts overwhelm knowledge (of their relationships). Facts are "objective"; they are not the product of judgment, and, therefore, they are amoral.

Pornography is one of the great discontents of masculine, perspectival civilization (meaning to be cultivated); it is a technologically enhanced war against Man's sexual drives and the perceived source of them—Woman. The resulting tension leads to guilt, fear, hate and violence (pornography)—not eros. The former is manifested as violent and directed lust (a very selfish emotion), the latter as a nebulous passion that annihilates the self—making "one" invisible within the orgiastic chaos.

The pornographic cultural milieu expresses the strident efforts of individualism to possess the Other as personal property—total conquest and remote control in slow motion, freeze frame, fast forward and reverse. The modern episteme constitutes a fetish of fixation itself, a permanent present purified of ambiguity, transcendentally removed from space and time. The burning desire of the modern attitude is for eternal youth/ beauty, eternal bliss and total privatized, yet value-free, isolation—the hyperreal (Baudrillard 1983).

The abstract realm of the hyperreal is the masturbatory paradise of modern technological alienation. Complex and confounding reality is rejected in favor of total and efficient control—with surround-sound and digital high-definition multidimensionality. The wilderness of space and time is conquered by *tele*communications. This is why pornography is so popular; the modern craves it. Pornography expresses the hypertrophic pursuit of immediate gratification, performance (power) on command.

The qualitatively different attitudes expressed by pornography and erotica are self-evident. Pornography isolates, purifies and insulates the viewer from what happens behind the cameras. Its videocentric realism is the great delusion, for videotape leads to the belief that what is seen with the eyes is "natural," "objective," "value-free." The danger of videocentrism is that it fragments reality, offering only a tiny slice of the world (perspectivism) as *fait accompli,* and these contextless data are confused with truth.

MODERN PORNOGRAPHY: DOMESTIC AND INTERNATIONAL TRENDS

If nothing else, pornography is a commodity that enjoys a huge market demand. In *The Beauty Myth,* Naomi Wolf reveals that pornography is the biggest media category (1991, 79). Estimates show that globally pornography generates over $7 billion a year. This amount is more than that generated by the worldwide nonpornographic commercial film and music industries *combined.* The pornographic motion picture industry (both video and film) grosses close to $400 million a year in the United States alone. Every month over 18 million men in the United States purchase nearly 200 different pornographic magazines, generating about half a *billion* dollars a year (Wolf 1991, 79). Clearly, pornography is a profitable industry, and the rates of consumption indicate that it is anything but culturally or economically marginal.

The typical age of the "adult" female performer suggests that the Lolita Complex (a fetish for very young females), which permeates practically all commercial media (Wolf 1991), totally dominates pornographic media images. Pornographers often hire performers in their late teens and dress them to look even younger (U.S. Department of Justice 1986, 855). Another aspect of the industry, actual child pornography, is often described by experts as a burgeoning "cottage industry," where parents sometimes appear in the movies with their own children (U.S. Department of Justice, 1986, 405–25; Rush 1980, 71). The United States is the largest consumer of child pornography in the world (U.S. Department of Justice 1986, 674).

Florence Rush describes this "Lolita" obsession as an issue of power: "I do not think it is an accident that the ideal of femininity is fast becoming the infantilized woman. Men are attracted to a woman who has the helplessness of a child. . . . Today our society either makes the child look like a woman or the woman look like a child" (1980, 70).

The woman-child syndrome is quite expressly at variance with ideals of beauty that were common not long ago, such as Mae West, Marilyn Monroe and Sophia Loren. Nicolas Bornoff compares the classical Asian beauty with her modernized counterpart thus:

> Ideally, according to Chinese Tang dynasty canons of beauty, she was plump and also wore make-up. She powdered her face an immaculate full-moon white, rouged her chubby cheeks and colored her lips with a paste made from brilliant red safflower. With two large round dots of charcoal gray just above where her eyebrows would have been had she not plucked them out, the rotund and diminutive Heian belle would fare none too well as a modern contestant for Miss Japan. (1991, 119)

The equation of "innocence" and passivity with inexperience (the fetish for the eternal virginal), physically presented as a girlish stature, is embodied by beauty icons. Stuart Ewen (1988) and Judith Williamson (1986) argue that such images generate a "body politic" that has led to an epidemic of anorexia and the overall anxiety about aging.

The message is simple: To be lovable, one must be subservient and controllable, a sex toy, not an equal partner. The feminine in "full bloom," like the fertility figure of the Venus of Willendorf, seems frightening to the modern male, who attempts to manage eros by containment or banishment (the desire for the prepubescent). Sexual relations with mature women raise the specter of pregnancy and domestic responsibilities (maturity)—the ultimate enemy of the highest value to the modern, individual freedom. Hence, the omnipresent icon of the cowboy-warrior, the social isolate who experiences pleasure strictly at his convenience and with "no strings" attached, is admired and loved (Kramer 1988). This is very different from the preperspectival male's role, even in polygamous social arrangements.

In Taiwan, in 1983–84, martial law under the Kuomintang was still in effect.[3] Sexually explicit media content was largely restricted. However, pirate pornography from Japan was very common. Portable book stalls run by street merchants during the day and in the mobile "night markets" appeared to sell only nonpornographic material. Innocuous looking books on computer programming or general fiction would have inserts of photographs of usually young, nude, Caucasian women. Books that had serial photographs of nude women, ostensibly for figure studies in art, were popular with young men. With the lifting of martial law on July 14, 1987, a fledgling pornography industry sprang to life. Since then, several publications mimicking Japanese and American titles such as *Playboy* have become prevalent, while the movie industry has altered its content to become more explicit, including some nudity.

In Britain, the pornographic magazine industry grosses £500 million (approximately 750 million U.S. dollars) a year (Wolf 1991, 79). Twenty million copies are sold annually at about £2 to £3 (about $3.20 to $4.80) each. In Sweden, half a million men purchase pornographic magazines each *week.* According to Wolf, by 1985, 13.6 million pornographic magazines were sold by the largest distributors from corner kiosks, and, by 1983, every fourth video rented in Sweden was pornographic (1991, 79). In Canada, the most widely read magazines are *Playboy* and *Penthouse.* By comparison, pornography makes up half of all video sales in Italy.

Meanwhile, in countries that typically have more of a collectivistic rather than an individualistic tendency, pornography is quickly taking root along with modernization. *Reform,* Hungary's revealing named first tabloid, read by one in ten Hungarians, has a topless or bottomless model on each page. In 1987, Cuba and Bulgaria held beauty contests, and the following year the Republic of China sent a contestant to the Miss Universe pageant. In 1988, the first Miss Moscow competition was held. In 1990, shipments of outdated women's glamour magazines and copies of *Playboy* began to flow into the Soviet bloc (Wolf 1991, 89).

Today, Asian pornography reflects trends first established in the United States and Europe. This mimicking is mostly in terms of novel uses of consumer telecommunications technology, such as VCRs and camcorders, for voyeuristic purposes. More recent examples also include computer and telephone sex, which are not yet heavily promoted in Japan, Thailand, the Philippines or Hong Kong. A recent development in Japanese voyeurism is a service that involves renting a nude model by the minute to pose for amateur videographers.

Furthermore, the sex-slave trade is probably best organized and tolerated in Japan. A post-colonial callousness is manifested, as poor neighboring countries are seen as "nothing other than gigantic brothels" (Bornoff 1991, 857). The slave trade of the 1990s is operated by "talent agencies" that are fronts for crime syndicates in various countries. These syndicates have international agreements with the Japanese *yakuza* (the infamous criminal organization) to create what Bornoff refers to as a "lucrative priapic co-prosperity sphere" (1991, 354).[4]

THE EROTIC ATTITUDE: THE FLOATING WORLD

In order to clearly demarcate modern pornography and premodern eroticism, it is necessary to briefly assess the classical world. Premodern Asian eroticism is expressed by such texts as *Records of the Bedchamber* by the Taoist sage Liu Ching, which details how to harmonize with a woman by rubbing and caressing her organs to get her yin flowing, and Tung'Hsuan's *Six Ways of Penetration.* These are basically medical books concerned with longevity and rejuvenation of vigor. According to these ancient texts, sex is healthy; indeed, done properly, it has healing benefits. Such texts strongly influenced the attitudes of the "idyllic" world of the Heian era in Japan, which copied the world of the Chinese Tang Dynasty (618–906). This era (794–1185), which is comparable to Camelot in the Western imagination, still engenders a nostalgic sense of true affection and a gentle beauty that depicts humans as extensions of cosmic forces. This is, of course, the opposite of the current modern attitude, which characterizes the technological world as an extension of transcending human power.

The predominant classical Japanese aesthetic is signified by an almost untranslatable phrase, *mono no aware,* which harbors strong Buddhist existential overtones. *Aware* expresses a sense of pathos and beauty. It connotes a sort of "gentle melancholy" that results from calm reflection on the beautiful, yet fleeting, nature of the world. Thus, Chinese poets often refer to the plum blossom, while the Japanese favor the annual blossoming of the cherry as metaphors for the brilliant, but fast-fading, splendor of youthful vibrancy and beauty. This attitude is much more "quiet" than the central issue of sublimity in Western romanticism, which expresses power as much as beauty. It is also characterized by indirectness and patience expressed by the use of translucent screens that encourage voyeurism without a direct gaze.

Only one example of romantic Heian erotic iconography exists. The *Koshibagaki-zoshi* scroll painting of sixteen frames depicts the amorous "exertions" of a couple in a very graphic way. But the Heian attitude persisted in the Japanese imagination and was expressed 600 years later in the great woodblock prints depicting the fabled "floating world," the *demi-monde* in the *yoshi* marshlands on Edo's northern boundary. Erotic novels of this floating world, known as *ukiyo-zoshi,* appeared along with Hishikawa Moronobu's (1618–94) woodblock prints of the pleasure quarters, brothels and teahouses of the *ukiyo.* Unlike the Western masters, who dwelled on Biblical subjects and idealized neoclassical nudes, the great Heian and Edo artists were not averse to depicting copulating couples, which they saw as perfectly natural.

Among the most famous books that tell the stories of the pleasure quarters, brothel lore and tales of courtesans are Fujimoto Kizan's *Great Mirror of the Yoshiwara* and Ihara Saikaku's *Life of an Amorous Man* (1682). These stories, along with the works of the great Tang poets of China (Tu Fu 712–70 and Li Po 701–62), demonstrate that romance is deeply embedded in these cultural traditions. Often the theme is love lost, leading to tragic suicide. These artists' expressions embody a world of "superficial dazzle and ritualized pleasure" populated with rogues, scheming courtesans, slumming samurai, horny nuns, ludicrous fops and fey spendthrifts. The floating world attracted samurai and monks, who wore commoners' clothing to enter the pleasure quarters forbidden to their class and cloth (Bornoff 1991, 175–76).

The history of Japanese eroticism dates back to prehistoric fertility cults and festivals (which only vanished from rural village life in the mid 1950s, primarily because the youth have moved to urban centers) (Bornoff 1991, 100). This change from a rural to an urban milieu leads to a fragmented and isolationistic life that is very different from village life. Modern corporate feudalism, with its demand for a highly mobile and regimented work force, now dominates Japanese life. However, it is believed that in a few isolated villages, the peasant custom of *yobai* ("night creeping") is still practiced today, as it was in Yin Dynasty China (as early as 1500 B.C.).

Bornoff (1991) refers to this event as a "ritual springtime romp" of which there are several reported versions. One version suggests that after their first menstruation, girls would "often" roam their villages "to offer themselves to local youth" (Bornoff 1991, 125). In rural Japan, women started reproductive activity as soon as possible. In fact, in Heian times, women who remained virgins for very long after puberty were suspected of being possessed by evil spirits.[5]

Another version of *yobai* has it that all the village bachelors gather at the headman's home for a party (Bornoff 1991, 137). After the party, the youths leave in groups to creep quietly (no carousing allowed) around the dark village. When they arrive outside a house where a young girl lives, they play *janken-pon* (scissors-paper-rock). The winner then enters the house where the girl has expectantly left her door open, not knowing who will join her. Meanwhile, the rest of the group makes its way to the next house.

This behavior has the tacit sanction of the parents, who may have found their mates in the same way. In the typical Japanese style of saving face by pretending (*tatemae* as opposed to *honne* or the true self or feelings), parents feign ignorance despite the fact that rooms are separated by thin partitions. It must be noted that although marital relationships sometimes emerge from such liaisons, this tradition serves more as a ritual "defloration" than a process of mate selection.

Many stories tell of girls who have enjoyed, or endured, more than one nocturnal visitor. Until quite recently, girls who were not thus visited by the "ripe old age of seventeen" were ritually "deflowered" by a Shinto priest wearing a wooden phallus or by an anonymous youth chosen by the parents. The anonymity of such sexual behavior is indicative of the general lack of importance of individualism and personality in this fast vanishing rural world. A sense of cosmic balance, rather than possession (even of self-identity), is an issue here. Such behavior is not an entertainment, but a necessity.

Reminiscent of ancient Greek Bacchanalia, rural Japanese peasants (the vast majority of the population until the Second World War) held orgies and phallic festivals (i.e., the *jibeta matsuri* and *utagaki*), which combined eating, drinking, merrymaking, parades of giant phalluses and sex. Put in proper perspective, the orgy turns out to be very appropriate for rural (more precisely preperspectival) communities, which are often extended families. With regard to this sense of unity, erotologist Georges Bataille (1957) expresses what Algis Mickunas (1990) calls the feminine "rescendent" (as opposed to the masculine "transcendent") attitude of a collectivistic tribal community where the individual is "obliterated by the group" (Bornoff 1991, 110).[6] Bataille explains:

> The orgy is the sacred aspect of eroticism, where human generation progresses beyond isolation to attain its fullest expression. Ultimately, the participants are lost in a confusing mass.... It is in fact a complete denial of the individual; it dictates equivalence between its participants.... The final significance of eroticism is fusion, the abolition of restrictions.... In the orgy, this object [of desire] becomes indistinguishable: sexual excitement herein is triggered by an exacerbated movement running contrary to habitual reserve. (1957, 27)

This is expressive of the preperspectival consciousness (attitude) that is exhibited by the *yobai* ritual (Gebser 1985). This fusion, which is the "essence of eroticism," is distinguished fundamentally from modern perspectival pornography. Pornography manifests a fundamental dualism that characterizes the modern Western (and fast westernizing) world. Pornography creates the vicarious *viewer* as an isolated masturbating monad—a hypertrophic ego separated from the action by a patriarchical transcendental attitude. Ironically, the more realistic the representation is, the more pornography draws attention to the gaps between the viewer and the viewed and between the simulation and that which is simulated and to the fact that realism is after all only a form of fiction.

As Japan becomes increasingly westernized/modernized, the sense of individualism emerges. Consequently, erotic rituals come to be seen as either grotesquely immoral or quaintly old-fashioned, a source of guilt (not shame). Guilt presupposes ego involvement. Likewise, as modernization rapidly occurs, eros is replaced by pornography and slavery, both of which manifest an emphasis on personal power, property and violence/domination (disharmony). Pornography is pragmatic, isolationist and expressive of a psyche that is possessive. By contrast, Bornoff notes that many peasants never bothered to marry; children "belonged to" the village (1991, 109). Thus, children born as a result of anonymous ritual and celebratory sex were assimilated into the communal "we." Today, the cult of marriage (possessive *monogamy*) has replaced the fertility cult, a worldwide trend that Mickunas (1990) and Kramer (1992a) attribute to the masculine effort to domesticate the wilderness forces of the feminine.

THE PORNOGRAPHIC ATTITUDE/WORLD: PERSPECTIVAL VIDEOCENTRISM

The word *pornography* itself is derived from the Greek *porne,* which means "harlot." Thus, pornographic material is technically that which represents or expresses a world (logos) of excess. Commodification, which is the essence of the "professional," expresses disinterested emotional neutrality. Unlike erotica, pornography is "obscene." The word *obscene* derives from the Latin *obscenus, obscaenus, obscoenus,* meaning "ill-looking" or "filthy" (*ob* + *caenum* filth). That which is obscene is offensive, foul, loathsome, disgusting. Obscene things are supposed to offend the chastity of mind or modesty and to violate purity and are seen as ill-omened—unnatural. Obscene utterances, and other actions, are impure. The word *coarse* also emerges in this discourse.

"Coarse" is that which is common, unrefined, vile, low, rude, gross, rough, sharp. The intrusion of technologically enhanced sharp focus manifests pornographic violation. Ironically, the realism exaggerates the gap between the viewer and the viewed—or draws attention to the medium and its powers of reproduction. Modern videocentrism is an obsession with the physical quality of the vision, the excessive or overdetermined definition of the phenomenon. Thus, it is vulgar, obscene. The technology itself expresses the modern perspectival obsession with making present what is absent—to banish the absent that ultimately leads to meaninglessness, the abolition of difference. Pornographic imaging is obscene in that it allows no ambiguity, no tolerance. It is fascist. Pornography dictates that everything must be violated to extreme, and only youth can exist. Excess to extremes becomes point-like. It is violent in depiction, not just in what is depicted.

The modern pornographic attitude is expressed well by Kaoru Kuroki (Fragrance Blacktree), the biggest porno star in Japan. Her tapes sell well despite, and also because of, the total lack of inhibitions that she expresses and that the cameras capture. Many Japanese men have complained that they find her "frightening," that her videos are "no good for masturbation" (Bornoff 1991, 423). This may seem strange since Kuroki, like many other arousing Japanese porno actresses, is also typically portrayed as being gang-raped, slapped, and generally humiliated. Her uniqueness is expressed by her "erratic" behavior during intercourse, which recalls the Asian view of women as having demonic tendencies, a belief that compelled the Heian courtesans to blacken their teeth so as to demonstrate their humanness and the Balinese to file off their canine teeth even today. This "demonic" aspect is manifested by her occasional self-assertiveness in her videos. It is this that bothers some of her viewers.

Because she is articulate, she appears on many TV chat shows and commercials and even is a spokesperson for a prestigious department store. Bornoff characterizes Kuroki as "Italy's Cicciolina, America's Doctor Ruth, and France's Brigitte Lahaye all rolled into one: social rebel, sex counselor and porno star turned thinker" (1991, 420). She sees herself as a modernizing liberator from social pressure, a champion of individualism and disinhibition. Although her parents are deeply disturbed by her profession, she rationalizes what she does as a declaration of independence.

Kuroki's attitude about what she does for a living is quite informative, for it illustrates the power of videocentrism (Kramer 1988; 1992a; 1992b) and the fundamental difference between modern pornography and classical erotica. Pornography is a celebration of the individual social isolate and self-indulgence. It also suggests the desensitization of not only the consuming viewers, but the producers as well. This may be an essential trait of industrialization, generally.

Of course, the commodification of lust is not a new thing. What is new, however, are the media used for presentation, which manifest a perspectival attitude. As Zillmann and Bryant point out (without adequate explanation):

> The principal reason for the apparent revival of concerns about unregulated pornography is simply the new technology. In the old days, a privileged few could, dependent on one's view, enrich or compromise their erotic imagi-

nations and experiences by reading about sexual engagements or by perusing drawings or paintings of such engagements. Nowadays, any conceivable sexual activity performed by others can be witnessed in living color and sound. The portrayal has "you-were-there" quality. In fact, video presentations are said to show sex that is "bigger than life" by closing in on the events in ways that go beyond the unarmed eye and ear. However, the social dimension of exposure to such super-iconic representations of sex is probably more significant. Pornography has gone truly public. It reaches all people. . . . The proliferation and distribution of pornographic materials are such that more and more children find access. Thanks to the new communication technology, pornography has become an affordable form of entertainment for all. (1989, xii)

Zillmann and Bryant wrongly reduce the availability, concerns about and affordability of pornography to sheer quantity. Demand develops before production can be sustained. Although they mention the qualitative difference between modern chemical (filmic) and electronic (video) representations from media of the "old days," they utterly fail to understand that this is not "simply" a technological change. There was a motive and an interest in developing such media before they came into existence. Telecommunications technologies are not naturally occurring phenomena. They are the consequences of the videocentric drive to presentiate and stimulate. Zillmann and Bryant only touch on the fundamental issue when they recognize the new "super-iconic," "bigger than life," "you-were-there," "living color" *quality,* missing the point that it is precisely this issue that is central to any explanation of the explosive growth in pornography production/consumption worldwide. Deficient perspectival (pornographic) Man admits no limits to self-satisfaction. Thus, he is insatiable. He wants to see/consume everything and believes he has a transcendental right to do so. In order to justify this desire, deficient perspectival Man attempts a pseudo-rationalization via dialectical jurisprudence and the democratic tradition. This explains the widespread support for large quantities of high-quality product. "Quality" means exaggerated presencing—videocentric reduction of the world to physical stimuli and their magnification.

At issue is why there has been a shift from an erotic attitude to a pornographic one and what this fundamental change in attitude means. The fundamental nature of this change in attitude pervades all manner of life, not just graphic depictions of sexual behavior. A pornographic world is distinguished from an erotic existence by a cosmic separation (and therefore invention) of the subject from everything else. Perspectival modernity is essentially a world of the viewer, where everything else becomes a view for consumption, a disengaged drama.[7] The modern looks upon the world as a play. Modern technologies are desired (rigorously pursued in research and consumption) because they enhance this distance, this purity. One can watch without being touched. Responsibility and reciprocity are not a part of this vicarious world.

Concurrent with the explosive rise in demand for pornographic expression is a concern about a correspondent increase in violent content and its effects (Zillmann & Bryant 1984; Malamuth & Spinner 1980; Smith 1976).[8] But the quality of the new pornographic vision is itself exaggerated and exaggerating (obscene). Separation of content from form wrongly presumes that the mode of presentation itself does not harbor any interest, motive or meaning. Videocentrism, the drive for ever greater visual (spatial) intrusion, such as measurement and other graphic simulations, manifests an essential characteristic (obsession) of the modern and his will to power (truth). Progress, for instance, can never achieve a goal, or it will self-contradict. Hence, it is by definition insatiable and beyond judgment, for there is no goal except continued progress itself (Kramer 1992a).

Everything in a pornographic world is overdetermined, exaggerated and obscene. An example is the propensity of the modern mentality, exhibited many times, to hunt another species to absolute extinction. Another example is the creation of ever more destructive weapons systems and their seemingly insatiable duplication. Yet another is the intolerant presupposition that endless economic expansion (development) is desirable. The singular reason for unbridled obscenity is the aggrandizement of the hypertrophic ego, which essentially distinguishes the modern perspectival human from other pre-, un- and aperspectival peoples (Gebser 1985). It even impacts on what it means to be "human." Egocentrism defines modernity and colors all physical and relational experience.

CONCLUSION

Clearly, production follows demand, and realistic renditions of sexual behavior have proven to be far more desirable than drawings and paintings. The new "highly motivated" iconography (with its emphasis on spatiality) panders to a logocentric prejudice that is rapidly spreading worldwide along with the technologies that enhance the metaphysics of presence. This is not mere simulation as in classical mimesis, for simulation implies a strict demarcation between fantasy/unreality and the Real. Rather, the images in pornography are pathetic and signalic, not symbolic (Jakobson 1958). At the pathetic (emotional or perhaps even instinctual-biological) level, there is no separation between the symbol and some reality for which it stands. A symbolic expression manifests a mode of being that is instrumental, that is to stand in for, to re-present or to simulate in a "secondary" manner a separate "primary" reality (Ong 1982, 26). Such symbolic expressions manifest a transcending consciousness, which is essentially patriarchical and signified by purity, ideality of law, detachment, vision, science and metaphysics.

These new technologies manifest the fundamental value of the modern attitude to simulate natural processes as graphically as possible. As more energy and time are spent living with simulations, building the technologies and producing and consuming the simulations, the simulacrum (the total simulation of the physical world) becomes our reality. The consequent hyperreality is preferred because of its total manageability. Man becomes transcendent god, at once king of his new self-made domain (culture) and hopelessly alienated from anything not simulation. The simulacrum—a total replication—heralds the final defeat of nature at the hands of culture. Indeed, "nature" becomes a cultural concept that is defined as a binary opposite of artificial (Kramer 1992a). Everything, including "nature," is under transcendental control—domesticated. This is the *universalis mathesis* dreamed of by Bacon, Galileo and Descartes. This is the era of domesticated "wild" sex and prepackaged fantasy/fetish. The wilderness of eros is brought under scrutiny by sharp focus, zoom and a host of "experts." Fantasy without mess on a cheap fifty-five-minute videocassette. What a marvel! What a modern convenience! Eros on demand and at several speeds, including slow motion and freeze frame! Pornography is a celebration of individuation and power, not eros, which submerges the individual in the surrender to *ekstasis.* Inherent in this process is the sense that the truth of the event is *captured* and rendered totally *privatized,* absolutely possessed.

Zillmann and Bryant (1982) have demonstrated that people repeatedly exposed to pornography exhibit a tendency labeled "desensitization" or "callousness." Zillmann (1986, 155) reinforces this position by summarizing the available research about the consumption of pornography, stating that "Habitual male consumers of common pornography appear to be at greater risk of becoming sexually callous and sexually violent toward women than occasional male consumers." Pornography is a violation of eros and its attendant behavioral manifestations. As industrial societies manufacture and export these technologically high-quality pornographic materials, they also export an attitude that proclaims the new vision (the hyperreal) to be good, entertaining, desirable, practical, efficient, even necessary and, more important, in line with the pseudo-religious dogma of "development" and "progress." The attitude behind pornographic software springs from the same logocentric obsession that drives the development and spread of new electronics hardware.

Magic identity is enhanced through modern technologies of presentation. When the viewer identifies with the perspective of a rapist, which predominates pornographic depictions, what results is a magical/emotive unity of excitation and motivation. Pornography is a catalyst for fantasy and animus (Green & Mosher 1985; Pilotta 1992). The fantasy is no less real than physical sex, but it is essentially different. Pornography is not a marginal simulation. Pornography is excitatory on the level of magical identity. In pornographic depictions, qualities—both quantitative physical (enlarged body parts, youthfulness, numbers of partners) and qualitative relational (subservient, incestuous)—are pushed to exaggerated levels as a constant infusion of animus to the fantasy work. Exaggeration is the essence of "obscenity." With the emergence of photography and the electronic media, "vulgarity" is manifested by the sharpness and bluntness of imaging that outruns the imagination.

The mass consumption of such material magic (technologically facilitated identification) exposes a vast uniformity of impulse and motive. Identification and solitary interaction (with images) manifest the prerational power of seduction—the seduction of power. This is the essential force of the hyperreal videocentric prejudice (machine magic). The Other is first split into subjective mind (independent will) and behavioral object and then the subjective fragment is denied existence. This facilitates the denial of the Other's feelings and one's own responsibility vis-à-vis those feelings. Since only visual (behavioral/material) phenomena are granted the status of reality, ethics are avoided. Excitation is precisely what makes pornography popular, what drives demand for ever more individual control over the pleasure-producing experience. Pornography panders to the demand for control. To the modern mentality, control *is* pleasure. However, in the process of achieving total control, the authoritarian mind completely banishes the authenticity of the Other as an autonomously acting (possibly resisting) subject. Isolation is the final consequence.

NOTES

1. Already in 1707 and 1708, Berkeley was formulating his response to Descartes's *Dioptrics* (1637). In his famous work *An Essay Towards a New Theory of Vision,* Berkeley borrows an argument from William Molyneux's work, which like Descartes's book is entitled *Dioptrics* (1692). This argument, which Berkeley used to refute Descartes's geometric explanation of sight, claims that distance, depth of field, cannot itself be seen. Elaborating on Molyneux's argument, Berkeley puts forth the theory that depth perception is constituted via the active mind's integration of all the senses. Depth is a synthetic phenomenon. The problem of depth perception is still debated. For instance, in many of his works, the preeminent neurologist-psychologist Karl Pribram has explored how a distorted (because the retina is actually a half-sphere, rather than a flat surface) two-dimensional image is perceived as having complex depth. The brain seems to integrate sensory data from all receptors to generate depth, or what Gibson calls visual (phcnomcnological) world, as distinguished from visual (retinal geometric) field. Memory from past experience (transactions with the world) also seems to play a role.

2. This compulsion to avoid maturity and domesticity is central to the modern phallocentric narrative. This narrative is expressed in countless television and film icons. In all of these narratives, women are portrayed as castrating enemies of freedom.

3. I wish to thank Richiko Ikeda, Annette Sun-chee Aw and Yayoi Yoshizawa for helping me to acquire samples of Asian pornography used in the preparation of this chapter.

4. Another business exploitative of poor women is the booming sex-tour business, whereby Japanese salarymen qua business samurai take holidays appropriate for the current overworked and, by many accounts, sexually frustrated corporate warriors. Their R&R takes the form of *kisaeng* tours. *Kisaeng* is the Korean equivalent of the Japanese *geisha*. These "professional unmarried ladies" were part of the spoils of the Japanese colonization of the Korean peninsula at the end of the nineteenth century. Many Korean women were enslaved and shuttled between Japanese brothels in Southeast Asian ports. Today, the word *kisaeng* is used by special tours to the various fleshpots of Asia. These tours are operated by the *yakuza,* Japan's infamous criminal organization. During the rise in economic power of the Japanese in the mid-1960s, these tours frequented the former colonial holdings of Seoul and Taipei. During the 1970s, prices in these places had risen, so the tours now favor the destitute destinations of Bangkok and Manila. Salarymen flock to these destinations for anywhere from three days to a week of cheap sex and booze. The general tenor of the situation is post-colonial arrogance, expressed by the phrase "raping foreign women with their money" (reporter for an Asahi newspaper quoted by Bornoff 1991, 350). Ever concerned for outward appearance, many Japanese are troubled by news documentaries in which these vacationers are described by the women, who are forced out of economic necessity to service them, as "sexual predators," "pigs," and "monsters" that act worse than Vietnam-era GIs. Some Japanese have attacked this business as a "sex invasion," stressing the analogy of warfare and the post-colonial mentality widely exhibited by brutish salarymen "without shame." Similar to clubs in Manila and Bangkok, there are establishments in Hawaii, Los Angeles and San Francisco that cater only to Japanese salarymen. It is likely that these are owned and operated by either *yakuza* personnel or local criminal organizations in cooperation with the *yakuza.*

5. Mickunas (1990) offers an extensive tracing of the phenomenon of the dangerous "she-fiend," which is "dirty" and beguiling; leading unsuspecting suitors into an intoxicating dissolution of the self. In Chinese tradition, the "she-demon" has the power to change into a fox, bewitch men and ghoulishly devour them. This ingestion implicates a rescendent dissolution back into the feminine origin.

6. Mickunas (1990, 10) describes rescendence thus:

> The striving toward the release from selfhood is reflected in melting reverie, and various functions are regarded as means for the attainment of this dissolution, this melting: wine, dance, song; it is no accident that Dionysus is a divinity of wine, eroticism, and orgiastic reveries. The excitement brought about by wine and dance has a disruptive effect, leading to melting and indeed dissolution. . . . In the grip of *ekstasis* the word rises to chant and the step to dance. The eros of Dionysus originates with dance, music, and reverie, and has an accepted reflective power of dissolution of personality, breakdown of cohesion. At the erotic level, every sign flows, breaks up, and leads on.

7. This is why the metaphor of dramatistics has now been elevated to the level of academic terminology by such scholars as Goffman and Garfinkle. The idea of

a participant observer, so much touted in ethnographic literature, and the related opposition of emic versus etic perspectives articulated by Pike indicate a hopeless confusion concerning the fundamentally incompatible attitudes manifested by each antagonistic position—an antagonism that is a constant source of animus in the human "sciences" today. To be a participant observer is to live a contradiction. It also indicates the mistaken turn taken by the Schutzeans away from the Husserlian solution, which is to bracket such metaphysical gamesmanship in favor of the realization that observation and participation are essentially integrated. Perspective is a result of the attitude of the participant. There are no nonparticipants or nonobservers, only differing attitudes. The idea of a privileged perspective that casts all the world as a drama, with the self as the sole audience member not following a "script," is purely Cartesian. As Nietzsche succinctly put it, there is no truth, only perspectives.

8. Increasingly liberalized community standards have led to a shift in focus away from nudity per se to behavior. Concern has focused on aggression, violence and the use of animals and children in sexually explicit contents. Detective magazines and "crime magazines," according to Dietz, Harry and Hazelwood (1986), generate monthly sales of over 1 million copies. These, plus more violent "adults only" films, videos and magazines, frequently portray women being intimidated into submissive roles by men threatening or enacting physical violence toward them. Likewise, Malamuth and Spinner (1980) found that many of the cartoons published in *Playboy* and *Penthouse* depict sexual violence against women. In the introduction to *Take Back the Night*, Laura Lederer (1980, 18) points out that until 1978 *Hustler* magazine published a cartoon featuring "Chester the Molester," who regularly molested a different young girl "using techniques like lying, kidnapping, and assault."

WORKS CITED

Apel, K. O. 1972. *Transformation der Philosophie.* Frankfurt, Germany: Suhrkamp Verlag.

Barthes, R. 1964. *Essais critiques.* Paris: Editions du Seuil.

Bataille, G. 1957. *L'erotisme.* Paris: Editions du Minuit.

Baudrillard, J. 1983. *Simulations.* Trans. P. Foss, P. Patton and P. Beitchman. New York: Semiotext(e).

Berkeley, G. [1708] 1922. *A New Theory of Visions and Other Writings.* Reprint. New York: E. P. Dutton.

Bornoff, N. 1991. *Pink Samurai: Love, Marriage and Sex in Contemporary Japan.* New York: Simon & Schuster.

Dietz, P. E., B. Harry and R. R. Hazelwood. 1986. Detective Magazines: Pornography for the Sexual Sadist? *Journal of Forensic Sciences* 31: 197–211.

Doubrovsky, S. 1967. Critique et existence. In J. Ricardou (ed.), *Les Chemins actuels de la critique* (pp. 261–87). Paris: Plon.

Dufrenne, M. 1964. Critique littéraire et phénoménologie. *Revue Internationale de Philosophie* 68–69: 193–208.

Ewen, S. 1988. *All Consuming Images: The Politics of Style in Contemporary Culture.* New York: Basic Books.

Gadamer, H.-G. 1975. *Truth and Method.* New York: Seabury Press.

Gebser, J. 1985. *The Ever-present Origin.* Trans. N. Barstadt and A. Mickunas. Athens: Ohio University Press.

Geertz, C. 1973. *The Interpretation of Cultures.* New York: Basic Books.

Gibson, J. J. 1950. *The Perception of the Visual World.* Boston: Houghton Mifflin.

———. 1962. Observations on Active Touch. *Psychological Review* 69(6): 477–91.

Giedion, S. 1962. *The Eternal Present: The Beginnings of Architecture.* 2 vols. New York: Pantheon Books.

Green, S. E., and D. L. Mosher. 1985. A Causal Model of Sexual Arousal to Erotic Fantasies. *Journal of Sex Research* 21: 1–23.

Habermas, J. 1968. *Erkenntnis und Interesse.* Frankfurt: Suhrkamp Verlag.

Hall, E. T. 1966. *The Hidden Dimension.* New York: Anchor Books/Doubleday.

———. 1976. *Beyond Culture.* New York: Anchor Books/Doubleday.

Heidegger, M. 1971. *On the Way to Language.* New York: Harper & Row.

Husserl, E. 1970. *The Crisis of European Sciences and Transcendental Phenomenology.* Trans. D. Carr. Evanston, Ill.: Northwestern University Press.

Ingarden, R. 1965. *Das literarische Kunstwerk.* 3d ed. Tubinger, Germany: Niemeyer.

Jakobson, R. 1958. Closing Statement: Linguistics and Poetics. In T. A. Sebeok (ed.), *Style and Language* (pp. 350–77). Cambridge: MIT Press.

Kepes, G. 1944. *The Language of Vision.* Chicago: Paul Theobald.

Kilpatrick, F. P. 1961. *Explorations in Transactional Psychology.* New York: New York University Press.

Kramer, E. 1988. *Television Criticism and the Problem of Ground: Interpretation After Deconstruction.* Ann Arbor, Mich.: University Microfilms (no. 8816770).

———. 1992a. Gebser and Culture. In E. Kramer (ed.), *Consciousness and Culture: The Thought of Jean Gebser* (pp. 1–60). Westport, Conn.: Greenwood Press.

———. 1992b. The Origin of Television as Civilized Expression. In J. Deely (ed.), *Semiotics 1990* (pp. 27–36). Lanham, Md.: University Press of America.

———. 1992c. Phenomenology of International Images. In L. Embree (ed.), *Japanese and Western Phenomenology* (pp. 1–18). Amsterdam: Kluwer Academic Publishers.

Lederer, L. (ed.). 1980. *Take Back the Night: Women on Pornography.* New York: William Morrow.

McLuhan, M. 1964. *Understanding Media: The Extensions of Man.* New York: American Library.

Malamuth, N. M., and B. Spinner. 1980. A Longitudinal Content Analysis of Sexual Violence in the Best-selling Erotic Magazines. *Journal of Sex Research* 16(3): 226–37.

Mickunas, A. 1990. Reflection, Gender and Power. Unpublished manuscript.

Mumford, L. 1934. *Technics and Civilization.* New York: Harcourt, Brace, & World.

Ong, W. 1982. *Orality and Literacy: The Technologizing of the Word.* New York: Methuen.

Pilotta, J. 1992. Media Power Working over the Body: Application of Gebser to Popular Culture. In E. Kramer (ed.), *Culture and Consciousness: The Thought of Jean Gebser* (pp. 79–102). Westport, Conn.: Greenwood Press.

Poulet, G. 1971. *La Conscience critique.* Paris: Librairie Jose Corti.

Rush, F. 1980. Child Pornography. In L. Lederer (ed.), *Take Back the Night: Women on Pornography* (pp. 57–70). New York: William Morrow.

Sapir, E. 1949. *Selected Writings of Edward Sapir in Language, Culture and Personality.* Berkeley: University of California Press.

Smith, D. G. 1976. The Social Content of Pornography. *Journal of Communication* 26: 16–33.

U. S. Department of Justice. 1986. *Attorney General's Commission on Pornography: Final Report.* Washington, D.C.: GPO.

Wellek, R. 1963. *Concepts of Criticism.* New Haven, Conn.: Yale University Press.

Williamson, J. 1986. *Consuming Passions: The Dynamics of Popular Culture.* New York: Marion Boyars.

Wolf, N. 1991. *The Beauty Myth: How Images of Beauty Are Used Against Women.* New York: William Morrow.

Zillman, D. 1986. Coition and Emotion. In D. Byrne and K. Kelley (eds.), *Alternative Approaches to the Study of Sexual Behavior* (pp. 173–199). Hillsdale, N.J.: Lawrence Erlbaum.

Zillman, D., and J. Bryant. 1982. Pornography, Sexual Callousness and the Trivialization of Rape. *Journal of Communication* 32: 10–21.

———. 1984. *Connections Between Sex and Violence.* Hillsdale, N.J.: Lawrence Erlbaum.

———. 1989. *Pornography: Research Advances and Policy Considerations.* Hillsdale, N.J.: Lawrence Erlbaum.

7

The Anorexic as Overconformist: Toward a Reinterpretation of Eating Disorders

Debra Gimlim

Anorexia nervosa, an eating disorder that causes women to starve themselves to the point of devastating weight loss, is becoming increasingly prevalent in modern Western societies. Hilde Bruch, one of the pioneering researchers studying anorexia, has called the disorder nothing less than an "epidemic" (1972, viii).

Currently accepted criteria for diagnosing anorexia include a series of somewhat vague symptoms: (1) onset before age twenty-five; (2) a loss of at least 25 percent of body weight; (3) a distorted attitude toward eating, food or weight that overrides hunger and threats; (4) no known medical illness accounting for the weight loss; (5) no other known psychiatric disorder; and (6) at least two of the following manifestations: amenorrhea, lanugo (soft, fine hair covering the body), bradycardia (persistent resting pulse of sixty or less), overactivity, episodes of binge eating and frequent vomiting (which may be self-induced) (Feighner 1973). These criteria, while generally accepted by the medical profession, reflect empirical observation and statistical frequency, rather than a rational ordering of causal mechanisms. Though not arbitrary, they reflect the uncertain and complex nature of the illness. While some controversy exists over whether early cases of self-starvation actually constitute the same illness as modern anorexia (Brumberg 1988, 41–60), numerous writers concur that anorexia nervosa existed as early as the seventeenth century. Furthermore, some researchers have claimed that the religious aesthetic of self-starvation among female mystics in the thirteenth century constituted an early form of the disorder (Bell 1985, 200–20).

Reported incidents of anorexia have increased considerably since its discovery, with the number of cases spiraling in the last twenty years. In

1973, when Bruch published her early work, she claimed that the incidence of the disorder was "very rare." However, by 1984, it was estimated that 1 in every 200 to 250 women between the ages of thirteen and twenty-two suffered from the illness and that 12 to 33 percent of college women controlled their weight through vomiting, diuretics and laxatives (Bordo 1985–86, 75). There is some evidence, however, that anorexia nervosa has become an increasingly popular diagnostic category, and this, quite apart from any increase in the real incidence, could have contributed to the considerable rise in reported cases (Crisp, Palmer & Kalucy 1976). Nevertheless, the increased incidence is certainly provocative, as is the fact that 90 percent of anorexics are women (Chernin 1981, 62–63).

Theorists working in a broad psychoanalytic tradition have suggested numerous possible sources of anorexia nervosa, including metabolic dysfunctions (Garfinkle & Garner 1982, 186–213), connections with depression (Cantwell, Sturzenburger & Burroughs 1977, 1089), hysterical neurosis (Lorand 1943), compulsiveness (Dubois 1949, 107–112) and obsessionality (Smart, Beumont & George 1976). In one variant, writers in the classical psychoanalytic tradition have situated the source of anorexia nervosa in the victim's inability to resolve a developmental crisis occurring during childhood or adolescence. In another variant, family systems theorists have looked primarily to the anorexic's dysfunctional interpersonal relationships as the source of her illness. Most important, both classical psychoanalysts and family systems theorists see the anorexic, or the anorexic and her family, as unhealthy. In some way, the anorexic has not matured correctly, either because of some personal failing or because of her family's dysfunctional nature.

In contrast to the psychoanalytic traditions, a group of observers, who might be called cultural theorists, understands the anorexic's condition as a response to social forces. In particular, eating disorders are viewed as a struggle against the dominant patriarchal order of modern Western society. For example, they have cited the religious aesthetic of self-starvation practiced by women saints in the thirteenth century as a response to the male domination of church and society. Addressing more recent conditions, cultural theorists consider popular models of ideal female beauty as evidence for the impossible demands presented to young women. Rather than attempting to meet these cultural imperatives concerning femininity, some adolescents rebel against them, sacrificing their bodies through self-starvation in an attempt to reveal the indecencies of gender inequality.

More directly, observers in the psychoanalytic tradition (in both its psychoanalytic and its family systems variants) treat the anorexic as a deviant, while, in contrast, those in the cultural school treat the anorexic as a virtual martyr for womankind. Yet neither of these images fully characterizes the anorexic. This chapter proposes a new model, which considers the problematic relationship to food, sexuality and nurturance shared by all women in this society. In this model, the anorexic is discussed in terms of her response to contradictory social norms concerning femininity. Rather than a deviant or a martyr for womankind, the anorexic actually embraces cultural ideals concerning feminine behaviors. The devastating symptoms of anorexia, then, arise as the anorexic overconforms to these ideals. But, at the same time, by overconforming to the social constructs of femininity, the anorexic resists this ideal. Before discussing this model, however, it will first be useful to more clearly define the opposing images of the anorexic. To do so, a more in-depth look at the theories is necessary.

form more

THE ANOREXIC AS DEVIANT: PSYCHOANALYTIC AND FAMILY SYSTEMS THEORIES

Psychoanalytic and family systems theories present the two dominant hypotheses for dealing with the anorexic. It is important to note that both schools view anorexia as a response to the developmental crisis of adolescence. Beginning with the work of Sigmund Freud, these theorists situate the origins of anorexia in the adolescent's struggle over self-determination, individuation and sexual development. The anorexic fails to deal with these issues adequately, as "normal" adolescents do; thus, a neurosis results. While never working explicitly with anorexia, Freud obviously came into contact with the condition, and he clearly believed that anorexia derived from a personal inability to deal with normal sexual development (Freud 1966, 106). Later clinicians have cited the underdeveloped sexuality of most anorexics as evidence for this interpretation (Bruch 1972, 250–55).

Since Freud, psychoanalysts have continued to examine internal sexual conflict as the possible source of anorexia. Centering the origin of anorexia in an unresolved oedipal crisis, Waller, Kaufman and Deutsch point to oral impregnation fantasies as an indicator of these conflicts (1940, 15). Conversely, Meyer and Weinroth claim that anorexia derives from a very early disordered mother-child relationship, rather than from internal sexual conflicts. Thus, these authors see the sources of this illness as pre-oedipal, rather than oedipal (1957, 394).

Likewise focusing on the emergence of anorexia during the advent of maturity, Bruch claims that the anorexic is unprepared to cope with the psychological and social consequences of adulthood and sexuality. The main conflicts in anorexia, according to Bruch, center around control, identity, competence and effectiveness (1972, 251). Specifically, Bruch claims that a sense of inadequacy is the essential component of anorexia. This feature stands in stark contrast to the life history of anorexics, who are overwhelmingly "good and quiet children, obedient, clean, eager to please, helpful at home, precociously dependable, and excelling in school" (1972, 255). The illness emerges, according to Bruch, when the onslaught of adolescence requires a new independence and self-awareness. The anorexic is unable to cope with these demands after a childhood of absolute obedience. Inability to perceive personal resources eventually gives rise to the anorexic's feelings of inadequacy.

In contrast to the individualistic bias of the classical psychoanalytic tradition, family systems theorists emphasize the interpersonal relationships of the anorexic, paying special attention to familial values and patterns of interaction. Salvador Minuchin describes four characteristics of the anorexic family. Specifically, the anorexic's family is highly enmeshed, overprotective and rigid, while attempting to appear "perfect" to the outside world (Minuchin 1978, cited in Edwards 1987, 64). The anorexic has learned to subordinate herself for the good of the family. Self-starvation becomes a form of silent protest, an "internalized struggle for individual identity and autonomy" (Edwards 1987, 65).

Within both psychoanalytic and family systems theories of anorexia, writers frequently emphasize the mother's role. Selvini-Palazzoli (1974) claims that anorexics model much of their behavior after their mothers, from whom they learn to center their lives around others. These mothers tend to be conservative, submissive and weight conscious and are unlikely to differentiate themselves effectively from their children. Similarly, Chernin, whose work will be dealt with more closely in a later section of this chapter, argues that eating disorders are rooted in the problems of mother-daughter separation and identity. According to Chernin, the interconnectedness of mother-daughter-food provides the foundation for modern anorexia (1985, 39–94).

It would be a mistake, however, to dwell on the differences between the psychoanalytic and the family systems theories. Both of these schools deal with the anorexic (or the anorexic and her family) as deviant. In the psychoanalytic framework, the anorexic's problems with food arise because she has dealt poorly with crises in adolescence, has failed to differentiate from her parents or suffers from an unresolved oedipal drama. In family systems theory, the anorexic's interpersonal relationships have dysfunctional outcomes. She is enmeshed with her mother, does not see herself as an autonomous individual and is unable to make her own decisions. When theorists in these schools fault parents for their daughter's eating disorder, they usually emphasize the mother's failings. These writers tend to characterize specific tendencies in the anorexic's mother that correlate strongly with the illness's occurrence. Seemingly, anorexia will arise most frequently among individuals whose psychological makeup lends itself to difficulties during adolescent development. Children with these predetermining factors will then be more likely to contract anorexia if their mothers are submissive, weight conscious and demanding. Overall, the picture of the anorexic arising from these theories is that of a sick adolescent, her illness arising from her inability to develop "normally."

While the theorists in these schools have had considerable success in predicting psychological and familial phenomena that correlate with the occurrence of anorexia nervosa, they have ignored the social forces that create these predictor variables. The social origins of personalities, relationships and family configurations are ignored. Questions such as why a mother is weight conscious and submissive, while a father is distant and emotionally rejecting, are not considered. Similarly, none of these writers adequately explains why families with such parents create anorexia in daughters, rather than sons. Overall, the psychoanalytic and family systems theories fail to adequately explain why women develop the disease nine times more often than men. This inadequacy arises because these schools question only the health of the anorexic, while ignoring the contradictions inherent in the feminine role to which she is directed. Most important, these schools fail to notice that the ideal woman in modern society must be mature, yet childlike; sexual, yet neutral; competent, yet passive. Specifically, the psychoanalytic and family systems theories never deal with the impossibility involved in meeting this ideal. Overall, the lack of attention to broader social issues leaves these schools' explanations of anorexia basically unsatisfying.

THE ANOREXIC AS MARTYR: THE INFLUENCE OF CULTURE

In an attempt to go beyond the limits of the psychoanalytic and family systems theories, a cultural explanation of anorexia nervosa provides an alternative model of this eating disorder. In particular, this model adds a consideration of broader social forces to psychological and familial variables in the making of the anorexic. Thus, while not completely disregarding the psychoanalytic and interpersonal factors that researchers in these schools emphasized, cultural theorists include social factors in the foundation of anorexia nervosa. Most generally, the cultural school views the anorexic as a product of society, rather than as a deviant.

Cultural theories insist that anorexia nervosa derives primarily from the overwhelming social imperative toward thinness and the resulting problematic relationship women have with food and appetite. Features of this imperative include veneration of the svelte female frame and the demands of fashion, stressing androgyny, rather than full-figured femininity, as well as an unceasing stress on restrictive dieting (Brumberg 1988, 51). According to the cultural model, modern visual media fuel the emphasis on female slimness, serving as a major impetus for anorexia. Because the cultural model begins to explain why women make up the overwhelming majority of persons inflicted with eating disorders, feminists have generally been the leading proponents of the theory. Feminist writers have dealt not only with anorexia, but also with bulimarexia and overeating. Because theorists of the cultural school typically view these problems as versions of the same obsession, I will deal with them simultaneously, under the term *eating disorder* (Counihan 1985, 78).

Writing about obesity, Orbach considers the social forces that lead women to overeat. She states that the problematic position of a mother in modern society, raising her daughter into inevitable oppression, is central to the onerous condition of contemporary womanhood, cripples the mother-daughter relationship and may give rise to eating disorders. Specifically, she claims that as long as patriarchical culture demands that women rear their daughters to accept an inferior social status, the mother's job will involve tension and confusion, which often surface in the way mothers and daughters interact over the subject of food (1978, 119).

While sharing Orbach's analysis of the ways in which the mother-daughter relationship is shaped by social forces, Chernin adds a discussion of the "tyranny of slenderness" as a product of the mind-body dichotomy characteristic of Western societies. This dichotomy equates men with the exalted mind, empowering them and allowing them the right to act, while linking women to the denigrated body, limiting them only to serving. Chernin argues that women's obsession with fat arises from an attempt to "control or eliminate the passionate aspects of the self in order to gain the approval and prerogatives of masculine culture," thus explaining "all those particular sensations of emptiness, of longing and craving, of dread and despair" that characterize anorexics, bulimarexics and the obese (1981, 178).

Counihan also combines aspects of family systems, psychoanalytic and cultural theory. She describes eating disorders in terms of four themes: (1) sexuality and sexual identity; (2) power, control and release; (3) solitude, withdrawal, deceit and competition; and (4) family strife. According to Counihan, the sexual nature of eating disorders arises from a discomfort with the developing female body and a rejection of adult sexuality (1985, 81). Thus, while anorexics flee from maturity by becoming childlike and androgynous, the obese remove themselves from sexual possibilities by violating cultural standards for female beauty (Millman 1980, 105–39). The second theme in eating disorders, according to Counihan, involves authority and capacity for action. Women with eating disorders generally find themselves unable to exert control over their lives. Food becomes an arena where control is played out, whether through extreme control or complete abandon. Counihan describes the third major characteristic of eating disorders in terms of the competition, deceit and isolation typical of these illnesses. Drawing from Orbach, she claims that women in this culture have difficulty coping with their feelings about competition. Getting fat, as well as isolating themselves through starvation or binging-purging behaviors, allows women to use the body as a socially permitted excuse for failure. Similarly, persons with eating disorders are able to hide their competitive feelings within private, food-related activities, rather than public ones (1985, 79). The final theme in eating disorders is that of family conflict. Here Counihan considers both social forces and familial organization. Within the family, food becomes a battleground on which the anorexic fights for autonomy and individuation. Anorexia can enable a previously "perfect" child to express her discontent, powerlessness and anger at her parents (1985, 87–88).

The cultural model, then, clearly adds to an understanding of anorexia and its sources by considering social phenomena, rather than strictly psychological and familial ones, in the making of such disorders. Moreover, by rooting its explanations in gender-differentiated social forces, cultural theory helps us understand why the overwhelming majority of anorexics are women. Nevertheless, the cultural school fails to provide an adequate explanation of anorexia in several very important ways.

Theorists in the cultural tradition emphasize the universality of women's problematic relationship to food, often venerating the anorexic and the obese as examples of modern women's shared experiences. Thus, not only do cultural approaches treat anorexia as fundamentally continuous with bulimia and obesity, but also they treat all eating disorders as fundamentally continuous with the experience of all women. Within these formulations, the anorexic appears not as a deviant, but as the purest expression of the more general dilemmas of womanhood in contemporary society. The anorexic is, in short, a martyr. For example, MacLeod views anorexia as "a statement" of such importance that the anorexic would "rather die than stop saying it" (1981, xi). Orbach claims that obesity is an attempt to break free of society's sex stereotypes and culturally defined experiences of womanhood. For her, getting fat becomes a "definite and purposeful act," aimed at challenging patriarchical society (1978, 18). This act expresses a rebellion against the powerlessness of womanhood, against social pressures to look and act in narrowly defined ways and against being evaluated according to the image one projects.

Feminists have attempted to dignify these predominantly female illnesses by equating them with political hunger strikes opposed to male domination and degradation of the female body (Orbach 1986, 23–31). Accordingly, anorexia is interpreted as a protest in which self-starvation is offered as a symbol of a culture that does not value femininity (Bordo 1985–86, 100). Even more explicitly, Bell, in his work on holy anorexic saints, frequently points to these women's need to battle dominant male clergy in their pursuit of holiness (1988, 135). While never stating that these women chose to starve themselves solely to defy male oppression, he implies that the disorder involves a male-female struggle, with holy anorexia indicating female triumph.

But this position is troubling. Do these theorists assume that the death of Saint Catherine of Siena from starvation is the ultimate female victory? Or that a teen-age girl throwing up by herself in a school toilet, tortured by guilt and anxiety, represents an effective protest against oppression? The anorexic's "protest" exists only within the individualized body of the anorexic. Rather than acting as a collective political strategy of resistance, anorexia fails to reflect a social or political understanding of women's plight. Furthermore, the very symptoms of anorexia actually serve to isolate the victim from any sort of social activity. Far from being socially oriented political actors, anorexics are deliberately political only in the highly restricted sense of rebelling against parents and self. Anorexics starve not with a consciousness of social goals, but rather in response to their personal needs and circumstances. While anorexia may be political in the sense that it provides evidence for the contradictory nature of the female role, it is a mistake to make the anorexic a heroine of a premeditated political martyrdom that exists only in the imagination of social critics.

In making the modern anorexic a martyr for womankind, cultural theorists assert that her disease derives from women's rebellion against the female role in Western society, including socially defined norms for female sexuality (Millman 1980, 105–8). As previously mentioned, however, the anorexic's reactions to the contradictions inherent in the socially sanctioned female role are more complex than simply rebellion against that role. Turner claims that these contradictions create confusion concerning the requirements of femininity because the ideal is defined in terms of opposites. Turner asserts that anorexia is the product of these contradictory social pressures on women, as these pressures prevail in societies centered around systems of consumption (1984, 93). In social systems that promote commodities with reference to a body aesthetic, a woman is valued for her appearance; body form becomes symbolic of her social worth and personal character. According to Turner, the obese woman is not simply fat; she is uncontrolled. The unrestrained female body makes a statement about unrestrained morality, so that to control women's bodies is, according to Turner, to control their personalities. This domination represents an act of authority over the feminine body in the interests of a public order organized around male values of rationality.

Anorexia, then, arises in consumption-based societies as a response to the impossibilities of meeting socially defined notions concerning femininity. The disorder, however, represents more than a simple physical illness; it is also a "dis-order" of social relations. For Turner, anorexia is an "alternative, disruptive regime, an anarchy within the domestic government" (1984, 196). Anorexia—and eating disorders more generally—is rebellion, but it is also adaptation and maladaptation.

Turner (1966) compares anorexia to Durkheim's egoistic suicide, and consequently reverts somewhat to family systems theories of the disorder. According to Durkheim, egoistic suicide appears to be an individual's subjective choice to end her life, but sociologically it is the result of collapsed social bonds linking the individual to the social group. The individual is no longer protected by group ties, but is exposed to the destructive suicidal forces of an individualistic culture (1966, 145–277). Contrasting anorexia to egoistic suicide, Turner claims that the suicide of anorexics results from a rebellion against familial bonds aimed at overprotective surveillance and discipline. Thus, the anorexic's suicide arises from oversocialization within the family structure, from too much, rather than too little, parenting (Turner 1966, 145–277).

In this perspective, anorexia is portrayed as an act of adolescent rebellion against parental, and primarily maternal, control. This rebellion, however, is set against the backdrop of a consumerist culture, which values a woman primarily for her physical attractiveness. Turner implies that while anorexia cannot be fully understood within the wider social context of a commodity-based culture, a consideration of women's historical social position is necessary for a complete understanding of the disorder (1966, 145–277).

AN ALTERNATIVE THEORY: THE ANOREXIC AS OVERCONFORMIST

The cultural and family systems approaches fail to capture the complexity of anorexia. Psychoanalytic theories predict which individuals will contract eating disorders, but ignore the larger social issues essential to an understanding of these diseases. Conversely, the cultural approach explains social trends, such as why women, rather than men, become anorexics and why the incidence of anorexia has increased so drastically in the last twenty years. The cultural model, however, cannot explain why particular individuals become ill. The incompleteness of both approaches implies an evaluative stance that fails to do justice to the anorexic. The psychoanalytic perspective, by focusing on the individual or her family, implies blame and thus victimizes the victim. Conversely, the cultural model intentionally removes blame from the victim, but at the same time romanticizes her, making her into a heroine in a manner that denies the immense suffering accompanying eating disorders.

A more complete approach to anorexia must make up for the failings of earlier approaches. First, so as not to blame her, a comprehensive approach must consider the social forces operating on the woman with an eating disorder and understand the disease as a strategy for dealing with these social forces. Doing so, this model recognizes the anorexic's agency.

This model should also acknowledge the very real suffering involved in eating disorders so as not to romanticize the victims of these diseases. This approach considers that, while individual variation exists, all women must struggle to accommodate a cultural model of femininity that is unattainable. Rather than emphasizing the reasons why specific women become anorexic, bulimic or obese, this model of eating disorders considers the various forms taken by all women's attempts to meet contradictory norms concerning female appetite. In this model, eating disorders become strategies for dealing with these norms.

In opposition to the psychoanalytic and family systems schools, however, this model would define the anorexic as an overconformist, rather than a deviant, and, in opposition to the cultural school, would not romanticize her behavior. Moreover, this perspective points out that in overconforming to social ideals concerning femininity, the anorexic illustrates the contradictory nature of the female role itself.

Feminists have rightly pointed to anorexia as evidence for the sexual inequality existing in modern society. Taking this stance further, it can be argued that the anorexic typifies one end of a continuum of women's problematic relationship to the contradictory norms of femininity; her disease can be seen as an extreme strategy for dealing with these norms. That is, every woman must negotiate the contradictory ideals that are culturally available to her in an attempt to meet the unattainable feminine role. The anorexic's inability to meet the contradictory aspects of femininity, despite her attempts to overconform to this ideal, calls attention to women's inability to fill the role.

The anorexic can be thought of as an overconformist because she negotiates the conflicting demands of the feminine role by overcomplying with one dimension of these contradictions. In several very specific ways, the anorexic fills the female role perfectly. For example, by practicing extreme control over her body, the anorexic suppresses the male, rather than the female, aspects of herself. Cultural theorists have argued that anorexia is an attempt to eliminate the passionate, female aspects of the self (Chernin 1981, 187), while others claim that the anorexic experiences herself as "woman-as-too-much" (Bordo 1985–86, 93).

In contrast, the anorexic may affirm social notions concerning femininity and feminine behavior. The aspects of herself that she attempts to suppress—competitiveness (Counihan 1985, 69), insatiability and drive (Bordo 1985–86, 77–81)—are characteristics revered in men, but criticized in women. The anorexic's strategy of rejecting and suppressing these characteristics is demonstrated via the devastating symptoms of the disease. She conforms completely to the social ideal of woman as helpless and dependent.

Psychoanalysts have argued that anorexics negate their female sexuality, attempting to withdraw back into childhood. However, a more complete perspective on this disorder sees that the anorexic actually overconforms, although in a distorted manner, to cultural notions concerning feminine sexuality. In addition, the anorexic overconforms by participating in and reifying the culturally prescribed hatred of the feminine. In another sense, the anorexic overconforms by affirming social notions of female sexuality by becoming submissive, androgynous and vulnerable in the most ultimate sense. That is, the anorexic complies perfectly with social ideals concerning female sexuality. Her strategy can be more fully appreciated, however, when this ideal is shown to include the contradictions of sexuality and neutrality, which arise when a woman is expected to be avidly erotic with her male partner, but sexually uninterested in her public life. Even while she attempts to meet cultural ideals of feminine sexuality, the anorexic's symptoms make her completely asexual. Once again, in her intention to overconform, the anorexic actually resists the contradictory nature of femininity.

The contradictory character of the role that the anorexic is trying to meet is reflected in the contradictory nature of her disease. The symptoms of the illness are counterproductive to the anorexic, so that while she is overconforming to cultural ideals of femininity, she ultimately exemplifies the impossibility of meeting those ideals. As suggested above, the anorexic, more than any other woman, meets social norms of passivity and vulnerability. The feminine ideal of passivity, however, is only one side of the norm that implies that women should be dependent on men in their private lives as lovers, while competent in their roles as mothers and workers. Because the anorexic has complied so completely with one side of the feminine norm of passivity, her death provides an unquestionable testimony to the flaws in these contradictory ideals.

In the same vein, discussion has been presented regarding the anorexic's overconformity to social notions of female beauty. To do so, she practices diet and exercise regimes that become more and more extreme as her illness progresses. The anorexic strives, more so than any other woman, to achieve the socially approved ideal of female beauty, which is largely unattainable. Thus, the anorexic overconforms to social notions of beauty by striving to be as thin as possible; yet in doing so, the anorexic loses control of her weight-loss tactics, so that she becomes grossly emaciated. While aimed at conformity, the anorexic's strategy takes a severe turn. Specifically, because her attempts to meet cultural notions of beauty act to make her far from attractive, the anorexic's tactics exemplify the impossibility of meeting social standards for female beauty.

The contradictions within anorexia reflect the inconsistent nature of the female role in modern Western society. A connection between anorexic symptoms and social imperatives can be summarized by relating these issues in terms of Merton's typology of modes of individual adaptation (1957, 131–60). The goals and means of the anorexic can be divided into two levels, that of the anorexic's intent and that of the social myth that she cannot attain. Specifically, the anorexic intends to conform to social ideals of femininity, but chooses radical methods to do so. Thus, in her overconformity to the norms of femininity, the anorexic must deviate from prescribed social means. However, in terms of the social myth of femininity, the anorexic emphasizes her physical self and so seems to adopt the most acceptable means for gaining approval as a woman. By adopting these methods so completely, however, the anorexic resists the social goals of femininity by proving that this ideal is unattainable.

In conclusion, anorexia nervosa presents a particularly difficult intellectual puzzle due to its peculiar and contradictory nature. While previous theorists have attempted to explain this disorder by characterizing its victims as either deviants or martyrs, the anorexic is more adequately characterized as an overconformist. Furthermore, her overconformity should be seen as one culturally available strategy for dealing with social contradictions. Like the anorexic's symptoms, her overconformity is paradoxical. Even as the anorexic woman overconforms to socially proscribed norms for femininity, she resists the contradictory nature of those norms.

NOTE

Thanks are due Dr. Robert Zussman and Dr. Michael Kimmel for extensive advising and editing.

WORKS CITED

Bell, R. 1985. *Holy Anorexia.* Chicago: University of Chicago Press.

Bordo, S. R. 1985–86. Anorexia Nervosa: Psychopathology as the Crystallization of Culture. *Philosophical Forum* 2: 73–103.

Bruch, H. 1972. *Eating Disorders: Obesity, Anorexia and the Person Within.* New York: Basic Books.

———. 1978. *The Golden Cage: The Enigma of Anorexia Nervosa.* Cambridge: Harvard University Press.

———. 1988. *Conversations with Anorexics.* Ed. D. Czyzewski and M. Suhr. New York: Basic Books.

Brumberg, J. J. 1988. *Fasting Girls: The Emergence of Anorexia Nervosa as a Modern Disease.* Cambridge: Harvard University Press.

Cantwell, D. P., S. Sturzenburger and J. Burroughs. 1977. Anorexia Nervosa: An Affective Disorder? *Archives of General Psychiatry* 34: 1087–93.

Chernin, K. 1981. *The Obsession: Reflections on the Tyranny of Slenderness.* New York: Harper & Row.

———. 1985. *The Hungry Self: Woman, Eating and Identity.* New York: Random House.

Counihan, C. M. 1985. What Does It Mean to Be Fat, Thin and Female in the United States? A Review Essay. *Food and Foodways* 1: 77–94.

Crisp, A. H., R. L. Palmer and R. S. Kalucy. 1976. How Common Is Anorexia Nervosa? A Prevalence Study. *British Journal of Psychiatry* 128: 549–55.

DuBois, F. S. 1949. Compulsion Neurosis with Cachexia. *American Journal of Psychiatry* 106: 107–12.

Durkheim, E. 1966. *Suicide: A Study in Sociology.* New York: Free Press.

Edwards, G. 1987. Anorexia and the Family. In M. Lawrence (ed.), *Fed Up and*

Hungry: Women, Obsession and Food (pp. 61–74). New York: Peter Bedrick Books.

Feighner, J. P. 1973. Diagnostic Criteria for Use in Psychiatric Research. *Archives of General Psychiatry* 26: 57–63.

Freud, S. 1966. An Infantile Neurosis and Other Works. In J. Strachey (ed.), *The Standard Edition of the Complete Psychological Works of Sigmund Freud* (pp. 1–122). Vol. 17. London: Hogarth.

Garfinkle, P., and D. Garner. 1982. *Anorexia Nervosa: A Multidimensional Perspective.* New York: Brummer Mazel.

Lorand, S. 1943. Anorexia Nervosa: Report of a Case. *Psychosomatic Medicine* 5: 282–92.

MacLeod, S. 1981. *The Art of Starvation: A Story of Anorexia and Survival.* London: Schocken Books.

Merton, R. 1957. *Social Theory and Social Structure* (revised edition). Glencoe, Illinois: Free Press.

Meyer, B. C., and L. A. Weinroth. 1957. Observations on Psychological Aspects of Anorexia Nervosa. *Psychosomatic Medicine* 19: 389–98.

Millman, M. 1980. *Such a Pretty Face: Being Fat in America.* New York: Norton.

Minuchin, S. 1978. *Psychosomatic Families: Anorexia Nervosa in Context.* Cambridge: Harvard University Press.

Orbach, S. 1978. *Fat Is a Feminist Issue: The Anti-diet Guide to Permanent Weight Loss.* New York: Paddington.

———. 1986. *Hunger Strike: The Anorectic's Struggle as a Metaphor for Our Age.* New York: Norton.

Selvini-Palazzoli, M. 1974. *Self Starvation: From the Intrapsychic to the Interpersonal Approach to Anorexia Nervosa.* London: Human Context Books.

Smart, D. E., P. J. V. Beumont and G. C. W. George. 1976. Some Personality Characteristics of Patients with Anorexia Nervosa. *British Journal of Psychiatry* 128: 57–59.

Sugarman, A., D. Quinlan, and L. DeVenis. 1981. Anorexia Nervosa as a Defense Against Anaclitic Depression. *International Journal of Eating Disorders* 1: 44–61.

Turner, B. S. 1984. *The Body and Society.* Oxford: Basil Blackwell.

Waller, J. V., R. M. Kaufman and F. Deutsch. 1940. Anorexia Nervosa: A Psychosomatic Entity. *Psychosomatic Medicine* 2: 3–16.

8

Female Bodily Perfection and the Divided Self

Catherine G. Valentine

S1: The question of the divided self. The constant battle we wage within ourselves of what we are and what our culture demands we be. Two months ago I began exercising again for the first time in many years. I had gained weight over the summer.... I felt obligated to lose the weight. Now I ask myself why? Have I accepted society's definition of my body, the all-powerful beer commercial, the beautiful object? ... I am beginning to understand my relationship with my body to be one aspect of my battle for self.[1]

Analysis of the intersections between self and social structure has long been central to the sociological enterprise. This chapter concerns one such intersection: that between the emotionally embodied self (Denzin 1985, 226) in women and the system of gender distinctions and inequalities. Based on analysis of central themes in journals written by female students, I offer some thoughts on the reach of the gender system into women's deepest sense of self. Specifically, I argue that women's moral identity incorporates definitions and feelings of self constructed in relation to an abstract ideal of bodily perfection and perfectibility, which is produced and disseminated by electronic and print media.[2] I submit that idealized images of female bodily perfection and messages of perfectibility exercise control over women's lives by constructing a self that is distorted and divided against itself, self-policing and self-destructive.

DATA ANALYSIS

Data for this chapter come from an analysis of core themes in journals written by female students in gender studies courses I taught from 1987 to 1990. In the first rounds of analysis, I examined seventy-seven women's and seventeen men's journals. Only women wrote about the themes that became central to this chapter. Of the forty-eight female students whose journals were the focus of analysis, all but one were white, most (78 percent) were of traditional college age and they were overwhelmingly middle or working class.[3]

Although standard caveats about generalizing from this type of data set apply—the feelings and experiences of these students cannot be taken as universal—it is important to remember that these students are authorities about their own lives and that their own written words help one to understand, in some depth, the salient themes of their lives.

THEORETICAL CONTEXT

Turner (1984), Bordo (1989) and others (Glassner 1988; Edgley & Brissett 1990) observe that analysis of the body in society necessarily involves the study of social control. The body, Bordo says, is both a symbolic form and a locus of social control (1989, 13). Similarly, Turner views the body as an important medium by which societal control over the self is carried out (1984, 39–40).

Since women are subject to greater social control than men (Glassner 1988, 107), the study of societal control of individuals via the body has focused on women's bodies. Social control of women involves a powerful imperative for bodily control. Women's bodies are the locus of rape laws, abortion and birth control restrictions, sexual harassment, wife beating, eating disorders and cosmetic surgery (Epstein 1988; Bordo 1989). Through these rules and practices, women's bodies are interpreted, ordered, regulated, restricted, shaped and reconstructed, mutilated, even destroyed.

To control women is to define women's moral worth, that is, their goodness or badness. Through body rules and practices, women are divided into polar moral types: good women and bad women, respectable women and unrespectable women, madonnas and whores (Lerner 1986; Sheffield 1987). These moral dichotomies revolve around the imperative for female bodily control: appearance, sexuality, reproductive capacity, movement in space and time. The body's outer surfaces and its activities are defined and interpreted as signs of a woman's character. The self, in a woman's experiences, is reduced to surfaces—public and observed—in particular, the body's appearance and activities; in other words, a woman's outer body is interpreted as a mirror of her "deep self" (Denzin 1985, 232–33). Turner, commenting on the social control of women via their bodies, says succinctly: "To control women's bodies is to control their personalities" (1984, 197).

Societal control of women via bodily control is heightened considerably in modern consumer societies in which the body is commodified, images of perfect bodies abound and body work has become a sign of moral worth for whole segments of society (Glassner 1988, 253–55). Women's lives, it is argued (Freedman 1986; Glassner 1988; Edgley & Brissett 1990; Wolf 1991), are increasingly dominated by what is variously termed the cult of the perfect body, the beauty myth and the tyranny of bodily perfection.

In consumer society, the electronic and print media act as the "mediated generalized other" in the development of individual identity (Meyrowitz 1985, 131–32). They instruct us about average and normal, often setting impossible standards and often doing so through homogenized images and messages of perfect and perfectible bodies. In consumer society, analysts argue, bodies are replacing selves (Edgley & Brissett 1990, 271), and image counts more than ability (Glassner 1988, 29).

It is in this cultural context that women's identities and deepest sense of moral worthiness are forged and are most clearly and consistently the locus of controlling images and messages of perfection and perfectibility. As Bordo observes, "femininity has come to be a matter of constructing the appropriate surface self" (1989, 17).

BODILY PERFECTION AND MORAL WORTH IN STUDENT JOURNALS

Given a cultural milieu that is inundated with gendered images of bodily perfection and messages of moral perfectibility through body work, it makes sense that the students' journals are filled with accounts of their efforts to achieve such perfection and the consequences of their inevitable failure to do so. The journals emphasize that women's identities and moral worth are defined by the outer body's appearance.

S2: I have noticed just recently I have been focusing my energies toward being thin and having "that" look. But what changed inside my "self" that makes me believe I have to look good to be happy? . . . The "way I look attitude" is engraved in my head every day of my life. Through commercials, magazines, clothing stores . . . I am made to believe that I have to be better looking, better everything.

S3: When I was bulimic and overeating, I wanted so badly to conform to what I believed society wanted me to look like that I was willing to destroy myself to attain such unrealistic standards . . . when other people, men and women, stress that women are not worthy if they are not thin and attractive, then many women will continue to destroy their minds and bodies while looking for acceptance. . . . Advertising helps to perpetuate the idea that beauty . . . gives a woman a better chance at happiness. Advertising makes women believe that certain products will make them more appealing on the outside which, in turn, is supposed to make a woman feel better about herself.

In line with Schur's observation that appearance norms are a "central element in the objectification and devaluation of females" and that "concern about meeting these norms . . . pervades women's lives" (1984, 66), accounts of the impact of restrictive and unattainable appearance norms and ideals on the inner perspective and everyday routines of the journal writers were among the most frequently told stories in the journals. The omnipresent image of the normalized, homogenized, idealized woman in the pages of magazines and on television and film screens is the model for the body work, such as dieting and exercising, and the self-abuse, such as starving the body, with which many women struggle.

The argument that it is care and concern for others by which women judge themselves and are judged (Gilligan 1982) stands in sharp contrast to what the women in this study say: namely, that conformity to appearance demands and the imperative for bodily control define women's worth to self and others. The journals are clear. Technologically generated and endlessly reproduced images of female bodily, that is, moral, perfection are the measuring stick against which the women in this study evaluate their own worth, find it wanting and feel worthless.

In the following excerpts, students describe the power of media-generated images of perfect bodies to shape their privately experienced feelings and their daily body routines:

> *S4:* I must admit that when I look through magazines and see cosmetic ads with flawless, perfect-looking models I feel somehow inferior, not as perfect or attractive—plain, not glamorous. . . . When I look at these ads I begin to feel down, depressed and upset that I do not look like that and I always fail starving myself to look like that.

> *S5:* I find myself anxiety-ridden at times, almost out of breath. I believe I may have a true problem that is blown out of proportion or maybe it's a low self-image. Whichever may be the case, I find myself deeply disturbed by most advertising on television. . . . Why the constant use of women? . . . All I find myself doing is comparing myself to those sexy, beautiful women. . . . I cannot seem to accept this pure feeling of inequality. I feel like an object.

In these accounts, negative emotionality is central to the students' self-concepts. From Hochschild's view of emotion as clue and comparison (1983, 28–31), the emotions experienced and described by the students—for example, guilt, shame, anxiety, self-loathing, depression—can be tied to the discrepancy they see between their own body's appearance and the images of the perfect body.

Connected to negative emotionality, the students' accounts point as well to distortion and internal division in their self-concepts. Both negative emotionality and the divided self are, I believe, integral to what Wolf calls the process of reflexive legitimation of oppression (1986, 218), that is, the process by which unprivileged people submit to subordination.

LEGITIMATION OF SUBORDINATION, NEGATIVE EMOTIONALITY AND THE DIVIDED SELF

Wolf argues that the legitimation of oppression relies on the internalization of inferiority and/or the acceptance of one's inferior position as appropriate by those who are devalued (1986, 222). Women's subordination, then, hinges on women seeing themselves from the viewpoint of men, as inferior and relatively powerless. What one sees in the words of the women in this study is the reflexive legitimation of subordination at work through the objectification of the self and the formation of a negative looking-glass self.

The journal accounts suggest that the construction of an emotionally divided self is at the heart of the process of legitimation of subordination. In his discussion of the divided self, Denzin (1984) maintains that the divided self is dominated by negative emotionality—for example, guilt, shame, fear, anxiety, self-loathing, self-destructiveness. The body of the person whose self is divided is a source of pain to her and an object of self-hatred. "Violence toward the self, in the form of self-destructive actions and thoughts" is characteristic of the divided self (1984, 202). Of great significance to this study, the divided self, Denzin says, is the product of impossible standards set by the dominant other and arises or is exacerbated in social structures that suppress parts of our potential and "maximize invidious comparisons with others" (1984, 227; see also Gilligan 1990, 522).

The journal accounts of the students flesh out both Denzin's work on the divided self (1984) and Wolf's analysis of legitimation of oppression (1986). The journals both suggest a firmer and more direct social organizational basis for the distorted and divided self than does Denzin and point to the process of reflexive legitimation of oppression as a gripping emotional experience.

In the first case, the journals suggest that the construction of a distorted, divided self in women is a central component of societal control of women. The divided self represents the reach into the self of gender distinctions, divisions and inequalities. It is useful to conceptualize the divided self of unprivileged peoples—women, in this study—as a micro-level analogue to the "divide and conquer" strategy employed by dominant groups to control subordinate groups at the macro-structural level. The inner struggle described in the journals is about the political battle for control over female bodies and identities. Bordo views the female body as a site of struggle on which a "battle is being waged for women's energies and resources" (1989, 28; see also 1990, 667–68). The journals indicate that this struggle is deeply emotional and internally divisive, a struggle in which women's dignity and self-respect are at stake.

In the next excerpts, the imperative for female bodily and emotional control is described as a continual assault on women's sense of dignity and moral worth, a struggle in which women often lose out to impossible standards of perfection. These excerpts illustrate the emotional reach and grip of images of perfection and perfectibility on the deep self, especially the confluence of negative and conflicting feelings that are critical to the divided self and its role in reflexive legitimation of women's subordination.

> *S7:* I hate society's images, yet I cannot force my mind to accept myself as I am. Society has too tight of a hold on my thoughts and feelings of acceptance. I can only hope someday I can break free of its grasp before I destroy myself trying to live up to my gender's expected role.

> *S6:* It is obvious that society gave birth to the perfect image of who we should all want to look like. In magazines, on billboards, in advertisements, television, we are bombarded with them—super slim, super toned, sexy female bodies. . . . Since we were little girls, society has molded us into who it thinks we should each be. Now we are left with images that show us what perfect is, and if we are too far from these images, then we are bad and ugly and made to feel guilty.

THE "MEDIATED GENERALIZED OTHER": IMPOSSIBLE STANDARDS AND THE BATTLE FOR THE BODY

It is striking, on the one hand, that the women in this study understand the controlling and shaping power of images of perfection and messages of perfectibility; yet, on the other hand, they feel powerless in the face of those images and messages. Why do they feel powerless? Why do the students experience images of perfection and perfectibility as objective and coercive? I think that the answer lies, in part, in what the women identify as the primary source of images of perfection—the electronic and print media or the "mediated generalized other." The imperative for bodily perfection and messages of perfectibility come less from direct interaction with other people and more from mediated relationships with the images of women on television, on billboards and in magazine ads.

Meyrowitz stresses that the "mediated generalized other" avoids "face-to-face encounters . . . and is shared by millions of others" (1985, 132). Homogenized and ubiquitous, images of female bodily perfection are shared widely and are, in a sense, inescapable in a world in which electronic media are merging differences of identity, perspectives and spheres of life. The "mediated generalized other" presents "a view from no place" (Meyrowitz 1985, 143–49). For the women in this study, a view from no place that is, in fact, everywhere and in every place is understandably experienced as overwhelming and coercive.

The journals emphasize the importance of the electronic and print media in the development of social selves in consumer societies. As discussed above, in the process of legitimation of subordination, women form a self-concept influenced strongly by the viewpoint of the dominant group. One important source of that viewpoint, according to the journal writers, is the "mediated generalized other," whose standards and images of perfection teach women (and men about women) that their outer body's appearance represents and reflects their moral value; to be beautiful is to be good, and to be both, one must suffer—the female body must be scrutinized regularly, privately as well as publicly, restricted and labored over continually.

SELF-SURVEILLANCE AND SOCIETAL CONTROL OF WOMEN

The ritual use of self-surveillance and discipline, self-policing and self-improvement, required by the ideal of the perfect and perfectible body has been widely documented and discussed (Turner 1984; Spitzack 1990; Wolf 1991). Schur asserts that visual objectification of women through appearance ideals, norms and practices means that women are seen as objects and, in turn, come to view themselves as objects (1984, 66). Here is the link between objectification and the legitimation of oppression in women. As women internalize their devalued position, they come to see themselves as objects to be scrutinized and evaluated. Indeed, daily life for many women in this study is described as a dizzying series of mirrored images of bodily stigma, of their failure to comply with beauty demands, a failure experienced as moral inadequacy and failure. The following excerpt illustrates the heightened self-scrutiny to which women subject their outer bodies and inner moral selves:

> S9: The point is that society puts so many pressures on us that we begin to have strange thoughts such as this. The other day I woke up with a pimple. ... I tried to cover it up, but nothing helped. I repeatedly looked in the mirror.... Everywhere I went I caught my reflection. Windows, toaster ovens, car mirrors, etc. all taunting me and teasing me with my reflection. The pimple was really ruining my day. It seemed as if everyone was staring at it and that everyone, but me, had a clear complexion. Why was this red bump bothering me so? ... Television, magazines and newspapers all make it seem as though one just isn't adequate, unless they use their "wonder-products" and look like the models who probably don't look as good in

person. . . . We begin to believe we are failures unless we can look like those models. We spend so much money and only beget disappointment. . . . Symbols of this frustration, such as a "sinful pimple," only encourage negative self-perception.

At first glance, a pimple seems a trivial matter. It is not. Complexion, body size and shape, and eye and hair color are but a few of the many outer symbols of women's worth. Morally flawless women are physically flawless. Bodily flaws, the students tell us, are sinful. To repeat, failure to comply with appearance demands, no matter that compliance is impossible, is experienced by the women in this study in feelings of self-hatred, self-recrimination and self-devaluation. They blame themselves.[4] The impossibility of compliance with beauty standards (and with the norms of femininity in general) is, I believe, essential to women's subordination. Achieving the ideal is at best momentary and illusory; thus, women must be ever vigilant. There is no time to relax, no time to feel comfortable and safe. Life if lived, say the women in this study, scrutinizing one's image and catching disappointing reflections of oneself in every shiny object.

SELF-POLICING AND SELF-DESTRUCTION

The bodily and moral scrutiny to which women subject themselves is vital to the maintenance of gender distinctions and inequalities. Social control of women works not only because men police women, but also because women watch other women and turn themselves into sights. Spitzack points out that the guard and the prisoner coexist in women and explains that "through internalization of male gazes and values, women evaluate themselves as they are evaluated by men" (1990, 53). Self-policing is a key form of social control. It is the system of social control internalized, a striking example of the process by which the "structures of society become the structures of our own consciousness" (Berger 1963, 121).

Destruction of the self is an understandable outcome of the self-policing, distorted and divided self; eating disorders are a poignant example. Eating disorders, especially anorexia, have received extensive consideration, which includes analysis of the suicidal path of the anorexic and the deep divisions within the anorexic's self (Chernin 1981, 1985; Turner 1984; Brumberg 1988; Bordo 1989). They are one of the most dramatic examples of internalized inferiority in women: the divided self dominated by the other's negative definitions of her, estranged from and hateful of her body, self-destructive.

Eating disorders belong on a continuum of self-destructive thoughts and actions which, except for the more dramatic anorexia and bulimia, are more commonplace and have similar consequences for women's identity.

Most commonly among the women in this study, self-destructiveness is expressed in negative, often unwanted feelings that overwhelm, consume and control their lives. Never becoming clear-cut self-violence, emotions such as guilt, shame and self-loathing are nonetheless self-destructive. Dieting, exercise and other body rituals are some of the practices by which the students try to contain, counteract or overcome these suffocating emotions. In the words of one of the journal writers:

> *S11:* Like the majority of men and women in our society, I am concerned with my physical appearance. . . . I realize that it is only self-destructive. . . . More seriously, my personal obsession with weight has led to bulimic tendencies, although they have as yet not been carried out. I avoid mirrors when stepping out of the shower or changing clothes for fear that I will once again be so repulsed that I want to vomit. So far I have been able to control myself, knowing the physical damage the binge-purge cycle creates. . . . I'm trying to learn to accept myself as I am, to omit "weight" from my definition of "self" as a valuable person. It's tougher than it may sound when you've constantly heard that physical shape and appearance are the key to whether you are a beautiful or ugly person.

This journal writer's habit of equating her worth with her weight is common. Embodied in her concern for her appearance and in her negative emotions is the institutionalized order of gender distinctions and inequalities, the continuing realities of female subordination. The women in this study have learned that their value depends upon the shape and shaping of their bodies, even through unpleasant, painful and dangerous routines and practices. Negative self-feelings accompany and fuel these body practices and are destructive of the individual's dignity and self-respect; they are integral to the divided self. Women's feelings of unworthiness are the emotional underpinning of the structure of gender distinctions and hierarchy and, according to the journals, are associated inextricably with the failure of the female body to comply with images of female bodily perfection.

CONCLUSION

My analysis of women's journals suggests that mediated images and standards of female bodily perfection, which fuse the surface of women's bodies with women's deepest feelings of self-worth, are a primary means of societal control of women. The imperative for bodily control defines women's moral identity and gives rise to a divided self whose self-distortions and self-destructiveness characterize the lives of women in this study.

It seems to me that the words of the women in this study insist that we turn our attention to earlier feminist concerns with the ways in which women's bodies, in the pursuit of moral worthiness through bodily perfection, are enjoined in the reproduction of gender distinctions and hierarchy (Bordo 1989; 1990). They remind us to examine carefully the pathways by which social controls, including a wide range of restrictive body practices, shape the identities of women and construct selves that are distracted, distorted, divided and self-destructive.

What better way to keep women in their place than with selves divided against themselves, awash in negative emotionality and engaged in self-surveillance. The inevitable failure of the female body to conform to images of perfection is experienced as moral stigma, producing a confluence of negative feelings that locks women into an unrelenting and unforgiving focus on the embodied self, a focus that ensures the continued social control of women by women as well as men and through self-policing.

Journal accounts focus, as well, on the power of images in everyday life in consumer societies. The "mediated generalized other" figures prominently as the source of the image and the message that bodily perfection equals worthiness.

NOTES

1. Quotations from the journals of the female students in this study are identified by an *S* (student) and a number (e.g., 1), indicating the journal from which a particular passage was taken.

2. This chapter challenges the central argument made by Gilligan, who claims that men define the self in relation to an abstract ideal of perfection and through separation from others, while women's self-perceptions are based on connection to others and an ethic of responsible caring (1982, 35).

3. The ratio of women to men at the college is approximately five to one and is reflected in enrollments in most majors and courses. Students are overwhelmingly white and middle or working class.

4. This no-win, catch-22 situation resembles the situation in which raped and incestuously assaulted women find themselves; as reported by Stanko, they end up blaming themselves "for not escaping an inescapable situation" (1985, 41).

WORKS CITED

Berger, P. L. 1963. *Invitation to Sociology: A Humanistic Perspective.* Garden City, N.Y.: Doubleday.

Bordo, S. R. 1989. The Body and the Reproduction of Femininity: A Feminist Appropriation of Foucault. In A. M. Jaggar and S. R. Bordo (eds.), *Gender/ Body/Knowledge: Feminist Reconstructions of Being and Knowledge* (pp. 13–33). New Brunswick, N.J.: Rutgers University Press.

———. 1990. Material Girl: The Effacements of Postmodern Culture. *Michigan Quarterly Review* 29: 653–77.

Brumberg, J. J. 1988. *Fasting Girls: The Emergence of Anorexia Nervosa as a Modern Disease.* Cambridge: Harvard University Press.

Chernin, K. 1981. *The Obsession: Reflections on the Tyranny of Slenderness.* New York: Harper & Row.

————. 1985. *The Hungry Self: Women, Eating and Identity.* New York: Times Books.

Denzin, N. K. 1984. *On Understanding Emotion.* San Francisco: Jossey-Bass.

————. 1985. Emotion as Lived Experience. *Symbolic Interaction* 13: 223–40.

Edgley, C., and D. Brissett. 1990. Health Nazis and the Cult of the Perfect Body. *Symbolic Interaction* 13: 257–79.

Epstein, C. F. 1988. *Deceptive Distinctions: Sex, Gender and the Social Order.* New Haven, Conn.: Yale University Press.

Freedman, R. 1986. *Beauty Bound.* Lexington, Mass.: Lexington Books.

Gilligan, C. 1982. *In a Different Voice: Psychological Theory and Women's Development.* Cambridge: Harvard University Press.

————. 1990. Joining the Resistance: Psychology, Politics, Girls and Women. *Michigan Quarterly Review* 29: 501–36.

Glassner, B. 1988. *Bodies.* New York: Putnam.

Hochschild, A. R. 1983. *The Managed Heart: Commercialization of Human Feeling.* Berkeley: University of California Press.

Lerner, G. 1986. *The Creation of Patriarchy.* New York: Oxford University Press.

Meyrowitz, J. 1985. *No Sense of Place.* New York: Oxford University Press.

Schur, E. M. 1984. *Labeling Women Deviant: Gender, Stigma, and Social Control.* New York: Random House.

Sheffield, C. J. 1987. Sexual Terrorism: The Social Control of Women. In B. B. Hess and M. Marx Ferree (eds.), *Analyzing Gender: A Handbook for Social Science Research* (pp. 171–89). Beverly Hills, Calif.: Sage.

Spitzack, C. 1990. *Confessing Excess: Women and the Politics of Body Reduction.* Albany: State University of New York Press.

Stanko, E. A. 1985. *Intimate Intrusions: Woman's Experience of Male Violence.* London: Routledge & Kegan Paul.

Turner, B. S. 1984. *The Body and Society.* Oxford: Basil Blackwell.

Wolf, C. 1986. Legitimation of Oppression: Response and Reflexivity. *Symbolic Interaction* 9: 215–34.

Wolf, N. 1991. *The Beauty Myth: How Images of Beauty Are Used Against Women.* New York: William Morrow.

9

The Frosting of the American Woman: Self-esteem Construction and Social Control in the Hair Salon

J. Greg Getz and Hanne K. Klein

APPEARANCE AND THE SELF

The psychological significance of beauty or self-adornment (Dion, Berscheid & Walster 1972; Freedman 1986; Cash 1988; Eagly et al. 1991) and the social history of beauty (Banner 1983) increasingly have become issues of concern for behavioral and cultural researchers. In general, this chapter addresses the functions of beauty-related action in contemporary American culture. It explores the connection between beauty production at the interpersonal level of analysis and the domination of women at the cultural level. A person's appearance is an identity claim that contextualizes any subsequent discourse and/or meaning production. Also, persons do not construct their appearential (appearance as self-identity) programs in a social vacuum, but tend to adopt culturally provided programs of appearential self-presentation to encode "beauty." As Stone (1962, 101) notes:

> By appearing, the person announces his identity, shows his values, expresses his mood, or proposes his attitude. If the meaning of appearance is "supplied" by the reviews others make of one's appearance, it is established or consensually validated . . . by the relative coincidence of such reviews with the program of the one who appears. . . . [W]hen one's dress calls out in others the "same" identifications of the wearer as it calls out in the wearer, we may speak of the appearance as meaningful. . . . [I]n fact, . . . this is the self.

While Stone's focus is on that element of cosmetic manipulation called dress, the present study focuses upon the element of hair manipulation and facial makeup application. In either case, the stability of both selves *and* culturally embedded social systems depends greatly upon the stability or clarity of social validation elicited by individuals' presented appearances. The approach taken here exemplifies the increasing interdisciplinary concern with the social significance of the body (Turner 1984; Suleiman 1985; Johnson 1987; Featherstone Hepworth & Turner 1991).

APPROACHING THE WORLD OF BEAUTY THROUGH THE HAIR SALON

The aim of this research was to elicit hairdressers' perceptions of their clients' beauty-related activities and motives. There are several reasons for addressing the social significance of attractiveness from the perspective of the hairdresser. Perhaps the most important is that the interaction between hairdressers and their patrons constitutes one interface between the institutionalized beauty industry and the beauty-specific cognitive maps or schemata of individual women. It is important to discover if or how these cognitive maps are created, reinforced or modified through social interaction within the beauty frame (Goffman 1974) defined by the hair salon. It is this relationship or bridge between the macroscopic beauty industry and the microscopic face-to-face and face-to-mirror activities of individual women that is explored in this chapter. To understand the sociological significance of beauty is to understand the structured process of information transmission across that bridge.

Another advantage in approaching an analysis of beauty from the perspective of hairdressers is that they are in a unique position to systematically observe and interpret the beauty-related habits, aspirations and anxieties of women. Hairdressers are more likely than other beauty-world staff (e.g., health spa employees and cosmetics salespersons) to have a representative and detailed picture of womens' beauty-specific cognitive maps because they get to know their patrons well and because patronage of salons cuts across age, racial, ethnic and socioeconomic lines, even though individual salons often cater to specific types of patrons.

PROCEDURE

First, all the hair salons (885) were enumerated in a large, southwestern metropolitan area, which included a major city and its contiguous suburbs. To eliminate interpretive complications produced by the differential significance of and criteria for beauty across racial/ethnic subcultures, we excluded all shops that served primarily either nonwhite or Mexican-American clients. From the remaining salons, a sample of 6.4 percent was drawn randomly, resulting in a list of fifty. The proprietor or manager of each was contacted via an introductory letter explaining the study in general and requesting an appointment to answer questions and to select at

random one stylist for an interview. Salons were then contacted by telephone to set up appointments. The acceptance rate was 42 percent
(twenty-one salons); to this list were added five additional stylists from
one of the salons within which the interview guide had been pretested.
Thus, the sample consists of twenty-six stylists. This is not a statistically
random sample of the hairdressers in the metropolitan area; but it seems
to be reasonably representative of at least the regional metropolitan statistical area (MSA) because the frequency distributions approached expected statistical normality on several measures: shop's socioeconomic
status, age of stylist, length of time as a stylist and average patron waiting
time. Also, variables with skewed distributions, for example, gender and
education, were skewed in expected directions. The majority of stylists are
female; most have not attended college.

THE INTERVIEW

An interview guide included both fixed-response and open-ended questions, with emphasis placed on the latter. Personal or potentially embar-
rassing questions were asked near the end of the interview, after rapport
had been established, or in the final two pages that were filled out by the
stylist and sealed in an envelope to assure confidentiality. Included were
questions regarding income, self-esteem, self-perceived attractiveness and
sexual preference. Only one stylist refused to fill out portions of these
pages, indicating that some questions were none of our business. All the
rest were very cooperative and candid after having been assured of anonymity and of the noncommercial nature of our study. Most of the stylists were genuinely interested, even enthusiastic, about participating.

Twenty-one of the interviews were conducted by the female author, six
by the male. Differential responses as a function of interviewer gender
were not apparent. The interview guide was designed to be employed
inductively, that is, not to operationalize theoretical constructs or test hypotheses. Spontaneous diversions from a question asked were not discouraged. Probes were made selectively, and responses to them were
recorded as probes. This is important to note because all responses reported here are stylists' initial replies to general questions (e.g., How
would you define a beautiful woman?). These general questions are examples of sensitizing concepts (Blumer 1955).

All interviews were tape-recorded. Content analysis and coding of each
tape were performed by both authors. After a systematic coding scheme
was constructed, all interviews were coded quantitatively, resulting in the
construction of 169 induced variables. Intercoder reliability was achieved
through constant feedback during the coding process on all problematic
responses. Also, each coded interview guide was checked visually a sec-

ond time by one of the authors, and any disagreements were resolved by discussing and re-listening to the appropriate portion of the tape.

The interview guide was organized to elicit beliefs and attitudes of the stylists in several areas. Finally, each stylist was asked to complete Rosenberg's ten-item self-esteem inventory (Robinson & Shaver 1973) and to answer some personal questions, including self-evaluations of face and body, height, weight, age, income and gender preference regarding sexual activity. The last question was important, since stylists not in the sample had indicated that about half of male stylists were gay. Although anticipating the possibility of systematic attitudinal differences, none was observed in the group of four gay and four straight male stylists.

FINDINGS

Demographics of the Sample

Demographically the sample was similar to samples of stylists described in other studies not conducted in the Southwest (Howe 1978; Schroder 1978). The following profile should serve as a background against which the beauty-specific cognitive maps of the stylists should be interpreted. Thirty percent (8) are male, half (4) of whom are either homosexual or bisexual. Fifty-nine percent (16) are thirty to thirty-nine years old, with 19 percent (5) under thirty. Forty-eight percent (13) are married. Forty-eight percent (13) are high school graduates, while 33 percent (9) have less than a high school education. Forty-eight percent (13) grew up in urban or suburban areas, while 52 percent (14) were from a small town or rural environment. Seventy percent (19) expressed a Protestant or fundamental Protestant religious preference, although 70 percent of those (12) also said that they attended church seldom or never. Forty-five percent (12) have a family income over $20,000 per year, with 30 percent below $12,000.

Stylists' Perceptions of Patrons' Motives: Self-esteem and Appearance Anxiety

Why do women go to a hair salon? In answer to this item, 41 percent said only that women wanted to look better. Probing could not elicit a more elaborate response; it was impossible for these stylists to explain what they meant by "look better." It is doubtful that this was due to the lack of experience or inarticulateness of the stylists. The association was low and inverse between elaborateness of response and year of schooling (gamma = −.27). Such answers reflect the extent to which the stylists themselves have been socialized relative to the beauty frame. Ninety-three percent said that their services were very necessary for women to achieve beauty. The necessity of commercial hair care is largely presumed by both male and female stylists.

Even when pressed, they cannot break out of their background assumptions, in spite of the fact that occupational socialization usually fosters the objectification of a clientele. Such objectification often includes generating client types with associated traits and motives. Thus, a we/they distinction is made. On some dimensions, such a distinction is made by hairdressers. The point is that, for most, "why women go to the salon" is not a dimension along which client types are abstracted. This finding extends to cosmetic use as well. All our respondents thought that women should use cosmetics: 63 percent felt cosmetic use should begin before age eighteen; 56 percent could answer only that it made them "more attractive." When asked why or how, 52 percent indicated that "it just does."

However, 59 percent of the stylists gave more elaborate opinions as to why women frequented salons; all of them involve the notion that having her hair done enhances a woman's *self-esteem.* Two important issues emerge. The first involves her self-perceived appearance as a result of the process; the second involves the process itself.

With regard to appearance, the phenomenological significance of hair that has been "done" can best be appreciated by considering the effects of its opposite, that is, hair that is badly done or not done. In discussing the importance of a woman being able to trust in the judgment and skill of her hairdresser, Schroder (1978, 133) quotes a salon patron, an unmarried professional woman: "I don't think a man has any notion of the terror a hairdresser can evoke in a woman's heart. I can well understand how a woman, once she finds someone she is satisfied with, she will stick to him all her life if she can."

This theme of *appearance anxiety,* coupled with a sense of dependence upon the hairdresser, is also reflected in our stylists' perceptions. Eighty-one percent said that their average patron changes salons at greater than three-year intervals or not at all. The explanation given was usually that women are very reticent, if not fearful, of having their hair done by anyone they do not know and trust. When a hairdresser moves to another shop, a large proportion of his or her patrons will follow. Twenty-two percent of the stylists made comments indicating that patrons seem to experience a "magical" transformation of self as a result of the hairdo. For example, one stylist relates:

A plain housewife will usually visit a salon, she needs a change, she's gained weight or she's frustrated in some way . . . she needs a redo.

Another stylist suggests:

> [A hairdo] helps your morale. It makes you feel good. You go out of here
> like I can go out and whip the world now, for a little while.

Clearly, stylists perceive a patron's sense of self-worth to be, at least in part, a function of her hair's appearance.

This inference may be generalized to include the appearance of a patron's face as this relates to cosmetic usage. In answer to the question concerning why women wear makeup, 44 percent of our sample gave an answer more elaborate than "it makes them more attractive." Of those, 83 percent gave explanations relating to appearance anxiety: to mask flaws, to counteract feelings of insecurity, to make them feel good and to fight age. Stylists indicated that virtually all of their patrons wore cosmetics, and 70 percent said that cosmetics were worn always or almost always as opposed to only when in public.

One question asked that stylists estimate the feelings of their average client without makeup in the following situations: at the supermarket, out to dinner, at a party and at church. Answers were coded on a seven-point Likert scale, ranging from very comfortable to very uncomfortable. Eighty-nine percent of the patrons were imagined to be uncomfortable. No patrons were anticipated to be at ease without makeup in any of the specified situations.

How might this attribution of appearance anxiety relate more generally to stylists' perceptions of their patrons' self-images? At the risk of belaboring a play on words already trite in the attractiveness literature, it is nevertheless instructive to invoke the metaphor of the beast in the beauty shop. To be a beast is to be uncivilized, or unpresentable to others in one of two senses. The first is one in which the woman feels her self to be less than whole or to be incomplete without makeup. The second sense is one in which the woman feels herself to be complete, but flawed, ugly and in need of a mask or disguise. Thirty-three percent of the stylists made explicit mention of the incomplete self or the flawed self in trying to assess the feelings of their patrons about cosmetics.

For example, one respondent said that if one were at a party or at church without makeup,

> [she would feel] not fully dressed. If I were going somewhere and couldn't
> find my makeup, I probably just wouldn't go.[1]

Another says:

> They all want to look their best. It makes them feel complete.

And another:

> Women who really have no character in their face should use makeup.

Flaw masking is reflected in the following remark, which equates physical with moral blemishes:

> The old saying that makeup covers a multitude of sins is correct. It covers lot of blemishes.

The beast metaphor lurks also beneath the following stylist's allusion to nakedness:

> [If out to dinner or at a party without makeup, she would] crawl under a table and hide if she sees a friend . . . because . . . she's embarrassed . . . because she feels naked.

And in this one's reference to deformity:

> Ninety percent feel they need to wear some form [of makeup]. Everyone feels deformed. They want to look like something they're not.

Apparently stylists perceive that the self-esteem and self-acceptance of women depend upon how women perceive their hair and face and that an acceptable appearance is impossible to achieve without hair styling and cosmetics. A stylist remarks:

> It's possible for any woman with the proper care, the proper self-concern, [to] put forth an illusion of beauty . . . that's what beauty is, an illusion . . . any woman can be beautiful if she creates the proper illusion of having a total look.

Some stylists attributed the instability of the woman's illusion of beauty to the cultural fetish surrounding youth. Thirty percent of the sample made explicit and unsolicited mention of a youthful appearance as linked to self-esteem. For example:

> [T]hey want you to make them look young. . . . It helps our morale.

> [T]he majority of customers are over thirty because that's when they're going through the period of age knowing they're not young anymore and that they've got to work harder at looking their best. . . . They are more steady and constant customers.

The sociological significance of the observation that beauty is a socially constructed and temporally precarious illusion will be dealt with later. Here the point is merely that appearance anxiety is engendered by the cognitive reification of that illusion.[2]

Regarding the perceived impact of the salon patron's appearance upon her self-esteem, a final inference can be made from our data: Appearance anxiety reflects not only a concern with attractiveness, but also a concern for the avoidance of appearential deviance. The two variables are conceptually orthogonal. When one's hairstyle is not unusual, that is, when it is within normative boundaries, and when cosmetics have been normatively applied, the result is that one's appearance has been standardized independent of her beauty. It may be that conformity to hairstyle and makeup norms is more critical for the self-esteem of "unattractive" women than for that of attractive ones, since counternormative hair and makeup styles, coupled with their unattractiveness, would mark them appearentially as double deviants. The value in American culture connecting beauty with goodness or moral worth (Dion, Bersheid & Walster 1972) was noted previously.

A related element of cultural ideology specifies that greater social approval should accrue to one who achieves a positively valued status than to one to whom such a status is ascribed. "Natural" beauty is a valued, but ascribed, status.[3] Appearential conformity to hairstyle and makeup norms is a valued, but achieved, status. Thus, we might expect considerable social approval to flow to women who are exemplary in their reflection of normative standards (e.g., "she has such good taste in grooming"). Conversely, we might expect stigma to be attached to those who violate normative standards ("she looks like a streetwalker") or for those who wear too little makeup ("she doesn't seem to care how she looks").[4] Here, the implications of ascribed as opposed to achieved appearential status have been separated for heuristic reasons. In the real world, appearential attributions made to women probably result from the interaction of ascribed and achieved looks.

Stylists' perceptions that patrons are concerned with deviance avoidance are reflected in the remarks quoted above in reference to patrons' feelings about makeup. The woman without makeup who feels "not fully dressed," or "naked," or like she "left her face at home" is manifesting a concern not for natural attractiveness per se, but for grooming norms. Apparently the distinction between beauty and conformity to grooming norms is not clearly defined in the beauty-specific cognitive maps of the stylists. Nevertheless, the stylists are keenly aware that manipulation of physical appearance constitutes what Goffman (1959) would designate a crucial impression management technique.

Anonymous Friendship and the Illusion of Loving

Thus far we have considered stylists' estimates of patrons' self-esteem as a function of styled appearance. Next we address stylists' estimates of patrons' feelings about the dynamic process occurring within the salon. Here the patron's self-esteem is related to anonymous friendship and the illusion of loving.

Forty-eight percent of the stylists made comments to the effect that patrons enjoy their experience at the salon because they find it therapeutic, or like to be pampered, or like the luxury, or need the social contact. Stylists believe a patron's tendency to feel good about herself is enhanced when the stylist interacts with her as if she or he cared, even in the midst of knowing that the relationship is relatively impersonal, utilitarian, temporally infrequent and of short duration, all of which are conditions militating against the development of intimate friendship. Consequently, most patrons' sense of intimate caring or loving can be understood as illusory, and, paradoxically, most patrons' experiences of friendship with a stylist are quasi-anonymous.

According to 56 percent of the stylists, either patrons' attitudes or the shampoo process was most important in retaining customers. A pleasant attitude and a willingness to communicate "personableness" were seen as important to patrons. One stylist put it in terms of

> being courteous and letting her know that you appreciated her business and you enjoy visiting with her. I always tell them that, make them feel wanted.

Others addressed the implicit sexuality in the interaction between male stylists and female patrons. One stylist said:

> Women in their 30s and 20s definitely have a sexual aspect, even if subconsciously—get a better input from men. As they get older, it diminishes and doesn't matter anymore.

The above remark was made by a male stylist. One female said:

> [They prefer] a male. . . . A woman feels like he can tell her how pretty she is. Even if I were to tell her that, it still wouldn't be the same thing. And the way they pamper her, even though I could pamper her the same way, it's just different when it's a man.

Perhaps for some women, receiving this kind of attention from a male stylist validates their femininity. Nevertheless, the two previous quotes do not validate implicit sexuality as a major axis of interaction between male stylists and their patrons. The large majority of hairdressers are female, and several stylists stated that women prefer female hairdressers. It can be argued that the sexual aspects of interaction semiotically invoke the sense of caring because of their intimacy. More than sexuality per se, the following comment seems to address some patrons' needs to be reassured that they are worthy of being cared about, that is, loved. This need merely manifests itself along the dimension of sexuality. Perhaps, also, this interpretation is not found explicitly in the comment below because of this male stylist's chauvinistic character.

> I think a man [stylist] has an advantage . . . because of the male/female sexual overtones in our relationships in life . . . it just carries into services . . . a lot of women are insecure . . . and they need to be assured at all times that they are sensuous . . . and sexually desirable . . . they need always assurance whether it's from their dentist, their doctor, their hairdresser, it's part of life. . . . Most women do it subconsciously.

Possibly the most sensual process within the salon is the shampoo. Its association with the perception of caring is expressed by this stylist:

> It is meaningful to them that I be there . . . that is why they stay with me— they will not let anyone else shampoo them.

And again:

> It has to do with the way they feel, too, about themselves. . . . Myself, I love to have someone shampoo my hair. It feels so good, it's just not the same to do it yourself. . . . It's the feeling, the attention that they get and that type of thing, to feel good, to feel important.

Explicit mention of the therapeutic function of the sensual experience is found here:

> A weekly shampoo and set is a psychological boost. . . . What keeps them going is not the looks that they're getting . . . it's a security feeling.

The "security feeling" is fostered by the shampoo not just because the shampoo feels good, not just because the shampoo giver's posture over the woman on her back and the enveloping warmth and wetness can signify sexual interaction, but also because the degree of physical intimacy necessary to give a shampoo is an encoding of positive affect, or a "loving" attitude—at least in American middle-class culture.

The significance of touching is not lost on the stylists, even though when probed on the issue of sensuality, they tend to evade elaboration. Stylists' sensitivity to the touch manifests itself in the analogy made between their occupation and the medical profession by 44 percent. For many stylists, the analogy rests on the recognition that both physicians and hairdressers experience a degree of physical and communicative intimacy that, in our culture, is rare in a professional relationship. Such intimacy is usually found only in primary relationships, that is, those marked by expressiveness and affectivity. Apparently patrons who are solicitous of this form of intimacy are not deterred by the fact that the revealing of self that is involved is not reciprocal; in fact, they do not want it to be. It is the lack of reciprocity that makes the loving an illusion and the friendship anonymous. As a matter of principle, the stylists (and physicians) tend not to share their whole selves with clients.

The stylist commenting below recognizes the importance of the illusion of loving in retaining customers.

> I've found that in a lot of cases you are very similar to a doctor and you get a lot of their personal problems. And they come to you because they want advice or they want to talk something out. So you may not be the best hairdresser in the world, but if you can talk to 'um and understand 'um on their level then . . . that's why they stay with you.

And from another stylist:

> I think they probably go [to the salon] for psychological reasons, and then, too, if they have any problems, we have become, we have to major in psychology, be psychiatrists because you do women so long and then they start confiding in you. I know all of the gyn-obs in town [laugh]. Women . . . trust what you tell them.

And another stylist remarks:

> [For patrons, the salon is a] home away from home. That's what you want them to feel like. . . . They are worked on personally. It's almost like a doctor's type of base you want to build.

The stylist quoted above observes that both doctors and hairdressers are engaged in doing body work on their clients. While the physician is repairing the physical body, the stylist is repairing the perpetually unstable capacity of the patron to create a coherent presentation of self (Goffman 1974). From the dramaturgical as well as Stone's (1962) perspective introduced earlier, it can be argued that the head and the body are the primary vehicles at one's disposal for engaging the social world. Thus, it is no surprise that the backstage repair of these empirically observable manifestations of self evokes affect toward those doing the repair. Twenty-six percent of the stylists made specific use of the repair-shop metaphor.

Getting one's hair "done" or one's face "fixed" means getting one's self "done." The patron places herself in a position in which she negotiates with a stylist as to what her presented self will be. She gives the stylist a tremendous amount of interpersonal power to construct an essential feature of her identity. The physical touch involved in the patron/stylist relationship is both an outcome of the negotiation for interpersonal control and a facilitator of the stylist achieving that control. As one stylist put it, "[A]fter you get them down in the shampoo bowl, they don't care what happens."

At this juncture, stylists objectify their patrons and make a we/they distinction, invoking professionalism to rationalize remaining aloof from their patrons, while giving an impression that they "care." Seventy-eight percent of the stylists said that they feel good about their patrons; 37 percent said that they encouraged friendship with their patrons. Fifty-two percent said that they felt good about patrons discussing their personal problems; only 7 percent said that they would discuss one of their own personal problems with a patron.

Thus, the intimacy of the touch is commonplace, tending to encourage social intimacy that is, in fact, pursued by many patrons—but only within the frame of the hair salon; the stylist rarely, if ever, socializes with patrons outside the salon. This social intimacy is not discouraged by most stylists as long as the patron does not expect the self-revelation to be reciprocated. Stylists strongly suggest that it is unwise to become close with a patron, but they do not object to allowing the patron to perceive a degree of closeness that the stylist does not feel. It is for this reason that the term *anonymous friendship* is appropriate.[5]

Dynamics of Social Control

Obviously, for the stylists, the beauty process is their business—the source of their income. Stylists are confronted then with several problems that they must recognize and handle pragmatically if they are to be successful. The first problem is drawing patrons; the second is retaining them; a third is creating a social environment within the salon that keeps the business running smoothly, that is, that allows stylists to process patrons with minimal negotiation, and keeps the rate of patron turnover profitable. Social rewards aside, stylists are there to make money.

As indicated above, the first problem is solved, in part, by the patrons themselves. They are presocialized to the necessity of coming to the salon. Elaborate advertising campaigns are not necessary to draw customers. Patrons under thirty may come less frequently and/or avail themselves of fewer services (e.g., they may exclude hair color or permanents), but this is because they perceive themselves as not yet needing to come as frequently, not because they are ideologically opposed to the values embodied by the salon.

According to 56 percent of the hairdressers, the second problem of retaining patrons is most effectively addressed via affective strategies and not necessarily skill as a stylist. As indicated earlier, most stylists liked their patrons; 37 percent encouraged friendship, and 56 percent indicated that they had close conversation with patrons. This "closeness," however, is quite one-sided because only 7 percent said that they often discussed their own personal problems with patrons; 67 percent never discussed their personal problems.

The third problem, efficient, profitable salon operation, also is addressed mainly within the expressive arena via techniques of impression management. Forty-one percent of the stylists made explicit mention of such techniques, many of which involved the manipulation or patronization of the customer's affect. Forty-one percent also made statements that indicated so conscious an objectification of the patron that they were coded "utilitarian manipulation." Recall that the phrasing of such remarks was not suggested directly via probes. Thus, the percentages reported here are probably conservative estimates of the extent to which stylists are conscious of the impression management techniques they employ.

All these references to patron manipulation suggest that the patron rarely controls the negotiation of the stylist/patron relationship, in spite of factors suggesting that she would.[6] One stylist related such manipulation in a medical analogy:

> If she's down . . . the hairstylist has to . . . bring her emotions up. If they're not up, you're not going to please her. You have to let her know that she's O.K. regardless of what you have to work with. . . . It's almost like being a psychiatrist without a license.

In response to the question "Do you try to create a particular emotional attitude in your customer?" 85 percent indicated that a moderately strong or very strong effort was made. Such efforts reflect social control of the patron, regardless of the benevolence of the stylist's motives.

With regard to the stylist's presentation of self, one remarks:

> You have to have a personality to suit all customers. . . . Some . . . want you to get them out with very little talk or they want you to listen a lot or they talk, you know, you have to be careful.

When asked if patrons should do more hair-care procedures by themselves, 63 percent answered with a "no" or "qualified no." One said: "No, because we'd be out of business." Another elaborated:

> [Customers should not do more procedures by themselves because] you want them to always be dependent upon you. . . . In fact, you often design something . . . you see a customer who's done a frosting a little by herself . . . you compliment her on that frosting, don't knock it . . . but . . . the next visit you say, "You know what would look good on you?" And you suggest something else. You get her off that frosting she can do herself.

Though 56 percent of the stylists felt that patrons should not have to wait more than fifteen minutes for their appointment to begin, some recognized the utilitarian advantage of the waiting period. For example:

> If it's their first visit, I do think they should spend time waiting.... Sometimes I make them, I find excuses to make them wait and say, "There are some magazines over there; there are some pictures over there. Go through it."... The majority, the first time, [are undecided about what they want]. ... [It has to do with], well, making money. Why waste time with something when you see a person and she's undecided, you know, while you could do someone else's hair.

When asked if she suggested styles to patrons, one responded:

> That's part of my selling technique. It's part of sales. I can convince her she looks better. I'd probably convince them that if they had their hair cut, how much younger they would look, how much their husband would like it on them.

The theme of patron manipulation was summarized quintessentially by one stylist who remarked:

> A good hairstylist can talk his or her customer into wearing a cow patty on the middle of her head. You need that kind of control.

The foregoing remarks have portrayed the stylists as skilled in the use of manipulative techniques that foster achievement of their consciously recognized economic interests. However, the stylist's attitudes and actions toward patrons are not exclusively a function of perceived economic interest. Quite the contrary; as a group, they believe sincerely that they are providing a necessary service to patrons. Ninety-three percent said that their services were "very necessary" in order for women to achieve beauty. Sixty-three percent said that they suggested specific hair and cosmetic products to patrons; 70 percent said that some or all of those products were sold in the salon. But only one stylist expressed a motive for selling such products that was exclusively self-interested; 74 percent expressed altruistic motives in that benefit to the patron was exclusively emphasized. The same percentage of stylists believed that patrons should have an appointment at least once per week, but again appearance of the patron was the rationale stated. The good rapport established with the stylists in the interview context minimized the tendency for such expressed altruism to be merely a reflection of social desirability.

Thus, typical of service sellers in an industrial capitalist society, stylists simultaneously exhibit altruistic and utilitarian attitudes toward their patrons. However, this is not perceived by them as a contradiction. They believe that the service they provide for profit contributes to their patrons' welfare. The prevalence of their use of the medical metaphor is instructive here. The stylists believe they are "doing well by doing good." They are not cynical, as a group, about their role in the production of beauty.

This lack of cynicism extends to their personal attitudes about beauty. Seventy percent felt their training as hairdressers had little or nothing to do with their attitudes toward beauty. Thus, the stylists seem to be as well socialized as the patrons; neither questions the legitimacy of beauty production as a necessity for women.

Social Psychological Consequences for Patrons: Child Role and Abdicated Control

There are several important social psychological consequences of beauty production for the patrons. First, the trip to the hair salon constitutes an institutionalized, legitimized break in the daily routine of the patrons. It is a temporary escape from the responsibilities of their everyday lives, roughly analogous to being sick in that it is a legitimate timeout for the essential repair of appearance. Proper appearance, like physical health, is a normative prerequisite for the performance of most social roles.

From the stylist's perspective, this escape may be a manifest function for some patrons. One said:

> I don't think beauty is just the number one reason. It's an escape.... I really think a lot of the reason they come up here is just to get away from their humdrum life and the routine of what they're doing.

And, similarly, another related:

> They enjoy being worked on ... it's their thing.... They enjoy someone else taking care of them instead of them having to do it.... They enjoy getting away from the house. They enjoy someone fussing over them.

Twenty-two percent of the stylists made explicit mention of this escape-from-responsibility function of the salon visit. It could be seen as merely a form of rest and recuperation. However, the quote above infers a less benign function in its emphasis upon the patron being taken care of and enjoying "someone fussing over them" because these possibilities interact with other aspects of the salon setting.

As indicated above, the social dynamics of the salon result in the stylist winning the negotiation for control of the patron/stylist relationship. An unanticipated consequence of the patron acquiescing in this negotiation is that she assumes within the beauty shop, as elsewhere in American society, the role of the child. This is the second social psychological result of beauty production. Escape from responsibility is, in fact, a central characteristic of childhood; the symbolic return to that state, even if temporary, involves placing one's self under the social control of a surrogate parent—in this case, the stylist.

The shampoo, for example, sets the stage for the abdication of self-control on at least two levels. On the physical level, it simply feels good; it is relaxing. On the social psychological level, it facilitates the production of the illusion of loving. And also it invokes the parent/child relationship. First, one is usually bathed in infancy by a nurturing mother. Second, the person administering the shampoo is standing above the patron, who is on her back, a signification of vulnerability or surrender. Third, dripping wet hair, in most contexts, is regarded as a private, backstage condition, the initial observers of which are one's parents.

Many techniques of impression management mentioned by stylists implicitly involve placing the patron in the role of the child in order to make her more malleable. For example, one female stylist says:

> If you get a new customer, they all have to be trained . . . they're a little disagreeable sometimes . . . "you're getting water in my ear, don't rub so hard, rub here," and that can be very irritating, and so after about the third time when they do that I put them down in the chair. I put my hands under their head and I hold them and I'm standing over them and I'm looking at them. I'll say, "Now you relax and you be quiet and enjoy this shampoo . . . when you want to holler and act like a child then holler . . . I'm not gonna hurt you. . . . " And after that, I don't have any more trouble with them.

The beauty salon is one context involved in the social construction of gender display. Goffman (1976, 5) links the structure of such ritualized gender displays in our society to the typical American parent/child relationship.

> Given this parent/child complex as a common fund of experience, it seems we draw on it in a fundamental way in adult social gatherings . . . in our society whenever a male has dealings with a female or a subordinate male (especially a younger one), some mitigation of the potential distance, coercion, and hostility is quite likely to be induced by application of the parent/child complex . . . which implies that ritually speaking, females are equivalent to subordinate males and both are equivalent to children.

In the beauty salon, the parent/child complex functions both to facilitate the stylist's dominance and to "cool out" the patron, that is, to ease control from her before she can define the situation as a confrontation over control.

Escaping from responsibility, as rejuvenating as this may be in some respects, carries with it a price, that is, the divestiture of control over self. This is the third social psychological consequence of beauty production in the salon. Earlier it was suggested that idealized physical beauty, at least for most women, is a socially constructed illusion. The achievement of this illusion is, at best, temporary. This temporariness of the illusion, coupled with its perceived necessity for patrons, keeps many women in a perpetual state of appearance anxiety. They are dependent upon their hairdressers for the bolstering of appearential self-esteem, but this self-esteem is achieved at the expense of not having equal partnership (i.e., power) in the social process through which selves are defined. Thus, for many, an unanticipated consequence of letting someone else "do" them is that someone else has control over a significant element of their identity and, hence, of their self-definition.

As symbolic interactionism asserts, *no one* can have complete control over the production of his or her self, and even as adults conscious of social influence processes, persons are often not the most powerful negotiators for control of their own self-conceptions. Here the attempt is to highlight one of the subtle ways in which women are *systematically* placed at a power disadvantage interpersonally *and* collectively.

Thus, a fourth social psychological consequence of the nature of beauty construction for patrons is that in subjecting themselves to grooming norms, they subordinate themselves to the social order in general. Women become objects of social control. Earlier it was argued that patrons have their hair and faces done not only to achieve beauty, but also to avoid being appearentially deviant, independent of the extent to which they become relatively more "beautiful." Avoidance of deviance achieved through putting one's hair or face under the control of others amounts to a public display of conformity that transcends the social psychological level of analysis. Such conformity functions to facilitate social integration and pattern maintenance at the societal level. The grooming ritual, whatever its unconscious psychodynamic significance (Leach 1958), is a social "structuring device through which other meanings can be expressed" (Herschman 1974, 296). One such meaning is that hair and facial grooming symbolizes the entering of society or "living under a particular disciplinary regime within society" (Hallpike 1969, 257). In American society, insofar as beauty production through hair grooming and cosmetic use is linked to femininity, it becomes a gender display symbolic of the subordination and domination of women within the patriarchy.

Sociological Consequences for the Beauty Industry: Co-optation of Self-esteem and Cash Flow

The main sociological significance of the dynamics of beauty production in the context of the hair salon is that achievement of self-esteem and avoidance of appearential deviance are accomplished through the expenditure of money. Patrons buy services from the salon operators, who in turn buy materials from corporate producers of grooming and cosmetic products. The beauty salon is but an intermediate institution that constitutes one of the links between individual women and the corporate structure. The beauty industry through sophisticated marketing adroitly creates and manipulates the appearance anxiety of women, transforming anxiety into a form of commodity fetishism necessary for corporate profit making.

The practice of self-adornment, of course, did not originate in corporate board rooms. However, in the context of an industrial capitalist environment, the practice of self-adornment has been transformed into a market-based activity. Landy and Sigall (1974, 2) speak of "the structure and consequences of late capitalist domination as it is internalized through the manipulation of human terror and desire, reproducing the system through its shaping of individual character." The empirical findings noted above demonstrate how the internalization of domination is achieved within one social-cognitive arena—that of beauty production. Landy and Sigall (1974, 10) refer to this internalized domination in terms of "1) the . . . manufacture of needs that find partial 'gratification' in capitalist production and consumption; 2) authority relationships which regulate interpersonal conduct; and 3) ideologies that disguise and mystify the capitalist system." Salon-based production of beauty is infused with each of these elements of domination.

First, patrons and stylists are socialized to the desirability and the necessity of hair styling and cosmetic use. The need for self-esteem is transformed into the manufactured desire for commodities, the consumption of which is believed to produce beauty, and hence lovability. But because physical beauty as articulated in American culture is an illusion only temporarily achievable, the perpetual repurchase of beauty-related commodities is necessary in order to reduce appearance anxiety. Through advertising, the beauty industry co-opts the sexuality of women (and men) into commodity consumption. Linking self-esteem first to industry-created fears and then to commodities ensures that gratification through product consumption will always be partial. Exploited by the industry is the fact that self-concept and self-esteem are dynamically connected. Unclarity of self-esteem (appearential anxiety in the context of this chapter) induces low self-esteem (Campbell 1990). Thus, the market for beauty-related commodities is reproduced internally as long as the appearential self-concepts of women can be kept unclear.

Second, the negotiation for control of the patron/stylist relationship results in the reinforcement of the traditional partriarchical authority structure in which females are the objects of physical and psychological domination. The fact that most hairdressers are female does not alter this dynamic. An authority relationship is established, which places the salon patron in the role of the child. This relationship further is reinforced when the patron's fears of appearential deviance are mitigated temporarily by the "expertise" of the stylist.

Finally, several ideological elements that perpetuate the mystification of patrons *and* stylists regarding their own domination have been discussed. One is the background assumption that the commodities in question do, in fact, make one physically attractive. Another is the notion that "experts"—in this case, stylists—are almost exclusively competent to construct that attractiveness. A third is the assumption that appearance anxiety, precarious beauty-specific self-esteem and precarious lovability are personal problems of individual women and not public issues linked to the structure of the economy. Marcuse (1964) designated such a constellation of cognitive patterns "one-dimensional thinking" because such patterns exist within a single ideological frame that precludes conscious consideration of alternative ideological frames. The advertising agents of the beauty economy play a large part in the construction of women's beauty-specific cognitive maps. The unfortunate result (for women in the beauty arena as for men in other arenas) is that many women are bound to beauty-commodity fetishism and to participation in their own exploitation.

SUMMARY AND CONCLUSION

Through the eyes of hairdressers, the meaning of attractiveness has been explicated for a sample of beauty salon patrons, both as individuals and as collectivity. The central phenomenological reality surrounding the appearance of individual patrons seems to be one of anxiety. The fear of being perceived as unattractive or as appearentially deviant is held at bay only through the frequent reconstruction of the mask produced through hairstyling and the application of makeup.

For the production of hairstyle, salon patrons rely heavily upon the hairdressers. Once in the salon, the interaction between patron and stylist is largely controlled by the stylist through various impression management techniques. The outcome of the process is a temporary bolstering of the patron's self-esteem at the expense of her control over self.

The goal of the stylist is to make a living by providing a service that they believe to be necessary and beneficial to the patrons—both appearentially and psychologically; many perceive themselves as lay therapists. They are not motivated by a desire to generate profit for the beauty industry beyond the boundaries of their salons. However, the social psychological dynamics of patron/stylist interaction tend to reinforce the dependency of the patron's self-esteem upon the purchase of a service or product. Thus, the interests of the larger beauty industry are served as a latent function of face-to-face interaction between stylists and their patrons.

Institutions are persistent patterns of social control. But too often in the macrosociological literature, we find the reification of institutions; the relationship between society and the individual is not merely one of interdependence, but also one of interpenetration. Thus, neither an understanding of the person nor an understanding of society is possible without addressing the conceptual overlap between the two. This overlap has most recently been conceived as the "micro/macro issue" (Alexander et al. 1987; Collins 1988; Wiley 1988; Huber 1991) and is an area of central concern in Giddens' "structuration theory" (Cohen 1987). The present research has addressed such overlap within one sociocultural arena—that of beauty production—which is an institution. The data have been interpreted with a sensitivity to how beauty-specific cognitive maps of hairdressers and salon patrons interpenetrate the beauty economy.

NOTES

1. Note that the respondent is expressing her personal feelings, rather than commenting as a stylist assessing the reactions of her patrons. This occurred frequently among female stylists, even though the questions were worded to refer to the respondent's occupational position and role. This can be regarded as further evidence for the pervasiveness of gender role identity, which assures that, for many women, femininity constitutes a self-attributed, master status, as well as one imposed on them by a sexist social structure.

2. Extreme appearance anxiety has been discussed as a psychiatric syndrome and labeled "dysmorphophobia" (Andreasen & Bardach 1977).

3. Exceptions to this generalization would occur for women who undergo cosmetic surgery and therefore acquire achieved statuses. However, the intent with these alterations is to disguise the achieved nature of the result. This is generally not true for makeup application.

4. The social psychological literature cited earlier, dealing with the effects of beauty, glosses the distinction made here between natural beauty and conformity to hair and makeup norms. For example, some studies operationalize beauty with stimulus persons whose faces are judged to vary along a continuum of attractiveness. Others measure beauty by varying the grooming of a single-stimulus person.

5. The phrase *anonymous friendship* was suggested as an interpretation of this situation by a hairdresser who was not part of our formal sample.

6. Hypothetically, the patron would assume control of the relationship for at least two reasons. First, she is a paying customer who is free to patronize another salon; second, she is frequently of higher socioeconomic status than the hairdresser.

WORKS CITED

Alexander, J. C., B. Giesen, R. Bunch and N. J. Smelser (eds.). 1987. *The Micro-macro Link.* Berkeley: University of California Press.

Andreasen, N. C., and J. Bardach. 1977. Dysmorphophobia: Symptom or Disease. *American Journal of Psychiatry* 134: 673–75.

Banner, L. W. 1983. *American Beauty.* New York: Alfred A. Knopf.

Blumer, H. 1955. What Is Wrong with Social Theory? *American Sociological Review* 19: 3–10.

Campbell, J. D. 1990. Self-esteem and Clarity of the Self-concept. *Journal of Personality and Social Psychology* 59: 538–49.

Cash, T. F. 1988. The Psychology of Cosmetics: A Research Bibliography. *Perceptual and Motor Skills* 66: 455–60.

Cohen, I. J. 1987. Structuration Theory and Social Praxis. In A. Giddens and J. Turner (eds.), *Social Theory Today* (pp. 273–308). Stanford, Calif.: Stanford University Press.

Collins, R. 1988. The Micro Contribution to Macro Sociology. *Sociological Theory '88* 6: 242–53.

Dion K., E. Bersheid and E. Walster. 1972. What Is Beautiful Is Good. *Journal of Personality and Social Psychology* 24: 285–90.

Eagly, A. H., R. D. Ashmore, M. G. Makhijani and L. C. Longo. 1991. What Is Beautiful Is Good but...: A Meta-analytic Review of Research on the Physical Attractiveness Stereotype. *Psychological Bulletin* 110: 109–28.

Featherstone, M., M. Hepworth and B. S. Turner. 1991. *The Body.* Newbury Park, Calif.: Sage.

Freedman, R. 1986. *Beauty Bound.* Lexington, Mass.: Lexington Books.

Goffman, E. 1959. *The Presentation of Self in Everyday Life.* New York: Doubleday Anchor.

———. 1974. *Frame Analysis.* New York: Harper & Row.

———. 1976. *Gender Advertisements.* New York: Harper Colophon.

Hallpike, C. R. 1969. Social Hair. *Man* 4: 256–64.

Herschman, P. 1974. Hair, Sex, and Dirt. *Man* 9: 274–98.

Howe, L. K. 1978. *Pink Collar Workers.* New York: Avon Books.

Huber, J. (ed.). 1991. *Macro-micro Linkages in Sociology.* Newbury Park, Calif.: Sage.

Johnson, M. 1987. *The Body in the Mind.* Chicago: University of Chicago Press.

Landy, D., and H. Sigall. 1974. Terror and Desire: The Social Psychology of Late Capitalism. Paper presented at the Annual Meeting of the American Sociological Association, Montreal, Canada, August 25–29.

Leach, E. R. 1958. Magical Hair. *J. R. Anthropological Institute* 77: 147–64.

Marcuse, H. 1964. *One Dimensional Man.* Boston: Beacon Press.

Robinson, J. P., and P. R. Shaver. 1973. *Measures of Social Psychological Attitudes.* Ann Arbor: Institute for Research, University of Michigan.

Schroder, D. 1978. *Engagement in the Mirror: Hairdressers and Their Work.* San Francisco: R&E Research Associates.

Stone, G. P. 1962. Appearance and the Self. In Arnold M. Rose (ed.), *Human Behavior and Social Processes: An Interactionist Approach* (pp. 86–118). Boston: Houghton Mifflin.

Suleiman, S. R. (ed.). 1985. *The Female Body in Western Culture.* Cambridge: Harvard University Press.

Turner, B. S. 1984. *The Body and Society.* Oxford: Basil Blackwell.

Wiley, N. 1988. The Micro-macro Problem in Social Theory. *Sociological Theory '88* 6: 254–64.

10

Young African-American Women and the Language of Beauty

Maxine Leeds

Black is beautiful. Those words were shouted in marches in the late sixties, along with "freedom now," "black power," and "off the pigs." "Freedom now" and "black power" were demands and "off the pigs" a threat. "Black is beautiful" was neither demand nor threat, but a redefinition of truth. Since this truth about beauty was contested, "black is beautiful" was a demand for respect and a threat to the racial order.

"Black is beautiful" called for pride in many facets of African-American culture. This chapter investigates one aspect of that call, the attempt to redefine physical beauty. The establishment of an Afrocentric beauty standard was a limited and problematic goal. It was limited because changing the definition of beauty would do little to restructure institutional racism. It was problematic because even a redefinition of beauty reinforced the exaggerated importance of beauty for women, upsetting the racial order, while validating gender hierarchies. Finally, even a new, black-centered beauty standard would define some African-American women as ugly. Just as the older standard placed women in what has been called a "pigmentocracy," extreme forms of the new standard defined some women's physical features as politically suspect.

Despite these inherent problems, the move to redefine beauty was important. Given the great value placed on female attractiveness, widespread acceptance of the words "black is beautiful" would have allowed African-American women to experience the advantages that come with beauty. Studies have shown that attractive people receive benefits ranging from sympathetic jury responses to a greater number of marriage proposals (Udry 1977; Webster and Driskell 1983). Men also had a stake in the words "black is beautiful." Lauding the black woman was imperative for a movement concerned with manhood (Fanon 1967; Grier and Cobbs 1968).

The "Afro" or "natural" became the definitive mark of a woman who embraced black identity. The first women who wore Afros risked ridicule, loss of employment and hostile reactions from family members, strangers and co-workers. At the same time, women wearing Afros were rewarded with praise and recognition by peers who understood that the hairstyle represented racial pride. In time, the natural hairstyle gained widespread acceptance (Goering 1971). The style continued to signify black pride, but no longer evoked strong reactions of support or hostility.

Did the acceptance of unstraightened hair in the 1970s represent a lasting change in beauty standards? Were activists successful in redefining the meaning of black? In this study, I looked for evidence of an enduring change in beauty standards by interviewing African-American girls aged twelve to fifteen.[1] I investigated both sides of the "black is beautiful" equation and will present findings on how these young women define (1) physical attractiveness and (2) black identity.

STUDYING BEAUTY

African-American women are absent from the majority of general studies of beauty (Banner 1983; Webster and Driskell 1983; Wolf 1991). The works of Lakoff and Scherr (1984) and Chapkis (1986) are notable exceptions. African-American and white women have intimately related, but distinct, historical experiences with respect to beauty standards. These different positions in relation to beauty standards parallel the relationships of white and black women to home life. Black feminist theorists hooks (1990) and Collins (1990) argue that for black women the home may be a site of gender oppression, but may also serve as a refuge from racism. Rituals of beauty are a part of this haven.

The concept that cultural practices can be acts of resistance has been applied to English working-class youth subcultures (Hall and Jefferson 1976; Hebdige 1979). The attempt to redefine beauty used the idea of beauty to consolidate black identity and to overturn a formerly Eurocentric set of standards.

Writing specifically on beauty standards and African Americans has two traditions. One form is the essay or novel (hooks 1988; Morrison 1970; Rushing 1988). The second builds upon Clark and Clark's (1947) classic study, which documented black children's preferences for white dolls. Replications conducted after the sixties, using the same or modified versions of the doll technique, found that African-American children prefer black dolls (Hraba and Grant 1970; Jones and Smith 1980). Fine and Bowers (1984) and Greene (1980) found no significant preference for black or white dolls among African-American subjects. The authors of these four studies attributed their results to the greater contemporary availability of black dolls and the gains won by the civil rights and black power movements.

The intricacy of the construction of beauty among African-American women cannot be seen in the limited information available in a child's choice of a doll. Studies that show that African-American children find black dolls attractive are indications that children are being exposed to positive images of African Americans. Keith and Herring (1991) documented the persistence of stratification on the basis of skin tone. Children's exposure to positive images of African Americans occurs in the context of a society that continues to reward lighter skin. I interviewed young women in order to reveal the complexity of their experiences with respect to beauty standards.

"KEEPING MY HEAD STRAIGHT"

> Yeah. I wanted to straighten my hair, but my mom, she says I should keep it natural for a while. . . . guess it's because she wants me to keep my head straight about it. . . . Everybody in my school who has hair like mine, black hair, is straightening it, and, I mean, I want to keep my hair natural, but it's not really sort of working out.

The majority of the young women I interviewed had straightened hair. Yet their ideals of beauty were often independent of and in contradiction to their personal beauty practices. The descriptions of beauty that they presented were an amalgam, drawing from personal memories, the appearance of favorite video stars, what they had heard their older brothers say, the opinions of peers and lectures from their mothers. My questions ranged from specific questions about hairstyles to broad queries about the meaning of beauty. Depending on the question, the respondents answered with different beauty ideals. These beliefs were often quite inconsistent. When I asked about the meaning of beauty in general, I usually received answers that reflected an ideology of beauty.

> I'm [cough] more into, um, my background and my natural looks. . . . Like I don't wear makeup any more, and, I mean, I'm really not into fashions and fads. Really as far as I'm concerned, beauty is in the eye of the beholder, and I think naturalness is the best beauty.

When a specific taste was referred to, it was almost always expressed as a description of what they considered to be the prejudiced standards of others.

> You know, girls these days, you know, they want to have long hair because, like boys only like long hair or something, and if you have short hair, people talk about you. They call you bald headed. It seems like a lot of black girls think that really light girls are pretty and stuff, but I really think that the darker girls sometimes, I sort of envy them. Because I like the chocolate color. It's so pretty and stuff.

Later in the interview, when I asked the last speaker if there was one thing she would change about her appearance, she said she would like her hair to grow in long ringlets and her eyes to be lighter.

Rarely did anyone express a preference for traits associated with white women. Yet these preferences arose repeatedly in claims about the standards of their peers. This tension was apparent when we spoke of skin color.

> You see, at like, at this school they be talking about dark people and stuff. Like talking about you look like charcoal and stuff.

The belief that dark complexions are beautiful is ardently held, but it uneasily wars with another standard expressed in taunts about dark skin. Skin-color prejudice among African Americans continues, and this engenders divisions and resentment. In every group I interviewed, someone told a story of a conceited light-skinned girl who was not especially pretty.

BEAUTY AS MORAL OBLIGATION

> You know I can't just let myself go. It's pressure.

> Let me tell you something, Diana Ross is butt ugly to me. I really think she is so fake. I said Diana Ross is butt ugly.

Just as these young women hold contradictory sentiments about the content of the beauty standard, their beliefs about what one must do to achieve beauty are inconsistent. Side by side with descriptions of beauty as natural, these young women expressed the idea that unattractiveness is evidence of a woman's failure to work hard enough. Such statements reflect the belief that anyone can attain beauty and the implication that all women should try to be beautiful.[2]

Hair is the feature most easily altered. It can be straightened, lengthened with artificial extensions, curled and cut. Its malleability makes it the focus of creativity, anxiety and display. These young women saw hairstyles that failed to meet the criteria for beauty as evidence of a woman's personal neglect. One young woman admitted feeling hopelessly unattractive.

The sympathy she received from one of her classmates took the form of encouragement and reproach.

> Well, can I give you like a little bit of advice and a little bit of a statement put together? . . . It hurts to be beautiful, you can't just ex [word not completed] . . . you know. So . . . I don't know. Just like, look in magazines and stuff. Maybe try to present yourself a little bit better, you know . . . I don't know. Just you know . . . 'cause if you try then I'm pretty sure you'll succeed.

These students called Diana Ross ugly because they thought her appearance was artificial. The same young women submitted to and considered reasonable hair-care procedures that required hours of preparation or the risk of scalp burns. Paradoxically, they considered hard work and suffering admirable and mandatory paths to attractiveness, while spurning artificiality. This moral code of beauty was applied when we discussed people who wore their hair short and unstraightened. This sort of hairstyle, which twenty years ago was esteemed as a symbol of racial pride, was generally rejected. Their rejections took the form of exaggerated accounts of the neglect such a hairstyle represents.

The coupling of nature and neglect could have been a strategy for overcoming the pain of rejecting styles that have been associated with black pride. This dilemma arose when one young woman, whose hair was straightened, discussed hair in the context of racial identity.

> But see, we all act white though, in a way because if we were going to be straight, just straight sisters we would straight have Afros because we wouldn't get our hair pressed or permed.

Later, she resolved her problem by redefining natural to mean dressing to please herself.

> You know it's not my natural hair. It's not my natural hair, but still, you know, I mean, you know, we, we, then again, it depends on, look at it, look at it in another perspective. If it makes you look good, you know, if you feel good about it, then it's not really trying to be like anyone else.

Her halting speech testifies to her uneasiness about defending her decision to straighten her hair. At another point in my interviews, the problem of desiring styles that can only be achieved artificially arose. This conversation was about Diana Ross.

> She has fake hair. It's stupid. If you ain't got no hair, just stay bald headed. If I didn't have no hair, I'd probably get a weave. I mean if it was that bad. She just wears too . . . she has too much.
>
> Yeah, it's too much!

It's just too much and she . . . does . . . the way she [imitates Diana Ross flinging her hair around].
Janet Jackson has real hair.
Don't Tina Turner?
She has a lot of hair though, but that's real.
She got human hair.
But it's cute though.

For readers who are not cosmetologically sophisticated, the distinction is being made between augmenting one's hair by weaving in artificial hair and, as these students claim Tina Turner does, lengthening hair by weaving in human hair bought from women poor enough to sell theirs. The latter is considered less artificial. This is one of the many ways to soften the dishonor of artificiality.

Weaves are both popular and the subject of ridicule. Their status is peculiar, in part, because the fashion is to incorporate them into cornrow braids, a traditional African hairstyle. In most of the group discussions, there was at least one young woman whose braids included artificial extensions. Weaves were criticized by students who ended with the chiding comment, "just stay bald headed." That comment crystallizes the dilemma of a young woman with short hair. She has the choice of being teased for having short hair or criticized for being artificial.

Most of these students felt that they should value their natural appearance, a lesson they had been taught by their mothers. Over and over again, when a young woman wanted to defend the beauty of dark skin or natural hair, she would quote her mother. Mothers provide the link with a beauty standard that appreciates black beauty.

Yesterday, when my mother was doing my hair, she was saying something that, um, a long time ago, white people made black people feel like they were ugly. Their face be dark and their nose being wide. Their hair not being combed and their lips wide. They probably did make them feel like that because they had them. They beat them and stuff. And they made them work for them, feed their babies and stuff.
Maxine: Do you think black people feel that way now?
Several voices: No!
Black is beautiful.
Amen.

"BEAUTIFUL"

In the course of my interviews, attractiveness was defined in varied and contradictory ways. These students frequently stated that there was a beauty standard that valued lighter skin and longer and straighter hair. They distanced themselves from that standard and articulated a more inclusive idea of beauty. Yet their own taunts about skin color and hair length indicate that they, to some degree, accept a Eurocentric ideal. These young women were aware that they ought to value darker skin and naturally curly or short hair, but they also accepted contradictory standards, which they helped to reproduce through their jokes and their everyday practices.

A moral language is used to discuss beauty. Hard work is aligned with beauty, while both carelessness and artificiality create ugliness. In the next section, I will discuss the first term in the "black is beautiful" equation and explore where black and white fit into the discourse of nature, authenticity, artifice and beauty.

"BLACK"

The black power movement did not create an identity. It embraced and redefined a preexisting identity. Black is an identity that people experience as both ascribed and natural. Being black appears as a self-evident fact, arising from the body. Yet, at the same time, the identity and its meaning are experienced as contingent and reinforced or lessened by behavior. The students I interviewed described both experiences of black: black as a fact of being and black as a way of being. The first was expressed by a young woman who dismissed the importance of racially identified styles:

> Well, you're black, no matter what you do to yourself. This is the way I think of it.

Others spoke of "dressing black," "acting black" and "acting white." With these students, I pursued the meaning of black and white. I brought fashion and women's magazines to my interviews, including one copy of *Essence* with a photograph of Diana Ross on the cover. Her image provoked the following jeremiad:

> She's just, she's just really really fake. I mean she looks like a typical white black Barbie doll. You know. I mean she's like, I mean, she, I mean, her eyelashes. I mean her body. Everything on her is just really really fake. OK. Look at her eyelashes. Her eyelashes look like you know, its just really really fake and that's.... It seems like she wants to be white sort of. You know. Her eyelashes. And she thins out her lips and um, her hair, it's not curled or anything. It's just straight.

Diana Ross's false eyelashes offend this young woman more than any other feature. She mentions them four times to illustrate what she considers Diana Ross's desire to be white. Of the qualities she mentions, only lip thinning can actually be described as an attempt to imitate a white woman's features. By contrast, naturally long eyelashes have never been associated with any racial group. False eyelashes are the height of artificiality. The unstated connection is that to be artificial is to be white. In the speaker's moral code of beauty and race, false eyelashes are artificial, ugly and white. Perhaps they represent a transformation too easily attained. Black is authentic and beautiful.

The student's objection to Diana Ross's hair—"it's not curled or anything. It's just straight"—indicates that hair that is straightened and then curled is acceptable. The use of artifice is not the issue. The dichotomy between white as artificial and black as authentic is too simple. In the following excerpt from an interview, a light-skinned young woman with long wavy hair explains her desire to straighten her hair as an assertion of her black identity.

> I had a really big conflict with my hair when I was younger. I was fighting with it all the time, and since I was raised out in Louisiana in Baton Rouge, I was like, I was, I was, really a funny person, you know. Because I was, like, am I going to stay this color forever? Because I was the only light-skinned person out there and I always wanted to press my hair.

She felt the need to affirm her racial identity. The way to "act black" and "be black" was to straighten her hair. One of her classmates repeated this sentiment later in our discussion.

> Like them Oakland girls, you know, they're straight up black. How they wear their hair.

"Oakland girls" were girls whose black racial identity was not in question. The speaker pointed to them to show that straightening one's hair is a way of being "straight up black." Being black is taking your lead from other members of the black community. It means remaining within the constraints of propriety. The language of authenticity and artificiality is used to define the boundaries of racial identification. However, the specific practices defined as white or black are not systematically more or less artificial. No behavior that is acceptable is considered an imitation of whites. This includes straightening one's hair. When an African-American woman presses her hair, she is not attempting to look white; she is meeting the standards of other African-American women.

A style, even one whose content is specifically about being African American, can lose its ability to express racial affiliation when it moves too far away from its roots in a community. Every time I asked about the wearing of African medallions, the wearers were ridiculed.

It started out that way. It started out as, um, a symbol of Africa. It ended up as a fashion. I mean they're everywhere now. You can go anywhere and buy one of those things.

The speaker was talking about the importance of black culture remaining the property of the black community. The symbol lost its expressive power when it became a commodity that could be purchased anywhere.

The language of race and beauty used by these young women revolves around the ideas of authenticity (described variously as "straight up black" or natural) and artificiality, where being fake is sometimes synonymous with acting white. This discourse has some continuity with the "black is beautiful" idea of the 1960s and 1970s. What was considered beautiful and black was what was closer to nature.

"GIRL"

Just as these young women talk about "acting black" and "acting white," they are very quick to admonish women for "acting like" or "looking like" or "wanting to be" a man.

It looks like she's a man or something, you know.
That's like a boy hairstyle.

Short, unstraightened hair at one time represented an expression of black pride. Even, however, at the height of the black power movement, the most popular version of the Afro was full, large and round. Today, the short natural represents nothing to these young women except evidence of the desire to be a boy. They considered short hair attractive only on women who compensated for the style's masculinity by possessing other symbols of femininity. The imperative to be feminine is so strong that it negates the importance of being natural. The lengthening of hair through the use of manufactured hair and the application of false fingernails are both ways of achieving femininity through synthetic products. The extremes of femininity are rejected as too false and are called "acting white." This association, even if it takes the form of rejecting exaggerated femininity, reinforces the stereotype that the true woman is the white woman. One of the students responded to a copy of *Sassy* I brought with me in this way:

It just doesn't do too much for me. *Essence* might do something. I mean, their [*Sassy's*] ideas on makeup is typical. I mean, it's not for black people or any other color. It's more like for typical thin-lipped white girls that you know, that wear pink lipstick and wear high clothes, high high heels.

Again, as in the discussion of Diana Ross's false eyelashes, extremes of behavior—in this case, fashion excesses such as "high high heels"—are "racialized"[3] and made to signify white. White is used as an epithet to delineate the boundaries of acceptable behavior. While this use of white denigrates white women, it, at the same moment, relinquishes femininity to white women. The moral language of race used by these young women divides behavior into "natural" (black) and "fake" (white). The moral language of gender sorts appearance into two groups, "like a man" (natural or, more to the point, raw, unstraightened, unkempt) and "like a girl" (sufficiently worked). The woman who works too hard at femininity, stumbling around in high heels, is the white woman. These young women shift back and forth between these poles, trying to achieve the impossible, being a girl, being "straight up black," being natural. The student who called Diana Ross fake also said:

> I gotta keep my hair done every two weeks. And then please get my nails done. Or something like that. I mean it's like really hard. I gotta keep up with all that.

The pressure she feels is exerted by her peers who, she says, "just steady talk about you." Her peers apply a moral code structured by the languages of race and gender.

During the 1960s, young women learned a new code, whose rules were summed up in the words "black is beautiful." The politically expressive styles of twenty years ago no longer have meaning for these young women. Big Afros are, for them, something hilarious from another generation. When I needed to liven up a discussion, I could ask if they or their parents ever wore Afros. Immediate loud laughter broke out, and voices screamed "yes," as hands shot up to tell funny stories about the immense dimensions of the Afros their relatives once wore. Natural hair is no longer viewed as a political statement. It is seen either as a neutral choice or as the mark of a woman who either "doesn't care about herself" or "wants to be a boy."

CONCLUSION: RACIAL IDENTITY

These young women, wearing straightened hair, frequently spoke with anger about racial injustice and expressed their love for African Americans.

> Every time something happens bad it's about the black kids. But then, when they do something good, they make something happen and it's good, they don't show them. Like they show Bush or something. If he did something bad, they wouldn't show him on TV. They'd show a black kid.

This critical reading of the mass media extended to fashion magazines. The students were familiar enough with white fashion magazines to dislike them. The most frequent complaint was that African-American models were not used enough and that when they were used, they were given unattractive outfits, clothes that were meant to make the reader laugh or lewd outfits. These were impressive critical judgments for students aged twelve to fifteen. Several of the students criticized the types of African-American models used. The magazines, they said, selected either women who looked white or very dark women who were used as exotica to draw attention to the advertisements.

These students hold an Afrocentric beauty standard, but only tentatively. They embraced African-American identity in other ways. There is a way of "dressing black" about which these young women feel pride. It is a pride in African-American creativity. It belongs to them. They resent the appropriation of African-American style.

> They're using black heritage just to get what they want. I think that's probably why a lot of people get these shirts that say "It's a black thing" because, um, because like, all these, like, all these white people and Mexican people, they always want to do all kind of things like we do. We're not trying to tell 'em not to but, um, we just do that. We just do that because we want to do it. It's, it's just like the shirt says. It's a black thing.
> It says, "It's a black thing. You wouldn't understand it."
> Let's put it this way. We're leaders and they follow [laughter].

The ideas expressed above were not subscribed to by all of the young women I spoke with. Some were sympathetic toward individual white students at school who adopted black styles. One student felt that her white schoolmates appreciated African-American hair more than her African-American schoolmates. However, feelings of resentment about whites imitating blacks were common.

These young women also appreciated and found pleasure in the difference of African-American speech. Most of the students used essentially standard American English during our discussions, perhaps because they always do or because of my presence or because we were at school. Every once in a while, a student would express something in black English. When this happened, someone would giggle or echo the last few words of the sentence. Black English is a language they enjoy, take pride in and play with.

In the context of a culturally hierarchical nation, valuing one's own black language and style can be seen as a form of resistance. It is not that the dominant culture in the United States insists on assimilation. On the contrary, American culture insists on racial differences. And black English itself cannot be viewed at all times as resistance, just as women's culture, taken in the abstract, cannot be seen as a challenge to a gender hierarchy. It can be seen as such only if the hierarchy of cultures is questioned.

The original challenge to the Eurocentric beauty standard sought to question this hierarchy of cultures, and some of this culture of resistance remains. It remains in the words "black is beautiful" and in the verbal rejection of "looking white" or "acting white." "Looking white" often meant being overly sexual or excessively artificial; this was posed in opposition to a presumably more authentic way of being black. Though these young women claimed to value natural beauty, they insinuated that African-American women who wore their hair naturally short might be lesbians. Women who refused to straighten their hair were suspect, unless they were exceptionally beautiful, because they were not doing enough to attract men. The discourse of femininity demands artificiality and heterosexuality. "Acting white" means being overly feminine. Rejecting white culture in these terms reinforces a Eurocentric ideology of beauty and femininity. A traditional discourse of gender thus undercut an attempt to establish a new discourse of race.

NOTES

1. Fifty-one subjects participated in individual interviews and focus groups conducted in 1989 and 1990 in the San Francisco area. Thirty-six of the young women were enrolled in public middle school. The majority of the public school students lived in single-parent homes, where the primary guardian was employed in a clerical or service position. The remaining fifteen young women were enrolled in private schools. No additional background information was available on these students.

2. Banner locates the American roots of what she calls the "democratic rhetoric of beauty" in the early twentieth century (1983, 206).

3. Omi and Winant developed the concept of racialization (1986).

WORKS CITED

Banner, L. 1983. *American Beauty.* New York: Alfred A. Knopf.

Chapkis, W. 1986. *Beauty Secrets.* Boston: South End Press.

Clark, K. B., and M. P. Clark. 1947. Racial Identification and Preference in Negro Children. In T. M. Newcombe and E. C. Hartley (eds.), *Readings in Social Psychology* (pp. 602–11). New York: Holt.

Collins, P. H. 1990. *Black Feminist Thought.* Boston: Unwin Hyman.

Fanon, F. 1967. *Black Skin, White Masks.* New York: Grove Press.

Fine, M., and C. Bowers. 1984. Racial Self-identification: The Effects of Social History and Gender. *Journal of Applied Social Psychology* 14(2): 136–46.

Goering, J. M. 1971. Changing Perceptions and Evaluations of Physical Characteristics Among Blacks. *Phylon* 33(3): 231–41.

Greene, P. 1980. The Doll Technique and Racial Attitudes. *Pacific Sociological Review* 23(4): 474–90.

Grier, W. H., and P. Cobbs. 1968. *Black Rage.* New York: Basic Books.

Hall, S., and T. Jefferson (eds.). 1976. *Resistance Through Rituals: Youth Subcultures in Post-war Britain.* London: Hutchinson.

Hebdige, D. 1979. *Subculture: The Meaning of Style.* New York: Methuen.

hooks, b. 1988. Straightening Our Hair. *Zeta Magazine* 1: 33–37.

———. 1990. *Yearning.* Boston: South End Press.

Hraba, J., and G. Grant. 1970. Black Is Beautiful: A Reexamination of Racial Preference and Identity. *Journal of Personality and Social Psychology* 16: 398–402.

Jones, R. L., and Y. Smith. 1980. Black Children's Associations of Class-descriptive Labels. *Journal of Black Studies* 10: 345–53.

Keith, V. M., and C. Herring. 1991. Skin Tone and Stratification in the Black Community. *American Journal of Sociology* 97: 760–78.

Lakoff, R., and R. Scherr. 1984. *Face Value: The Politics of Beauty.* New York: Routledge & Kegan Paul.

Morrison, T. 1970. *The Bluest Eye.* New York: Washington Square Press.

Omi, M., and H. Winant. 1986. *Racial Formation in the United States.* New York: Routledge & Kegan Paul.

Rushing, A. B. 1988. Hair Raising. *Feminist Studies* 14: 325–35.

Udry, J. R. 1977. The Importance of Being Beautiful: A Reexamination and Racial Comparison. *American Journal of Sociology* 83: 154–60.

Webster, M., and J. E. Driskell. 1983. Beauty as Status. *American Journal of Sociology* 89: 140–65.

Wolf, N. 1991. *The Beauty Myth: How Images of Beauty are Used Against Women.* New York: William Morrow.

11

Nothing to Lose: A Naturalistic Study of Size Acceptance in Fat Women

Cheri K. Erdman

Praised be to Allah who made me stout and stuffed cushions in my every nook and corner; nor did He neglect to lard my skin with fat that is fragrant as the spicebush.

> (*The Arabian Nights* [10th century] in Sternhell 1985, 66)

Heavy women are a drag on the dating market, and they know it. . . . It doesn't matter a bit how pretty your face is, what a terrific personality you have, what a good person you are—everything in this world, for women, boils down to body size.

> (Edelstein 1977, 38)

To me, a happy ending is when someone can accept her body as it is.

> (Susan C. Wooley in Sternhell 1985, 146)

These three quotes demonstrate varying viewpoints on the social acceptability of women who are fat. Acceptance of women's body size and shape has been influenced by many factors, including culture, aesthetics, medicine, economics, fashion and the media. Numerous analyses have been written on this topic from the viewpoint of history, anthropology, psychology and feminism. This topic stirs opinions from professionals and the general public alike. Given this, it is understandable why there is so much confusion about size and weight from a medical, psychological, fashionable and individual point of view. Any woman who can find her way through the maze of the various experts' opinions to her *own* sense of knowing what is right for her performs a remarkable feat indeed.

Numerous studies conducted about the fat woman have focused on how to assist her in attaining an acceptable weight through various diet, exercise, and psychotherapy programs. A basic assumption underpinning these studies is that fat is physically and psychologically bad and that almost *any* means to get rid of fat is desirable. A second assumption is that a woman who is fat does not accept her body, so she desires ways (new diets, more exercise, a different therapy) to reduce and reshape her body.

Motivated by these assumptions, researchers continue to study the dieting population, even though there is a dismal 95–98 percent failure rate. People who have dieted for weight loss usually return to their former, or even higher, weights (Sternhell 1985; Stunkard & McClaren-Hume 1959). Yet in spite of the high chance of failure, the diet industry, along with the medical and the psychological communities, continues to try to sell the public on even more and better ways to lose their unwanted fat. And the public, for the most part, continues to buy into the very solution (dieting) that has become the problem.

In fact, body size is determined not only by diet and exercise, but also by numerous other factors such as genetics (Stunkard et al. 1986), setpoint (Bennett & Gurin 1982), age, gender, nationality, social class (Atrens 1988) and environment (Beller 1977). Researchers have obviously overlooked a viable population to study: fat women who accept and care for their bodies without dieting or weight loss as a goal.

I am a non-dieting fat woman who has chosen to study other women like myself. We are the women whom other researchers have ignored because our existence has contradicted their assumption that fat women are not well adjusted physically and psychologically. In order to do this study, I change that assumption: We non-dieting fat women are well adjusted, and for that reason we are worth researching. I define a well-adjusted fat woman as one who has given up her obsession with dieting and body size and who has refocused that energy onto other dimensions of her life.

There are other guiding assumptions for this research. First, the "fat is bad" paradigm is a socially constructed reality. Second, fat is more of a problem for women in the contemporary culture. And, third, the profession of therapy has contributed a share of the discrimination toward fat women under the guise of a helping process.

The "fat is bad" paradigm is a contemporary social construction, with the agreed-upon language and research to verify this "truth." If this paradigm is changed to "fat is acceptable" or to "fat is a part of a natural diversity in sizes in the collective human experience," a variety of implications are obvious. Blame is shifted away from the individual woman and placed largely on current social and cultural arrangements. The experiences of the women in this study corroborated the idea that what is bad about being fat is the social interpretation of this body size, not the fat itself. Consequently, attempts to ameliorate fat must be viewed as means to impose culturally specific norms and values regarding body size. In this context, the physician or the therapist would be forced to look at her/his own biases when encountering the fat woman. And, once again, the personal is political.

Second, fat, or fear of becoming fat, is a more critical problem for women. Numerous studies support the idea that a woman's sense of self is based on how she looks, rather than on what she does. A few years ago, when public opinion pollsters asked women to name their greatest fear, 38 percent said "getting fat" (Sternhell 1985, 66). In another survey conducted by Dr. Susan Wooley for *Glamour,* 75 percent of the 33,000 women who replied said that they were "too fat," including 45 percent who, in fact, were underweight by the conservative 1959 Metropolitan Life Insurance Company Height and Weight Table (Sternhell 1985, 68). On any given day, a high proportion of females is dieting—nearly half of ten-year-olds, two-thirds of high school girls and one-third of adult women. And women over sixty report that gaining weight is the second most serious concern for them, with the first being memory loss (Freedman 1989).

The final assumption of this study is that when women with body-image concerns consult therapists, they often encounter more fat discrimination. Therapists have tried to provide psychological explanations of and treatment for what is clearly a cultural problem (Wooley & Wooley 1980). While clinicians have critiqued their own biases with respect to the many stigmatized groups that they try to engage in therapeutic relationships—disabled, gay and lesbian, elderly and cross-cultural clients—this profession has not begun to recognize its own prejudice about fat. This area of discrimination is socially and psychologically sanctioned because being fat continues to be seen as the woman's fault.

Irvin Yalom, M.D., clearly expresses this attitude in his book *Love's Executioner and Other Tales of Psychotherapy* (1989). He describes ten patients who pose difficult questions for him. Yalom devotes a chapter to one, Betty, whom he calls "The Fat Lady." He asks himself this question: "Could I possibly form an honest and a caring relationship with a fat lady whose physical appearance repelled me?" (14). Yalom focuses on the therapeutic issue of countertransference—irrational feelings that the therapist has toward the patient: "I have always been repulsed by fat women. I find them disgusting . . . *everything,* everything I like to see in a woman, obscured in an avalanche of flesh. . . . How dare they impose that body on the rest of us?" (88). He goes on to say:

> Of course I am not alone in my bias. Cultural reinforcement is everywhere. Whoever has a kind word for the fat lady? But my contempt surpasses all cultural norms. . . . When I see a fat lady eat, I move down a couple of rungs on the ladder of human understanding. I want to tear the food away. To push her face into the ice cream. "Stop stuffing yourself! Haven't you had enough, for Chrissakes?" I'd like to wire her jaw shut. (88–89)

Yalom works with his feelings of contempt and repulsion while he treats Betty. Her treatment issues emerge, while Yalom manages to keep his judgmental feelings to himself until termination of the therapy. He begins to care for this woman, but she also diets and loses eighty pounds during therapy. Yalom articulates the feelings that a fat woman may provoke in therapy. Whether a client's fat is a self-identified issue or not, it will probably be an issue for the therapist. I am acutely aware of this prejudice because not only am I a fat woman, but also I am a member of this profession.

This study then is significant. First, fat is considered a cultural problem of "truth" construction. Second, fat is viewed as a women's problem. Third, discriminating attitudes of the members of the psychological community are explored and challenged. A well-adjusted fat woman, therefore, challenges cultural norms and/or a therapist's view of her problems by insisting that they are not related to her weight.

RESEARCH BACKGROUND

Because I am a well-adjusted, non-dieting fat woman, I consider myself to be a part of this study. My experience of living in a fat body most of my life affects the way I have constructed this research. The study involves a naturalistic design and a phenomenological approach to explore the commonalities of fat women who accept their body size. This approach was used in order to respect the behaviors and perspectives of those under study. This is important because women's lives are interpreted within the context assumptions of culture, medicine, fashion, language and the media, all of which equate fat with shame and guilt. This study, however, focuses on body-size acceptance from the perspective of those who are experiencing it—fat women.

Eighteen women from the Chicago area were interviewed. Each one met these basic criteria: was at least thirty years old, was 40 percent and over on the Metropolitan Life Insurance Company Height and Weight Tables, had not dieted for weight loss for at least one year and considered herself to have accepted her weight and size and to be leading a satisfying lifestyle. The choice of these particular criteria is based on my experiences and perceptions that age, weight, dieting and self-perceptions of having a satisfying lifestyle are important indicators of a well-adjusted fat woman.

It is important to understand that these eighteen women do not represent all women who have accepted their size. Most of the respondents were white, middle-class, educated and in their thirties and forties; weighed between 185 and 357 pounds; and lived in the Midwest. The research results reflect the thoughts and experiences of these particular women and, therefore, are not especially generalizable to all other communities of women. This indicates that future research is needed to explore the common nature of these themes.

Each woman was asked, first, to give an overview of her weight history and, second, to expand upon the period of her life during which she came to accept her body size.

Six themes are reflected in their collective experiences:

1. personal realities of fat, weight and dieting that are in opposition to the public conceptions

2. self-perceptions

3. body image

4. involvement in something larger than themselves, whether it be spirituality or political activity

5. the role of support

6. evolving processes and methods of size acceptance

I will report the findings on each theme, along with a discussion of the implications for therapy.

Personal Realities versus Public Misconceptions of Fat

The first theme is supported by an examination of the cultural context of these women's lives. The cultural history of body size counters the assumption that thinness has always been valued (Beller 1977; Schwartz 1986; Seid 1989). Two main ideas are culled from an examination of the cultural values and norms.

First, when examined from a historical point of view, standards regarding body size and shape appear arbitrary. The appearance of being arbitrary is somewhat misleading because the relegation of women's body size can be contextually connected to patriarchical economics and politics. However, for the purposes of this research, a cursory look at women's changing body images over time gives a perspective that is initially liberating.

Second, research that has revealed a considerable amount of misinformation about fat, dieting, health and body-image issues has not become part of the public discourse on these topics. The popular views of medical and psychological information about fat, weight and dieting can be challenged. For example, fat people do not eat more than thin people (Wooley & Wooley 1984); fat people can be healthy (Ernsberger & Haskew 1987); obesity has health benefits and, therefore, is not a disease (Ernsberger & Haskew 1987); weight is not always controllable by diet and exercise because it is predetermined by genetics (Stunkard et al. 1986); diets are often the reason that people get fatter (Bennett & Gurin 1982); exercise will increase your level of fitness more than it will decrease your weight (Lyons & Burgard 1988); and fat and thin people score similarly on psychological tests, making fat people emotionally as diverse as thin people (Wooley & Wooley 1980, 1984).

The popular cultural, medical and psychological discourse that fat is bad is countered by the personal realities of the women interviewed. Through their decision to *not* diet, they make a cultural and political statement. This statement defies stereotypes; shows belief in their own body truths instead of the authority of the medical, diet and insurance industries; and positively re-visions fat as a simple variation in human size.

One woman sums up defying the stereotypes:

> Even with being overweight, I've pretty much done everything I've set out to do and gotten everything I've wanted to have.

Another woman describes believing her body truth, rather than medical "truths":

> My fear was that if I gave up dieting, I would just never stop getting larger and larger. That has not come to be.

And this woman talks about her re-vision of fat as positive:

> To me fat meant that I was noticed, and I was a presence that people had to contend with. So when I was able to identify those positive aspects of being fat, I was able to reclaim them as parts of my personality, and not something that was simply a facet of my physical appearance. So now it doesn't matter what size I am, or what I weigh.

Self-perceptions

The second theme is self-perceptions. This is a self-description of each woman's view of her personal characteristics, attitudes and behaviors.

These women tend to perceive themselves to be inner-determining, rather than externally determined. This means that they consistently make decisions about their lives in reference to their own inner voice, rather than relying upon others to decide for them. This is especially true in regard to their body size. One woman describes her inner-determining quality:

> My counselor helped me stay in touch with who I am and being centered in myself. So that has been important, almost like little jewels that you take and decorate the inside with. I have a lot of little jewels that are creating a

wonderful brilliance for me, that has enlightened me to take it one step further.

Other personal characteristics support this inner-determining quality. These women are knowledgeable about weight, dieting and health issues, and they are introspective about what this means in their daily lives. They are also assertive, independent and accepting of diversity in others. One typical assertive statement is this:

My doctor does not bother me about my weight, and if he did, I would go somewhere else. I'm the same way with him that I am with everybody else: "My body, my business."

They live in the present, doing things they want to do now, rather than letting their weight determine the timing of their activities or accomplishments. One woman talks about living in the present moment:

At one point I made a list of what I would do if I were thin and resolved to do some of those things right now. I had three things on my list: buy a new wardrobe, get my pilot's license and become more active at sports. I have done all those things.

All of them find ways to focus on the positive aspects of being a large-size woman.

I don't want to lose weight. If I lose weight, fine, but I am always going to be a weighty person, a substantive person.

Finally, there is a sense of being competent, confident and, in some cases, even empowered. Often their size contributes to these feelings.

I have an attitude, and that attitude is "Damn, I'm good!" And I'm so fortunate that there is even more of me to be good!

Body Image

The third theme, body image, plays an important role in these women's self-perception. Hutchinson (1985) says that body image means a visual, auditory and kinesthetic sense of one's body. Body image is also influenced by cultural discourse.

The women in this study reported a variety of body-image interpretations. In most cases, they underestimate their body-image size. Hence, they are not always comfortable, for example, with photographic images of themselves. However, this underestimation of size is positive, since these women can act as a size 14 (or 12, or 10) body-image allows, unencumbered by their own or others' fat stereotypes. A number of studies support the idea that positive distortion of body image is psychologically healthy. One study found that depressed individuals distort their body images in a (culturally) negative direction (i.e., thin to fat), while nondepressed individuals distort their body images in an enhancing manner (Noles, Cash & Winstead 1985). Depressed persons have been found to exhibit greater perceptual accuracy or realism as compared to the nondepressed, who display more enhancing distortions of self (Lewinsohn et al. 1980).

In this study, the underestimation of size appears to function as a "creative" body image. The respondents' body images allow them to discourse creatively in a cultural context that is critical of their size. They have adjusted their body-image size (instead of their body) to reflect the lifestyle of someone who is comfortable with her body. One woman says:

> I am deliberately choosing to have a smaller image of my physical body so that I can act out my *idea* of myself.

Some of the women interviewed *do* see themselves exactly as they are reflected in the mirror or camera. They have not only experienced size acceptance, but also recognized advantages to their size. Their perception of body image is "transfigured" because they transform the meaning attached to their size without criticism and reject the traditional negative stereotypes. One woman describes her transfiguration:

> I am thirty-eight years old with two children, and my body looks pretty matronly. Society says to look like a thirteen-year-old boy would be acceptable, rather than looking at my body and saying that it looks appropriate for someone my size and age.

Involvement in Something Larger than Herself

The fourth theme is involvement in something larger than herself, defined as either the expression of her spirituality or political activism. This interpretation considers the importance of encompassing a wider and larger view of the world and ourselves beyond body size.

The women interviewed in this study understand that they are large in body. This understanding reaches beyond the largeness of the body to the largeness of the inner spirit. They may have constructed a definition of their personal spirituality that includes appreciating nature's diversity, being open to others who are different or exhibiting generous behavior.

At other times, this spirit is attached outwardly in political actions. "Going public" might mean being successful in a profession, having leadership ability, being a role model for other large women or being a public spokeswoman for size acceptance. This is the ultimate in taking the original stigma of being fat and transforming it into something that is worthwhile and meaningful for the individual woman and for the culture. This quality is reminiscent of having a purpose, being directed or being self-transcending (Buhler & Allen 1972).

One woman talks about this quality from the perspective of her personal spirituality:

> I can't define it real well, but I have a sense of it. I have a sense of connectedness when I ask for help from something bigger than myself. I also need to feel a connection to women wherever they are who are needing to express themselves. I think that the power is there, and I think that primarily it generates within ourselves. It leaves me searching.

Another woman talks about going public with her attitude of size acceptance:

> When you meet another fat woman, if you come across confident, if you come across like "Yes I can," there's a good chance that some of it is going to rub off on this woman.

Support

The fifth theme is support—the tendency of these women to seek out support for the value of size acceptance and how they support other large women by their attitude and actions. This connection to others allows them to feel less isolated, less stressed about being large and more capable of being involved in something larger than themselves. In one woman's words:

> Working with other large women was probably my first positive experience, and I suppose that we have provided models for each other in that sense.

Process and Methods

The process and methods these women use in their experiences of size acceptance comprise the last theme of this study. As I conducted the interviews, I noticed that some women appeared "more accepting" than others, even though they all met the basic criteria of the study. Without judgment, I uncovered a four-phase continuum of acceptance. These are not linear steps or stages. The stories of acceptance have a more fluid quality to them.

These women often had no clear sense of the progress toward a new acceptance of their size. This is understandable, since there are so few role models for size acceptance. Intuitions, personal experiences and gathering support are the dynamics of this process. There are three major ways in which the women in this study move through their individual process of acceptance. They talk to themselves in positive ways, they perceive their experiences in positive ways and they "act as if" they have the same rights as their thinner sisters. Using these methods provides a base from which they meet the everyday challenges of being a large woman.

There are four phases of acceptance revealed by the women who participated in this study. I have termed these the pre-acceptance, initial acceptance, medial and decisive phases. Pre-acceptance is marked by ambivalence and passivity about being large. The woman in this phase is not dieting, yet she thinks she might diet at some time. She is not familiar with the current research about fat, weight and dieting. She does not like being fat, nor does she like other fat people, and she holds some beliefs around the cultural stereotypes of weight.

Initial acceptance is characterized by an active acceptance of size. In this phase, the woman appears to still have traces of issues around food, since she has not yet made the transition from dieting to responding to a natural physical hunger. For example, she might occasionally compulsively eat or worry about eating certain kinds of foods. However, she stops dieting because she knows dieting does not work for her. She stops weighing herself and using the scale as a measure of her self-worth. She develops a creative body image, which has a positive effect in that it allows her to act as if she is a "normal-size" woman who can do "normal" things. She lives in the present more than the future by experimenting with doing things that she was waiting to do after she lost weight. She begins to see that she can have the life she wants to have right now, even if she continues to be large. She begins to build a supportive consciousness by reading research that validates her dieting experience.

The medial phase involves more outward signs of acceptance. Dieting and scales are no longer used or considered. Eating and exercise are now seen as methods of maintaining health, not losing weight. The woman in this phase uses a creative body image, but there is less discrepancy between her image and the mirrored reflection. She lives in the here and now and is more inclined to be inner-determining. Intentionally or unintentionally, she is also a role model for other women.

Decisive acceptance is characterized by public displays of the decision to accept body size in a resolute and determined manner. The woman who moves into this phase has taken the power to determine the meaning of her size. She displays publicly her decision to accept what is culturally devalued. She has no issue with food or dieting because she now responds to her natural physiological hunger. She has a transfigured body image—she sees herself as being as large as the mirror or camera reflection. This is perceived as positive and even desirable. This woman infuses her experiences back into the culture by influencing others in a more public way.

She gives support as a role model or leader for size acceptance, which is also a form of self-support.

DISCUSSION AND IMPLICATIONS

Why did I bother to do this research? What contributions did I hope to make to the knowledge already existing about these issues?

In studying size acceptance in fat women and in listening to their stories, I see a way out for all women, fat or not, who struggle with body-size acceptance. The women studied here have experienced the processes of relinquishing obsessions with food, dieting and body size. Accepting themselves as they are, they have moved courageously away from cultural and personal traditions. They have managed to not listen to the popular messages that their embodiment is wrong. They have learned to trust their own experiences and voices and to accept their bodies as simply a part of the diversity of human sizes.

Listening to these women's perceptions and experiences is worthwhile for other reasons beyond this specific research. Consider that women's experiences in a patriarchical culture are devalued because women are devalued. Consider that many psychological studies concerning women have been based on research done with males and that these models are viewed as the epitome of mental health. This puts women's experiences outside the patriarchical mainstream, thus pathologizing women. By listening to and valuing their own voices and by making room to describe their own experiences, women can develop their own models of psychological health. Women need this perspective for validation, for building a healthy self-respect and for living with greater self-esteem.

Another significant issue that this study addresses is the attitude of the therapeutic community toward not only its fat clients, but also any woman who has body-image and body-size concerns. Brown and Rothblum (1989) are feminist psychologists who also recognize fat as a culturally constructed problem. They comment, "We challenge the notion that fat equals pathology . . . [We] approach fat oppression, not fat, as the problem" (2). This is quite a radical departure from Dr. Irvin Yalom, quoted earlier, who is "repulsed" at the sight of a fat woman.

As a fat woman, a researcher of fat women and a therapist, I propose the following objectives for therapists who are interested in the issue of fat acceptance.

1. We must become knowledgeable about the historical, fashionable, medical and psychological roots of valued body size. By reflecting on the cultural standards, we can view this issue from a larger perspective. This can expand the contemporary viewpoint regarding the "ideal" body size to include a diversity of sizes.

2. We must become introspective about this issue not only as it relates to our clients, but also as it relates to our feelings about our own bodies. It is imperative that we engage in an ongoing examination of our attitudes about fat, dieting and body image to ensure that we are not proliferating a prejudicial climate toward fat, fat people or ourselves.

3. Those of us who decide to work with fat women should consider alternative treatment approaches besides offering the typical dieting advice or viewing the fat as a problem of psychological repression. I believe that any therapist who is not willing to deal with fat and body-image issues as a cultural issue for women is not in a position to act ethically on behalf of her/his clients. Having a broadened perspective of this issue is essential.

4. Using the information from this study, we can design interventions that encourage the development of the qualities that the women of this study possess. The phases of size acceptance could be used as a guide through the territory.

This study has relevance to us all, whether we are fat or thin, therapists or not. It forces us to look at another socially sanctioned form of discrimination. It forces us to ask whether this discrimination is relevant in a day and age in which diversity is being acknowledged and celebrated. Let all women celebrate their bodies as beautiful, functioning and healthy, no matter what the shape or size.

WORKS CITED

Atrens, D. M. 1988. *Don't Diet.* New York: William Morrow.

Beller, A. S. 1977. *Fat and Thin: A Natural History of Obesity.* Toronto: McGraw-Hill Ryerson, Ltd.

Bennett, W., and J. Gurin. 1982. *The Dieter's Dilemma.* New York: Basic Books.

Brown, L. S., and E. D. Rothblum. 1989. *Overcoming Fear of Fat.* New York: Harrington Park Press.

Buhler, C., and M. Allen. 1972. *Introduction to Humanistic Psychology.* Monterey, Calif.: Brooks/Cole.

Edelstein, B. 1977. *The Woman Doctor's Diet for Women.* Englewood Cliffs, N.J.: Prentice-Hall.

Ernsberger, P., and P. Haskew. 1987. Rethinking Obesity: An Alternate View of Its Health Implications. *Journal of Obesity and Weight Regulation* 6: 58–137.

Freedman, R. 1989. *Bodylove.* New York: Harper & Row.

Goldblatt, P. B., M. E. Moore and A. J. Stunkard. 1965. Social Factors in Obesity. *Journal of the American Medical Association* 192: 1039–44.

Hutchinson, M. G. 1985. *Transforming Body Image: Learning to Love the Body You Have.* New York: Crossing Press.

Lewinsohn, P. M., W. Mischel, W. Chaplin, and R. Barton. 1980. Social Competence and Depression: The Role of Illusory Self-perceptions. *Journal of Abnormal Psychology* 89: 203–12.

Lyons, P., and D. Burgard. 1988. *Great Shape: The First Exercise Guide for Large Women.* New York: Arbor House.

Noles, S. W., T. F. Cash, and B. A. Winstead. 1985. Body Image, Physical Attractiveness, and Depression. *Journal of Consulting and Clinical Psychology* 53: 88–94.

Schwartz, H. 1986. *Never Satisfied: A Cultural History of Diets, Fantasies and Fat.* New York: Free Press.

Seid, R. P. 1989. *Never Too Thin: Why Women Are at War with Their Bodies.* New York: Prentice-Hall.

Sternhell, C. 1985. We'll Always Be Fat, but Fat Can Be Fit. *Ms* 13: 66–68, 142–46, 154.

Stunkard, A. J., and M. McClaren-Hume. 1959. The Results of Treatment for Obesity. *Archives of Internal Medicine* 102, 79–85.

Stunkard, A. J., T. I. A. Sorenson, C. Hanis, T. W. Teasedale, R. Chakraborty, W. J. Schull and F. Schulsinger. 1986. An Adoption Study of Human Obesity. *New England Journal of Medicine* 314 (4): 193–97.

Wooley, S., and O. Wooley. 1980. Eating Disorders: Obesity and Anorexia. In A. Brodsky and R. Hare-Mustin (eds.), *Women and Psychotherapy* (pp. 135–158). New York: Guilford Press.

———. 1984. Should Obesity Be Treated at All? In A. J. Stunkard and E. E. Stellar (eds.), *Eating and Its Disorders* (pp. 185–92). New York: Raven Press.

Yalom, I. 1989. *Love's Executioner and Other Tales of Psychotherapy.* New York: Basic Books.

Selected Bibliography

Ahmed, L. 1992. *Women and Gender in Islam: Historical Roots of a Modern Debate*. New Haven, Conn.: Yale University Press.

Banner, L. W. 1983. *American Beauty*. New York: Alfred A. Knopf.

Bartky, S. L. 1990. *Femininity and Domination*. New York: Routledge, Chapman and Hall.

Bell, R. 1985. *Holy Anorexia*. Chicago: University of Chicago Press.

Berkhofer, R. F. 1978. *The White Man's Indian: Images of the American Indian from Columbus to the Victorians*. New York: Alfred A. Knopf.

Berry, K. 1979. *Female Sexual Slavery*. Englewood Cliffs, N.J.: Prentice-Hall.

Bordo, S. R. 1985–86. Anorexia Nervosa: Psychopathology as the Crystallization of Culture. *Philosophical Forum* 2: 73–103.

———. 1989. The Body and the Reproduction of Femininity: A Feminist Appropriation of Foucault. In A. M. Jaggar and S. R. Bordo (eds.), *Gender/Body/Knowledge: Feminist Reconstructions of Being and Knowledge* (pp. 13–33). New Brunswick, N.J.: Rutgers University Press.

———. 1990. Postmodernism and Gender-scepticism. In L. J. Nicholson (ed.), *Feminism/Postmodernism* (pp. 133–156). London: Routledge, Chapman and Hall.

Bornoff, N. 1991. *Pink Samurai: Love, Marriage and Sex in Contemporary Japan*. New York: Simon & Schuster.

Brownmiller, S. 1984. *Femininity*. New York: Fawcett Columbine.

Brumberg, J. J. 1988. *Fasting Girls: The Emergence of Anorexia Nervosa as a Modern Disease*. Cambridge: Harvard University Press.

Chapkis, W. 1986. *Beauty Secrets*. Boston: South End Press.

Chernin, K. 1981. *The Obsession: Reflections on the Tyranny of Slenderness*. New York: Harper & Row.

———. 1985. *The Hungry Self: Women, Eating and Identity*. New York: Times Books.

Croutier, A. 1989. *Harem: The World Behind the Veil*. New York: Abbeville Press.

Daly, M. 1978. *Gyn/Ecology.* Boston: Beacon Press.

Donnerstein, E., D. Linz and S. Penrod. 1987. *The Question of Pornography: Research Findings and Policy Implications.* New York: Free Press.

Eco, U. 1986. *Art and Beauty in the Middle Ages.* New Haven, Conn.: Yale University Press.

Edgley, C., and D. Brissett. 1990. Health Nazis and the Cult of the Perfect Body. *Symbolic Interaction* 13: 257–79.

Epstein, C. F. 1988. *Deceptive Distinctions: Sex, Gender and the Social Order.* New Haven, Conn.: Yale University Press.

Ewen, S. 1988. *All Consuming Images: The Politics of Style in Contemporary Culture.* New York: Basic Books.

Featherstone, M., M. Hepworth and B. S. Turner. 1991. *The Body.* Newbury Park, Calif.: Sage.

Freedman, R. 1986. *Beauty Bound.* Lexington, Mass.: Lexington Books.

———. 1989. *Bodylove.* New York: Harper & Row.

Gebser, J. 1985. *The Ever-present Origin.* Trans. N. Barstadt and A. Mickunas. Athens: Ohio University Press.

Gimbutas, M. 1991. *The Civilization of the Goddess: The World of Old Europe.* New York: Harper Collins.

Glassner, B. 1988. *Bodies.* New York: Putnam.

Goffman, E. 1976. *Gender Advertisements.* New York: Harper Colophon.

hooks, b. 1988. Straightening Our Hair. *Zeta Magazine* 1: 33–37.

———. 1992. *Black Looks, Race and Representation.* Boston: South End Press.

Hraba, J., and G. Grant. 1970. Black Is Beautiful: A Reexamination of Racial Preference and Identity. *Journal of Personality and Social Psychology* 16: 398–402.

Kinsley, D. 1986. *Hindu Goddesses: Visions of the Divine Feminine in Hindu Religious Tradition.* Berkeley: University of California Press.

Kobylka, J. 1991. *The Politics of Obscenity.* Westport, Conn.: Greenwood Press.

Lakoff, R., and R. Scherr. 1984. *Face Value: The Politics of Beauty.* New York: Routledge & Kegan Paul.

Lederer, L. (ed.). 1980. *Take Back the Night: Women on Pornography.* New York: William Morrow.

Mascia-Lees, F. E., and P. Sharpe (eds.). 1992. *Tattoo, Torture, Mutilation, and Adornment, The Denaturalization of the Body in Culture and Text.* Albany: State University of New York Press.

Mernissi, F. 1987. *The Veil and the Male Elite.* New York: Addison-Wesley.

Millman, M. 1980. *Such a Pretty Face: Being Fat in America.* New York: Norton.

Rushing, A. B. 1988. Hair Raising. *Feminist Studies* 14: 325–35.

Schroder, D. 1978. *Engagement in the Mirror: Hairdressers and Their Work.* San Francisco: R&E Research Associates.

Schwartz, H. 1986. *Never Satisfied: A Cultural History of Diets, Fantasies and Fat.* New York: Free Press.

Seid, R. P. 1989. *Never Too Thin: Why Women Are at War with Their Bodies.* New York: Prentice-Hall.

Sheffield, C. J. 1987. Sexual Terrorism: The Social Control of Women. In B. B. Hess and M. Marx Ferree (eds.), *Analyzing Gender: A Handbook for Social Science Research* (pp. 171–189). Beverly Hills, Calif.: Sage.

Spitzack, C. 1990. *Confessing Excess: Women and the Politics of Body Reduction.* Albany: State University of New York Press.

Suleiman, S. R. (ed.). 1985. *The Female Body in Western Culture.* Cambridge: Harvard University Press.

Turner, B. S. 1984. *The Body and Society.* Oxford: Basil Blackwell.

Udry, J. R. 1977. The Importance of Being Beautiful: A Reexamination and Racial Comparison. *American Journal of Sociology* 83: 154–60.

Webster, M., and J. E. Driskell. 1983. Beauty as Status. *American Journal of Sociology* 89: 140–65.

Wolf, N. 1991. *The Beauty Myth: How Images of Beauty Are Used Against Women.* New York: William Morrow.

Zuhur, S. 1992. *Revealing Reveiling.* Albany: State University of New York Press.

Index

About the Contributors

KAREN A. CALLAGHAN is Assistant Professor and Chair of the Department of Sociology and Criminal Justice at Barry University.

CHERI K. ERDMAN is a Professor of Education and counselor at the College of DuPage, Glen Ellyn, Illinois. She also operates a private counseling practice.

J. GREG GETZ is a Research Associate in the Department of Psychiatry and Behavioral Sciences, Baylor College of Medicine. His current research interests include gender role socialization and the medicalization of social problems.

DEBRA GIMLIM is a doctoral candidate in the Department of Sociology, State University of New York–Stony Brook.

HANNE K. KLEIN is a freelance hairstylist who lives and works in Dallas, Texas.

ERIC MARK KRAMER is an Assistant Professor of Communication at the University of Oklahoma. He has recently edited a volume entitled *Consciousness and Culture: An Introduction to the Thought of Jean Gebser* (Greenwood Press, 1992).

MAXINE LEEDS is a doctoral candidate in the Department of Sociology, University of California, Berkeley.

BEN LOWE is an Assistant Professor of Early Modern European History at Florida Atlantic University in Boca Raton. He has published numerous articles in medieval and early modern discourse and is currently completing a book on the emergence of a peace ethic in medieval and Tudor England, *The Problem of War and Ideas of Peace in England, 1337–1558.*

ALGIS MICKUNAS is a Professor of Philosophy at Ohio University. He has written several books, including, with David Stewart, *Exploring Phenomenology: A Guide to the Field and Its Literature* (1974); translated works by Jean Gebser; and published numerous articles.

JOHN W. MURPHY is a Professor of Sociology at the University of Miami. He has published numerous articles and books dealing with contemporary social issues, including *Postmodern Social Analysis and Criticism* (Greenwood Press, 1989) and, with Jung Min Choi, *The Politics and Philosophy of Political Correctness* (Greenwood Press, 1992).

AMIRA SONBOL is an Associate Professor of History at the University of Cairo and a Visiting Assistant Professor at Georgetown University.

CATHERINE G. VALENTINE is a Professor of Sociology and the founder and Director of the Women's Studies Program at Nazareth College of Rochester in New York. She has coauthored *Field Research: A Sourcebook and Field Manual* (1982) and *Women and Symbolic Interaction* (1987), and her articles have appeared in *Urban Life* and *Symbolic Interaction.* Her recent research focuses on "bodies and emotions" in the classroom and on the relationships among body, emotion and gender hierarchy.

USHA ZACHARIAS is a doctoral student in communication at Ohio University. She worked for several years in India as a professional journalist.